RAF TANGMERE
— IN —
100
OBJECTS

'Tangmere was Shangri-La in the air force in those days. It was the most desirable station in the whole of the UK … It just was a jolly good station.'
Eric Marsden
Fitter, 'B' Flight, 145 Squadron, RAF Tangmere in May 1940

'There never was and never will be a station so attractive as Tangmere.'
Wing Commander H.R. 'Dizzy' Allen DFC

RAF TANGMERE IN 100 OBJECTS

The History of a Battle of Britain Fighter Base

MARK HILLIER & MARTIN MACE

AIR WORLD

First published in Great Britain in 2025 by
Air World
An imprint of
Pen & Sword Books Ltd
Yorkshire – Philadelphia

Copyright © Mark Hillier and Martin Mace

ISBN: 978 1 52670 641 6

The right of Mark Hillier and Martin Mace to be identified as the Authors of this work has been asserted by them in accordance with the Copyright, Designs and Patents Act 1988.

A CIP catalogue record for this book is available from the British Library.

All rights reserved. No part of this book may be reproduced, transmitted, downloaded, decompiled or reverse engineered in any form or by any means, electronic or mechanical including photocopying, recording or by any information storage and retrieval system, without permission from the Publisher in writing. NO AI TRAINING: Without in any way limiting the Author's and Publisher's exclusive rights under copyright, any use of this publication to "train" generative artificial intelligence (AI) technologies to generate text is expressly prohibited. The Author and Publisher reserve all rights to license uses of this work for generative AI training and development of machine learning language models.

Typeset by Mac Style
Printed and bound in the UK by CPI Group (UK) Ltd, Croydon, CR0 4YY.

The Publisher's authorised representative in the EU for product safety is Authorised Rep Compliance Ltd., Ground Floor, 71 Lower Baggot Street, Dublin D02 P593, Ireland.
www.arccompliance.com

For a complete list of Pen & Sword titles please contact

PEN & SWORD BOOKS LIMITED
47 Church Street, Barnsley, South Yorkshire, S70 2AS, England
E-mail: enquiries@pen-and-sword.co.uk
Website: www.pen-and-sword.co.uk

or

PEN AND SWORD BOOKS
1950 Lawrence Road, Havertown, PA 19083, USA
E-mail: uspen-and-sword@casematepublishers.com
Website: www.penandswordbooks.com

Contents

Introduction vii
Acknowledgements viii

SECTION ONE – THE EARLY YEARS 1
1. Early Ordnance Survey Map 2
2. Lieutenant Geoffrey Dorman's Letter 4
3. Photograph of a Veteran's Return 6
4. Airfield Guardroom 8
5. An Early Tangmere Pilot's Memoir 10
6. War Graves in Oving Churchyard 12
7. Slindon Sopwith Crash 14
8. Government Surplus Advert 16

SECTION TWO – A LEGEND IS CREATED 19
9. Land Acquisition Maps 20
10. Date Stone from Building No.25 22
11. Gloster Gamecock Replica 24
12. Training for Hendon Air Pageant 26
13. Royal Visit Press Photo 28
14. Hawker Fury Mk.I K5674 30
15. Empire Air Day Programme 1938 32
16. 'Tangmere Tonic' Cartoon 34
17. Jeffrey Quill's Pilot's Logbook 36
18. Air Ministry Fuel Depot, Portfield 38
19. Newspaper Cutting of No.1 Squadron Accident 40

SECTION THREE – A SECOND WORLD WAR 42
20. 'Fighter Pilot' 43
21. New Spitfires at Tangmere 45
22. The World's Oldest Surviving Hurricane 47
23. RAF Westhampnett 49
24. Tangmere's Battle Headquarters 51
25. The Medals of Air Vice-Marshal Lott 55

SECTION FOUR – THE BATTLE OF BRITAIN 57
26. Squadron Leader Max Aitken's Flying Boots 58
27. Tangmere's 'Scramble' Bell 60
28. German Bomb Fragment 62
29. Bomb-Damaged Centre Punch 64
30. A Tangmere Military Cross 66
31. Military Medal Gallantry 68
32. Stained Glass Window, Boxgrove Church 70
33. 'The Glorious 16th' Cartoon 72
34. Fontwell House 74
35. 'Tangmere Hurricanes' 76
36. Last Letter Home 78
37. Hawker Hurricane Mk.I, P261 80
38. Plaque to Squadron Leader Caesar Hull DFC 82
39. Memorial to Pilot Officer Własnowolski 83

SECTION FIVE – THE ROAD TO VICTORY 85
40. Presentation Biscuit Barrel 86
41. Spitfire Mk.IIa P7350 87
42. Night Fighter Crew at Tangmere 89
43. RAF Merston 91
44. Tangmere Defence Map 93
45. Gumber Decoy Site 95
46. Douglas Bader'S PoW Photograph 97
47. Tangmere's Role in Operation *Anthropoid* 99
48. Caterpillar Club Pin 101
49. Lysander Replica 103
50. Squadron Leader H.E. Bates' Tunic 105
51. Flight Lieutenant Ball's Album 107
52. The Night Hawk 109
53. C-Type Flying Helmet 111
54. Tangmere Cottage 112
55. Tangmere's Main Gate 114
56. Luftwaffe Reconnaissance Photograph 115
57. Typhoon Squadron First Day Cover 117
58. Tangmere's Watch Office 119
59. Avro Lancaster 'S' For 'Sugar' 121
60. Handley Page Halifax Crash Memorial 123

61.	Flowers Picked by Resistance	125	84.	Supermarine Spitfire Mk.LF XVI TE311	173
62.	D-Day Order of Battle	126	85.	RAF Javelins Gather at Tangmere	175
63.	The Ale Runs	128	86.	Donald Campbell's Bluebird-Proteus CN7	177
64.	Bishop Otter College Drawings	130	87.	Freedom Scroll	179
65.	Newspaper Cutting of Rear-Gunner's Survival	132	88.	The Unicorn Public House	181
66.	Special Duties Pilot's Maps	134	89.	Hawker P.1127 Crash-landing	183
67.	Royal Visit to RAF Tangmere	137			
68.	Operation *Exodus*	139		**SECTION SEVEN – THE END OF AN ERA**	**185**
69.	Captured Junkers Ju 88 Night Fighter	141	90.	Slides of Tangmere's Whirlwinds	186
70.	Tangmere's 'Enemy Aircraft Circus'	143	91.	Royal Flying Lesson Images	189
71.	Wartime Legends Meet Again	145	92.	Champagne Glass From a Guest Night	191
	SECTION SIX – THE COLD WAR	**147**	93.	A 'Royal Tangmere Incident'	193
72.	Tangmere's Type T2 Hangars	148	94.	Tangmere Closure Programme	194
73.	RAF High Speed Flight is Reformed	150	95.	ATC Cadet's Logbook	196
74.	Gloster Meteor F4, EE549	153	96.	A Sedbergh T21 of No.623 Gliding School	198
75.	The 'Tangmere Times'	155	97.	Building 116	200
76.	Portrait of Colonel Robin Olds USAF	157	98.	The Former Spitfire Club	202
77.	Hurricanes Return to Tangmere	159	99.	RAF Tangmere Memorial	204
78.	'Fighter Station Supreme'	161	100.	Tangmere Military Aviation Museum	205
79.	RAF Tangmere's Badge	162			
80.	Hawker Hunter WB188	164		*Source Information and Notes*	207
81.	Rustington Memorial	166			
82.	Tangmere's Headline Departure	168			
83.	Gloster Meteor Pilot's Logbook	171			

Introduction

On 16 November 1916, Lieutenant Geoffrey Dorman took off from Shoreham in a Royal Aircraft Factory FE2b with the intention of heading west along the South Coast to the airfield at Gosport. Not long into the flight, however, a dense sea fog formed and, as his engine was also 'misbehaving', Dorman decided 'it would be best to try and land'.

Spotting a suitable area of farmland, Lieutenant Dorman put his aircraft down near the West Sussex village of Tangmere. Evidently aware of what he had stumbled across, Dorman's subsequent report on the incident included a suggestion that the site would be eminently suitable for an aerodrome. Within twelve months, construction had started – and so was born the legend of RAF Tangmere.

Over the years that followed, Tangmere became one of the best known and strategically most important fighter stations in the United Kingdom. From its connections with the highly-polished air displays given at various RAF pageants in the 1920s and 1930s, through to numerous royal visits, or for its role in the post-war record-breaking speed flights or as a Cold War air-sea rescue base, Tangmere was a vital part of the nation's defences.

It is, however, for its service on the front line in the Second World War that Tangmere is best remembered. Not only was the airfield itself bombed and blitzed, its aircraft and pilots also found themselves in the thick of the fighting in the Battle of Britain, before turning to an increasingly offensive role whilst led by Wing Commander Douglas Bader. Operation *Jubilee*, the Combined Operations raid on Dieppe, and the D-Day landings in 1944 all required RAF Tangmere to play its part.

As well as overt offensive sorties, Tangmere was involved in the secretive world of covert warfare, when, during the full moon periods, 'A' Flight of 161 (Special Duties) Squadron would move its Lysanders forward to Tangmere. As well as delivering SOE agents, wireless operators, wireless equipment and weapons to assist the Resistance, these aircraft often returned with agents, VIPs and even Allied escapers and evaders.

The development and role of RAF Tangmere from 1916 until its closure in 1970, and beyond, is explored through the intriguing collection of 100 fascinating objects that follows.

Mark Hillier and Martin Mace
West Sussex, 2025

Acknowledgements

The authors are indebted to Dudley Hooley, without whose early patronage and encouragement this book would not have been started. Thanks must also go to David Coxon, who, along with Reginald Byron, wrote the highly recommended *Tangmere – Famous Royal Air Force Fighter Station* which was published by Grub Street in 2013, and Charles Hutcheon, who continued the support and co-operation begun by Dudley Hooley. Andy Saunders and Matt Field have readily fielded questions and tolerated their knowledge being tested, for which the authors are most grateful.

In terms of the images that appear in this book, every effort has been made to contact the copyright holders to ensure that full and appropriate acknowledgment is made in every case. In the event of any omissions or oversight, please do contact the authors through the publisher so that future editions can be updated accordingly. The authors would particularly like to acknowledge Andy Saunders and Chris Goss for access to their remarkable archives. Thanks must also go, in no particular order, to Dave Cassan, for the maps, David Cole, for allowing use of his images of Prince Charles during his flying lessons at Tangmere, Chris Budgen, Peter Amos, Edward McManus of the Battle of Britain Monument, and Chris Lofting. A particular mention must be made of the long-suffering Robert Mitchell – not only for his work in the field taking some of the pictures included in this book, but for all his efforts on many of the other images.

Lastly, we need to acknowledge Tangmere Military Aviation Museum and the unwavering support of those who manage and run this remarkable institution. Without access to its archives and collection, which was so readily offered and provided, putting this book together would have been impossible.

Section One

The Early Years

1: Early Ordnance Survey Map

Tangmere at the Start of the First World War

Situated under the foot of the South Downs on fertile plains leading to the English Channel is a village that dates back to 680AD – Tangmere. Originally a Saxon community, it grew and developed on land a mile south of the Roman road of Stane Street.

In 677 the Bishop of York, Wilfrid (later Saint Wilfrid), came to Selsey and converted the South Saxons to Christianity. In 680 a charter, which was possibly issued by the then king, that states: 'I Caedwalla ... have granted his brethren serving God at the church of St Andrew ... the land of 10 hides which is called Tangmere.' Though its exact origins are unclear, the name is thought to originate from the words 'Tang', meaning forked or serpent's tongue, which may well be a reference to a fork in two paths or streams that existed in the area, and 'mere', suggesting a pond or small lake.

The original church in Tangmere, St Andrew's, was constructed in the 11th-century and is mentioned in the Domesday Book. At this point in time, Tangmere had a population of around 120.

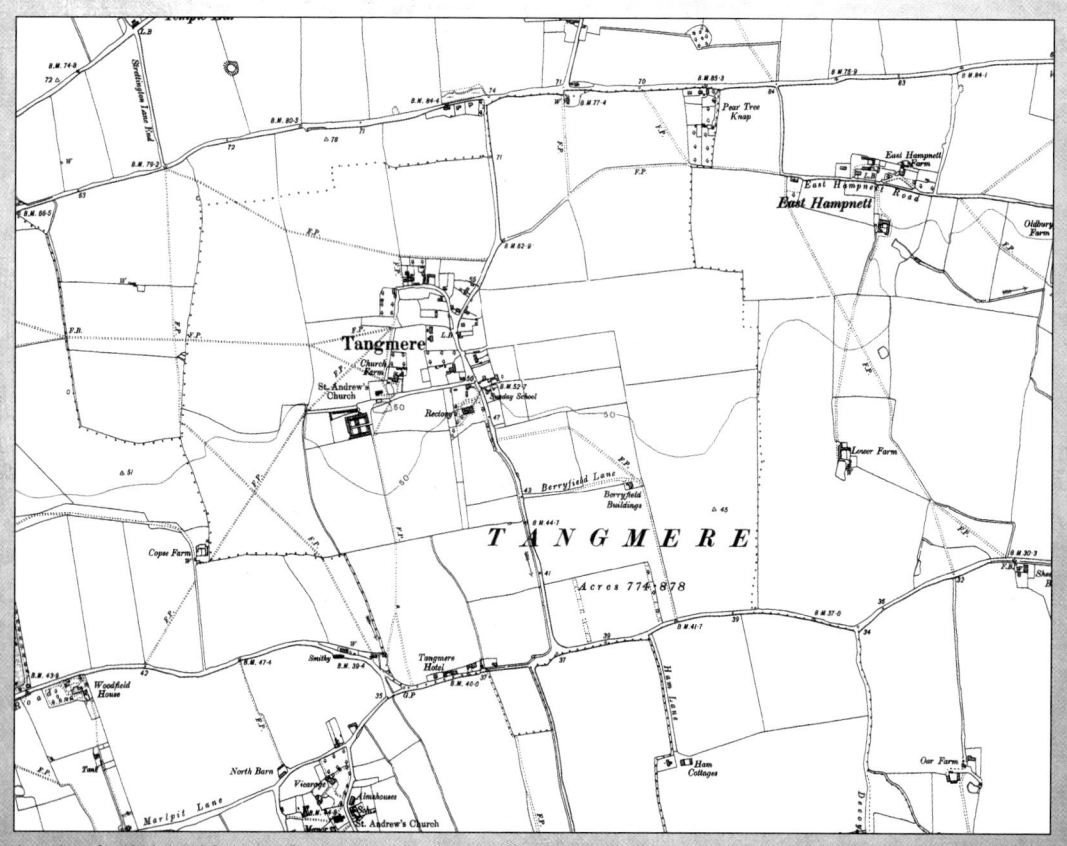

A section of a 1914-dated Ordnance Survey map of Tangmere. (*Historic Military Press*)

1: EARLY ORDNANCE SURVEY MAP

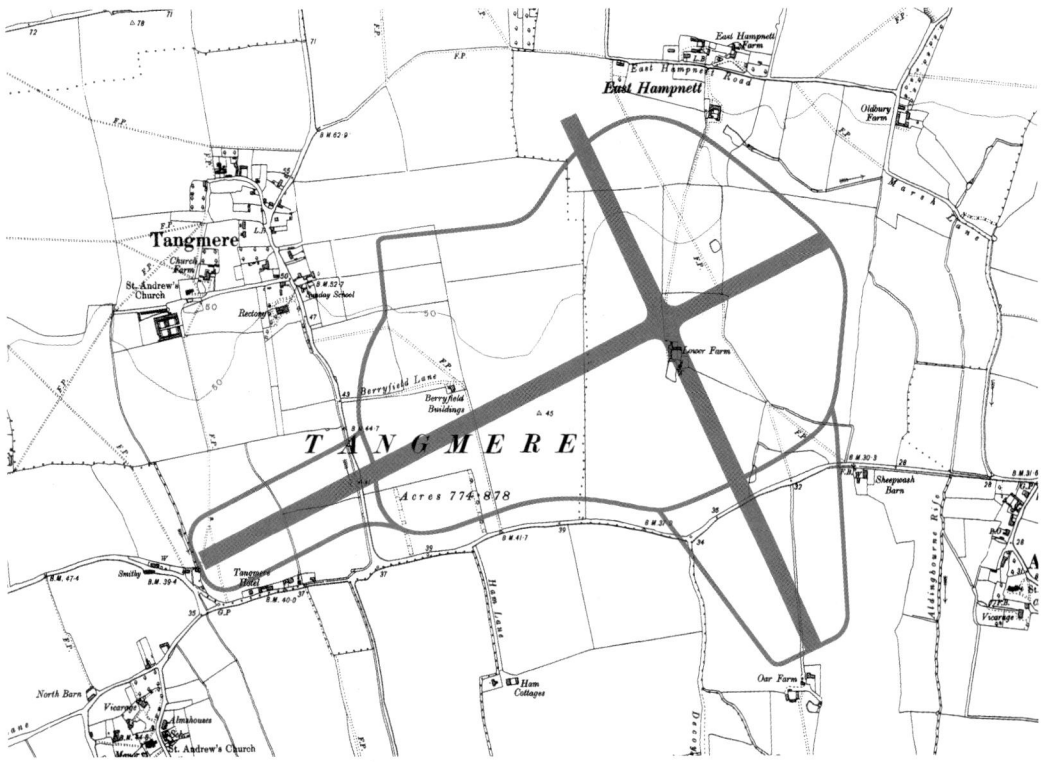

The same section of Ordnance Survey map with the RAF Tangmere's runways, as they would have appeared at the end of the Second World War, superimposed on it. (*Historic Military Press*)

In 1341, King Edward II granted the new Archbishop of Canterbury the right to hold a fair at Tangmere on St Andrew's Day. The event is still held by the church every autumn.

The Manor of Tangmere was owned by the Archbishop of Canterbury until 1542, at which point it was claimed by Henry VIII. It later passed to Cardinal Archbishop Pole, before reverting back to the Crown. In time, the community was granted by Elizabeth I to Richard Baker and then Sir Richard Sackville. In 1579 the manor became part of the Halnaker Estate, which was later acquired by the 3rd Duke of Richmond.

Predominantly an agricultural area, the land to the south of the village was also used for rearing pigs and livestock. The animals would be taken up through the village to market in Chichester, the pond in the village being used for watering the livestock.

It was the outbreak of war in 1914, when the Ordnance Survey map on the opposite page was published, that changed the nature of Tangmere and its surrounding area forever. From then on, the village would be associated with one of the most famous fighter stations in the history of the Royal Air Force.

2: Lieutenant Geoffrey Dorman's Letter

The Beginning

Tangmere aerodrome owes its existence to a chance event, the result of what should have been a routine flight for one RFC pilot, Lieutenant Geoffrey Dorman.

Having previously served in a Balloon Section on the Somme, Dorman returned to the UK in the summer of 1916, being posted to a training unit at Gosport. He takes up the story in his own words: 'With my previous training [I] soon passed out on "Rumpeties" (as Maurice Farman aircraft were sometimes called) and was posted to No.28 Squadron, also at Gosport, for advanced training on FE2b aircraft … The pilot sat in a robust throne, rather like a bishop's seat in a cathedral and the unfortunate observer sat or knelt in a round nacelle about the size and shape of a foot-bath right in the front. He had a Lewis gun there fixed to a tall pole and had to stand to use it, the sides of the foot-bath came to his knees. Most observers firmly anchored themselves by a home-made harness to the pole after one or two had been ejected. This was before the days of parachutes. We had to do 25 hours flying to qualify for wings and on 19 November 1916, I just had two hours and a cross country flight to get them.

'So, the CO, Major A Shackleton, instructed me to fly to Shoreham, land there and return. That was a route that I felt capable of tackling, especially as it was a nice fine day when I started, but with an East wind of about 20mph.

'After passing behind the prohibited area of Portsmouth, I turned out to sea a bit and flew inland again over the South Downs to fill in time, never loosing sight of the coast. I had plenty of time when I reached Shoreham, so I flew on over Brighton and landed at Shoreham after 1 hour and 45 minutes, with still 15 minutes needed for my wings. I had as a passenger Lieutenant Taylor, who was also under instruction but not as far advanced as I was. The FE2b aircraft was No.4875.

'After lunch I took off for Gosport and after circling round a bit, my 15 minutes for my wings had passed so Taylor turned round in his foot-bath and we shook hands and no doubt I looked pleased and smug. But pride cometh before a fall.'[1]

Dorman later revealed what happened next in a letter he sent to Tangmere's Commanding

A portrait of Second Lieutenant Geoffrey Dorman that was taken for his Royal Aeronautical Club Aviator's Certificate, in effect his pilot's licence. It was No.44, which was issued on 22 September 1915. (*Royal Aero Club Trust*)

2: LIEUTENANT GEOFFREY DORMAN'S LETTER

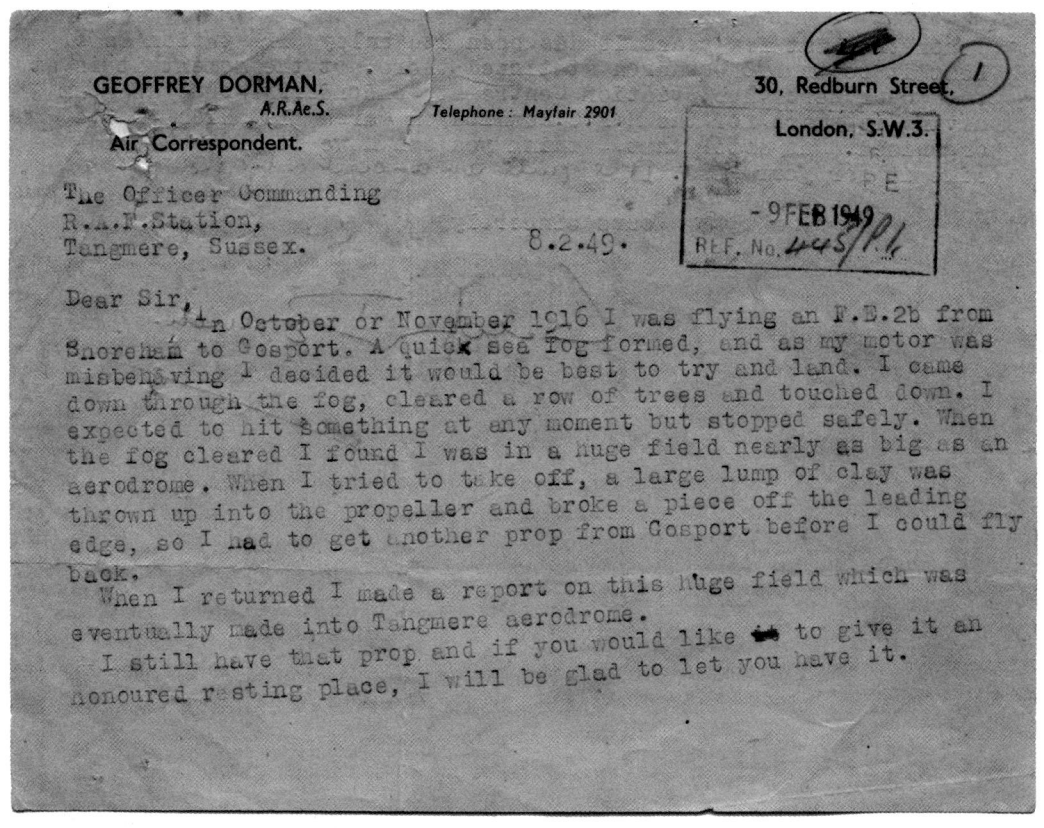

The first page of Geoffrey Dorman's letter detailing his unintentional landing at Bayley's Farm, Tangmere, on 19 November 1916. At the end of the letter, Dorman pointed out that he still had the damaged prop from the landing – and offered it to the Station Mess. It would seem that the gift was accepted, as the historian Andy Saunders notes the prop duly hung in Tangmere's Mess until the station closed in 1970. (*Historic Military Press*)

Officer on 8 February 1949 – the first page of which is seen above: 'A quick sea fog formed, and as my motor was misbehaving I decided it would be best to try and land. I came down through the fog, cleared a row of trees and touched down. I expected to hit something at any moment, but stopped safely. When the fog cleared I found I was in a huge field nearly as big as an aerodrome. When I tried to take off, a large lump of clay was thrown up into the propeller and broke a piece off the leading edge, so I had to get another prop from Gosport before I could fly back'

In his other account, Dorman also recalled the immediate aftermath of his landing, which occurred on land at Bayley's Farm, Tangmere, on 19 November 1916: 'We walked up a lane and came to a railway where there was a halt and a signal box from which I was allowed to telephone Gosport. In due course a tender was sent with a fitter and a new prop.

'I was driven into Chichester for the night where I stayed at the Dolphin & Anchor. The next morning the tender picked me up again and drove me to the "Bee". The fog had now cleared and I found I had landed in a field several hundreds of yards square.

'I took off from Tangmere village and flew back to Gosport, where I was told by the CO I could put up my wings. He told me to make a report on the forced landing, which I did. I wrote that the field would make a good aerodrome.' The rest, as they say, is history!

3: Photograph of a Veteran's Return

Another Early Landing

Whilst it is often stated that Geoffrey Dorman was the first pilot to land at Tangmere, he was not the only person who claimed to do so in November 1916. At around the same time, another RFC pilot, Lieutenant Eric Robbins, reported making an almost identical force-landing on the same field at Bayley's Farm. As the aviation historian Ken Rimell points out, 'who landed first is uncertain for both men claim to have landed there in the same month'.[2]

Like Dorman, Robbins had also been serving on the Western Front, and over the Somme, when he was permitted to return back to Britain

Eric Robbins pictured on his return to Tangmere in 1983, standing on the spot where he had landed his Avro 504, following engine failure, almost seventy years earlier. (*Courtesy of the Andy Saunders Collection*)

on leave. Ken Rimell takes up the story: 'It so happened that an old Avro 504 was to be flown back to the UK and a new aircraft brought back. His request for leave being granted, he was told to fly to RFC Upavon in Wiltshire where he was to deliver the old aircraft and collect the new one and fly it back to France a few days later.

'It was at first light the following morning [when] he set off from his base in Northern France and after crossing the coast over Calais took the shortest sea route over the Channel to Dover. He was by now low on fuel so noting a small roadside garage he made a landing in a field nearby where a very surprised garage owner filled his aircraft's tanks.

'Safely back in the air his plan was to follow the coastline to Portsmouth where he would track north to Upavon. It was over Bognor Regis that the engine in his aircraft started to misfire, [and] finally to die. Its last splutter was to cover the pilot in caster [sic] oil.

'[Robbins] had the advantage of height and his aircraft had a favourable gliding ability, so the search for a flat piece of ground was now foremost in his mind. Not wishing to end up in the sea he turned inland, noting Chichester Cathedral's spire in the distance and, to his joy, below a long flat piece of grass. He glided down to make a perfect landing at Bayley's Farm.'[3]

Having climbed out of his cockpit, Robbins' next actions were almost the same as those of Dorman – he set off to seek help. Rather than heading in the direction of the railway line, he set off towards the farmhouse.

'[There] the friendly farmer, after recovering from the surprise of this unexpected arrival on his farm,' continues Ken, 'suggested to his equally stunned wife to offer tea and cake, while a farm boy ran to Chichester where a message was sent to his HQ at Upavon for help. The following day an RFC lorry arrived and the aircraft was dismantled and taken away for repair.'

It would appear that the news of Robbins' and Dorman's landings at Tangmere, as well as the latter's report, 'had an immediate effect at higher levels', as the Tangmere historians Reginald Byron and David Coxon reveal: 'The Goodwood estate papers include a letter dated December 1916, only a month or so later, from HM Comptroller of Lands, War Office, sent to Mr. R. Hussey Freke, the Duke of Richmond's land agent, referring to the proposed establishment of an aerodrome at Tangmere.'[4] The journey to a front line fighter station was about to begin.

4: Airfield Guardroom

Relic of A First World War American Airfield

By September 1917, 200 acres of land at Tangmere, not only from Bayley Farm but also the neighbouring Church and East Hampnett farms, had been requisitioned under the Defence of the Realm Regulations (1914) with a view to construction of an airfield. However, the proposed aerodrome was not intended, as you might think, for the Royal Flying Corps.

When America declared war on Germany on 6 April 1917, the US Army Air Service (USAAS) found itself ill-equipped to play a large and decisive role in the air war in Europe. As part of its expansion plans, which were drawn up in 1917, the British Government was asked to assist with the provision of airfields, aircraft and pilot training. These schemes led to an agreement for the formation of thirty night-bombing squadrons which were to be equipped with the Handley Page O/400 twin-engine bomber.

During 1917 and 1918, construction began on a series of five Training Depot Stations for the USAAS, each of which was to be used for training American aircrew on the O/400. All bar one of the air stations were located close together in West Sussex, namely at Ford, Rustington, Goring-by-Sea and Tangmere – the fifth was to be established further west near Emsworth. Assembly of O/400 bombers would also take place at some of the sites.

All five airfields were to be constructed to similar plans. The American government sub-contracted most of the airfield construction work to the British authorities, and agreed to pay all material and labour costs, as well as a percentage of the general overheads. Intended to be built on empty fields between Limbrick Lane and Field Place, work on the aerodrome at Goring had not started by the time the Armistice was signed on 11 November 1918.

On the other hand, located in the general area of Station Road and the Sea Estate, Rustington Aerodrome is stated to have been finished just ten days before the end of the war, the grass runways running north to south along the direction of Sea Avenue. It is a unique survivor of the construction programme that included Tangmere which can be found hidden away behind some bushes at the north end of Sea Avenue in Rustington – the airfield's guardhouse.

Both Ford (known to the pilots as Yapton and officialdom as Ford Junction) and Tangmere had been completed and were ready for occupation by US personnel by the summer of 1918.[5] For its part, Tangmere officially opened on 1 August 1918.

However, in terms of Tangmere, delays in delivery of men and equipment prevented the start of training before the Armistice. Though American personnel moved in from Ford with a few smaller aircraft types in the weeks that followed, they soon left to return to the USA.

At that time, the American-owned airfield at Tangmere had a grass airfield, seven Belfast Truss hangars and one large Handley Page shed.

4: AIRFIELD GUARDROOM

Two views of the former guardhouse for the USAAS airfield at Rustington, which can still be seen today at the north end of Sea Avenue. This provides an example of what was, or would have been, constructed at Tangmere. (*Historic Military Press*)

5: An Early Tangmere Pilot's Memoir

'A Yankee Ace in the RAF'

One of the many Americans who flew from Tangmere at the end of the First World War was Bogart Rogers – though he did so as a member of the RAF and not whilst serving in a US unit.

Bogart Rogers was born in Los Angeles, California. After he and four friends travelled to Canada to train as pilots, Rogers enlisted in the Royal Flying Corps in the spring of 1917. With his initial training complete, he was posted from

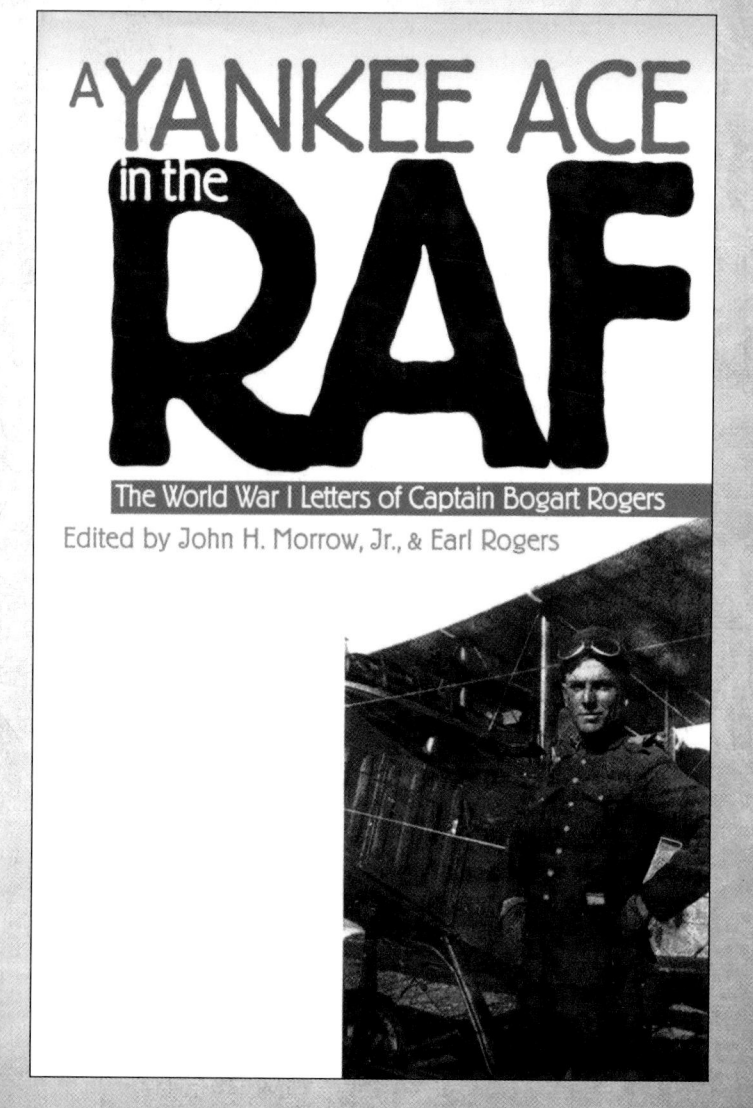

The front cover of the book containing the collected letters of Captain Bogart Rogers DFC.

Chattis Hill on Salisbury Plain to Tangmere in March 1918.

Rogers was prodigious letter writer, and it this correspondence that formed the basis of the 1996 book *A Yankee Ace in the RAF*. A number of the letters provide an insight into his time at Tangmere, though on 16 March 1918, for example, he revealed that he was not entirely enthusiastic about his move to Sussex: 'From all reports Tangmere – the new camp – is nothing to look forwards too.'

Rogers arrived at Tangmere at some point in the next four days, for in a letter dated 20 March he provided a brief description of the embryonic aerodrome: 'We've been working all morning putting up hangars as the camp is only about half finished. The hangars come with a pile of girders, several rolls of canvas, and a box of bolts and metal fittings. Getting them together is like working out a jig-saw puzzle. However, when they are up, they make fine large sheds.

'We have a fine large mess hall with lounging rooms and electric lights and our quarters are not all that bad. But both are only half finished, and the plaster is still damp. The aerodrome is large and level as a tennis court and covered with turf like any front lawn ... Tangmere is merely a hamlet situated back of the camp.'[6]

Whilst at Tangmere, Rogers' daily training routine included 'three or four hours of flying from 06.30 to 13.00 three days a week, and from 12.00 until dark on the other three days'.[7] However, this final part of his flying training paid off, and by 28 March 1918, he had become a graduated service pilot: 'Yesterday afternoon, by the grace of God and the skin of my teeth, I became a graduated service pilot by the simple process of flying a real service scout [S.E.5a] around the place, taking it off, riding it around and landing it without busting any of the essential portions.'

A photograph of Captain Bogart Rogers taken at Serny, France, in March 1919, the backdrop provided by his 32 Squadron S.E.5a.

In May 1918, by which time the RFC had become the Royal Air Force, Rogers was posted to 32 Squadron in France. Promoted to Captain on 4 November 1918, by the end of the war he had attained the status of 'Ace', being credited with six 'kills'. For actions, he was awarded the Distinguished Flying Cross.

Rogers remained in the RAF until May 1919, at which point he returned to the United States to begin a career in the film industry.

6: War Graves in Oving Churchyard

Early Tangmere Aircrew Casualties

As we have already seen, though the aerodrome at Tangmere was being built for, and funded by, the United States, the majority of the early pilots and aircraft that flew from it were from the RFC and, in due course, the RAF. As Reginald Byron and David Coxon discovered in their research, some of the first evidence of an operational unit's presence at Tangmere is provided in the form of a letter which, dated 24 March 1918, was sent by a Captain A. Broomer to, once again, the Duke of Richmond's land agent.

Giving his address as 'Tangmere Station, Royal Flying Corps', Broomer was the Adjutant of 92 Squadron. Formed at London Colney on 1 September 1917, working up as a scout squadron with Sopwith Pups, Spads, and SE.5as, the squadron moved to Tangmere Aerodrome in March 1918. As well as providing some of the first airmen to fly from Tangmere, 92 Squadron, however, also has the distinction of suffering some of the earliest aircrew casualties during flights from the airfield.

The last resting place of two early RAF casualties. The standard Commonwealth War Graves Commission headstone on the left is the grave of Second Lieutenant Craigie, while the private grave marker to the right is that of Captain England. (*Historic Military Press*)

It was only six days after the formation of the RAF when tragedy struck 92 Squadron in the form of a deadly flying accident over the airfield. Such events were sadly uncommon; out of a total of 14,166 RFC/RAF casualties in the First World War, 8,000 were the result of training flights or other similar accidents.[8]

The full story of what happened on 7 April 1918, was revealed at the subsequent inquest, which duly reported on by the *Chichester Observer* in its edition of 10 April: 'Two flying machines came into collision in the air near Chichester on Sunday, resulting in the death of three officers of the Royal Air Service – 2nd Lieutenant Norman Herbert England, age 31, Clifford Hackman, 20, and Victor Raleigh Craigie, 26. The story of the accident was told to the Chichester Coroner, Mr. J.W. Loader Cooper, and a jury at the Chichester Barracks on Monday afternoon.

'Captain Arthur Coningham, Royal Air Force, said all three officers were stationed at —. England was an instructor and a skilled flyer, and Hackman was up with him receiving instruction. They left the ground in a two-seater training machine at 12.55 p.m. Craigie had left five minutes earlier in a scout – a single-seater – it being his first trip in a scout machine.

'At 1.15 England's machine was planing in for landing and was about 300 feet above the edge of the aerodrome, when the scout came in at right angles from the right hand side, and his left wing tips almost knocked off the tail of England's machine. The two-seater at once spun round, followed about 200 feet away by the scout, and came to the ground.

'Witness [Coningham] did not actually see the collision, nor the fall. The whole explanation to his mind was that the man in the scout was watching his instruments instead of looking about him, which was one of the things they had to guard against. The scout could not see much above him and the two-seater flew down in front of him. He had seen Huns do the same thing in a scrap. There was no-one to blame at all; it was a chance they all took. He did not think the scout machine was going to land at the time.

'John Oliver, foreman to Mr. Bowley, Oar Farm, and living at Aldingbourne, said at 1.15 he was having dinner when he heard two crashes. On going out he saw one machine about 100 yards from his house, with a man on the ground. He moaned as he turned him over, and then he saw that he was dead. That was the double-seater machine, and on looking round he found another man with his head downwards. He thought at the time he was dead too.

'About fifty yards away there was the scout machine, and on going to that he found Lieutenant Craigie, with his head downwards and doubled up. He was quite dead.

'An ambulance arrived from the aerodrome about four minutes after the accident, a doctor coming at the same time. Dr. F.L. Dickson, Medical Officer at — Aerodrome, said the ambulance was always ready from sunrise to dusk. He was just beginning lunch when he was told there had been a crash and he went at once. He met the ambulance bringing Lieutenant England, who was alive but unconscious; he had fractured the base of his skull. Lieutenant Hackman was dead, having broken his neck. Lieutenant Craigle was entangled in the machine and they had to cut part of the machine to get him free. He was dead, the cause of death being a fractured skull.

'Lieutenant England was sent to Graylingwell War Hospital, but died on the way. Acting-Corporal Archibald Roberts R.A.M.C., stationed at —, spoke to accompanying Lieutenant England to Graylingwell. He died a few minutes before reaching the hospital. The jury returned verdicts of Accidental death".'

Both Captain England, who had been in an Avro 504, serial number B986, and Second Lieutenant Craigie, flying Sopwith Pup B5269, were buried in the graveyard extension of St Andrew's Church, Church Lane, Oving. Craigie was an American who hailed from Boston, Massachusetts. The third casualty, Second Lieutenant Hackman, was buried in Winchcombe (Greet Road) Cemetery, Gloucestershire.

7: Slindon Sopwith Crash

Another of Tangmere's Early Casualties

In a quiet corner of Chichester Cemetery is the last resting place of 25-year-old Lieutenant Alfred Theodore Wyman, an American who, buried thousands of miles from home, was another of Tangmere's early aircrew casualties.

Born in Fitchburg, Massachusetts, on 23 December 1892, Wyman was a university graduate who had travelled extensively in France and Italy during 1913, before returning to the United States to begin his career as an architect. During the First World War, he journeyed to Britain and volunteered for the RFC. In due course he was posted to 91 Squadron, which, at the time, was based at Tangmere Aerodrome alongside 92 Squadron.

It was on the afternoon of 27 May 1918, that Wyman undertook his final, fateful flight. At the controls of what was described as a 'Sopwith Scout', he took off from Tangmere and headed west, climbing up towards Slindon and the RFC balloon station located there. A witness on the ground, a Mrs Aylwin of Courthill Farm, Slindon, subsequently recalled how 'she heard an aeroplane flying rather low and making more noise than usual. After coming up south-west against the wind it turned east; then it turned on its side and commenced to fall. When about 100 yards up, it nose dived to the ground. When she arrived on the scene the pilot was being taken from the machine.'[9]

Still alive, Wyman was rushed to hospital in Chichester. One of those who treated him there was Major Pearson RAMC, who noted that when the 'deceased was admitted he was suffering from multiple injuries to the face and head, fractures to limbs and extensive fracturing of the skull. He was unconscious and died two hours later from shock and laceration of the brain.'

Speaking at the subsequent inquest into Wyman's death, Flight Sergeant Matthew Tomalin advanced the theory that Wyman, 'in turning at a low speed … side slipped and got into a nose dive too near the ground to get out'.

Answering questions raised by the Coroner, Major Strugnell RAF explained how he had 'examined the machine after the accident, and the cause was certainly not due to a defect in the machine. He (witness) had flown in it from Bournemouth the previous day and it was perfectly all right. The deceased was a very good flier for a pupil. He had done 60 hours' flying, including 3½ hours in a similar type of machine.' Wyman was buried in Chichester Cemetery on 31 May 1918.

It might never be possible to establish beyond doubt the identity of the first aviator killed while flying from Tangmere. Research by the authors, however, suggests that this could in fact be Captain Maurice D.G. Scott MC. A veteran RFC pilot with twelve official victories, Scott was killed on 17 March 1918: 'On Saturday afternoon he left Tangmere Aerodrome near Chichester, to visit some brother officers at Shoreham Aerodrome, Brighton. On arriving he went up some 900 feet and looped the loop. Then the machine got into a spin, and it was thought Captain Scott misjudged the exact moment when he reached the safety height for he failed to recover himself, and the machine crashed to the ground and was wrecked. Captain Scott was conveyed to a military hospital at Brighton, and died within a few hours, never recovering consciousness.'[10]

7: SLINDON SOPWITH CRASH

Courthill farmhouse at Slindon, from where Mrs Aylwin witnessed Lieutenant Wyman's fatal crash on 27 May 1918. (*Mark Hillier Collection*)

8: Government Surplus Advert

The Bentley Connection, September 1919

A short distance from Tangmere is the former Battle of Britain fighter station of RAF Westhampnett. It is located in Goodwood, a community that enjoys an important and lasting relationship with Rolls-Royce, the latter having opened an award-wining manufacturing facility in the village on 1 January 2003. Less well known is the fact that Tangmere also has a link with a major British marque – albeit one that was not so enduring.

Before the outbreak of war in 1914, Walter Owen Bentley and his brother Horace Milner Bentley owned a business in Cricklewood, North London, selling French-made motor vehicles. W.O., as Walter was generally known, had long harboured a desire to design and build his own car. With his plans interrupted by the Great War, it was not until after the Armistice that the brothers, together with a group that included Frank Burgess (formerly of Humber) and Harry Varley (formerly of Vauxhall), set about designing a high-quality sporting tourer for production under the name Bentley. In August 1919 W.O. finally registered Bentley Motors Ltd., and a few weeks later the brothers exhibited their first prototype at the London Motor Show.

As the design of the first ever Bentley was coming to fruition, so the hunt for a site for a factory grew in urgency. As the search increasingly consumed more of H.M.'s time, he turned to a friend, A.F.C. Hillstead, for assistance. 'A thorough search was now being made for suitable premises already in existence, and, somehow, I became involved,' Hillstead later wrote.[11]

It was about this time that Tangmere Aerodrome, all 198½ acres of it,[12] was one of eight airfields being advertised for sale by

MINISTRY OF MUNITIONS.
By Direction of the Disposal Board.

Tangmere Aerodrome Sussex.

Area : about 198½ acres.

For disposal as an Aerodrome.

Accommodation for 3 squadrons.

Buildings are mainly of brick.

Water Supply, Electric Light Plant and Sewage Disposal. Macadam Roads.

Decauville Railway from Drayton Station (1½ miles).

The site is occupied by the Government under the Defence of the Realm regulations, and can (if necessary) be purchased under and subject to the provisions of the Defence of the Realm (Acquisition of Lands) Act 1916.

For full particulars apply to the

Disposal Board, Room 135, Charing Cross Buildings, Villiers St., London, W.C.2.

Note :—For "SURPLUS" the detailed list of surplus Government property for sale, apply at the nearest bookstall or to a local newsagent (to whom a standing order should be given). Compiled by the Director of Publicity, Ministry of Munitions, Whitehall Place, London, S.W.1. Price **3d.**

An advert that appeared in the edition of *Flight* magazine dated 4 September 1919, announcing the sale of Tangmere Aerodrome. (*Historic Military Press*)

8: GOVERNMENT SURPLUS ADVERT

A photograph of the interior of the Handley Page shed at Tangmere taken during Hillstead's and H.M.'s tour of Tangmere.

the Ministry of Munitions, which, in turn, was operating under the direction of the Disposal Board, presumably on behalf of the US Government. These airfields, which also included nearby Ford, were listed in whole page adverts that, entitled 'Government Surplus', appeared in newspapers throughout the UK in September 1919. It may have been these notices that brought Tangmere to the attention of the Bentley brothers.

'The original plan had been to build the car in the country away from the manufacturing centres,' continued Hillstead, 'and, as H.M. had heard from the Air Ministry that Tangmere Aerodrome in Sussex was for sale, one fine morning we both set off to see what it was like. To say that we were impressed would be to describe our feelings mildly – we were staggered. One of the Handley Page sheds alone would have given us most of the space required, but no piecemeal sale would be considered; it was the whole aerodrome or nothing.

'I think it would have taken the best part of a day to make a complete tour of the entire estate; it was a small town complete with power station, several miles of railway, four canteens, innumerable lesser buildings, and enough open ground to provide a testing circuit that would have rivalled Brooklands. "It's rather large," I remarked, wishing that I had brought a pair of binoculars. "Rather more than we require," H.M. replied. "But we might be able to dispose of some of the surplus buildings."

'I took a few photographs, including the interior of one of the Handley Page sheds, and we returned to London to report to W.O.

'I think we were all a little mad at the time, for incredible as it now seems, not only did we make an offer for the entire aerodrome, but it was accepted, and solicitors were instructed to prepare the necessary contract. And so, for a day or two we were quite pleased with ourselves. The works problem appeared to have been solved, and everything was set for production to go ahead as soon as the car had passed its final tests, and machinery had been installed.

'Then, very slowly, our pleasure began to evaporate. At odd moments H.M. and I would say to one another, "Do you realize we have bought Tangmere Aerodrome?" … And in the cold light of reason it became all too apparent that, instead of providing the company with a works, we had involved it in a liability of gigantic proportions. Where was labour coming from? What arrangements could we make for its housing? How would the womenfolk do their shopping, and what facilities were there for recreation? As for electrical energy, admittedly the power station was most impressive, but how did we know it was in running order, and what would be the cost of maintenance?'

Having reconsidered their plans to purchase Tangmere airfield, the Bentley brothers decided to extract themselves from the deal. 'We were lucky to get out of it with only trifling legal costs,' concluded Hillstead, 'but most unlucky in so far as we were back exactly where we started'. By the spring of 1920, however, work had started on the construction of a factory in Oxgate Lane, Cricklewood.

An aerial view of the airfield buildings, including hangars and the Handley Page shed (in the foreground), at Tangmere circa 1930. (*Historic Military Press*)

Section Two

A Legend Is Created

9: Land Acquisition Maps

Tangmere is Purchased by the Crown

With Bentley's purchase of the Tangmere site having fallen through, and no other suitable purchaser having completed a deal, Tangmere Aerodrome remained in US Government ownership until 1923.

When the responsibility of Britain's air defence was switched from the War Department to the Air Ministry in the early 1920s, it led to a re-assessment of the facilities available, with the result that an expansion plan was agreed.[13] Tangmere, with its strategic position on the South Coast and relatively complete facilities, became one of the first beneficiaries of the new scheme. Negotiations promptly began with the American government to agree the terms of a purchase.

On 9 July 1923, Captain M.C. Elwell wrote to the Assistant Military Attaché at the American Embassy in London to confirm the price that had been agreed for Tangmere Aerodrome: 'I have received an offer from the Air Ministry to purchase the Land and Buildings with landlord's fixtures, together with Plant and Machinery for the sum of £18,000 … It was understood after explanation that this offer was acceptable to you and it would be convenient if your written acceptance could be received early please.'[14]

Elwell, however, was not finished. He went on to point out that 'since our interview I am informed that a commission of 5% is payable to the Disposal Commission in respect of negotiating the sale on the same basis as a charge is made to British Government Departments for disposing of their properties.'

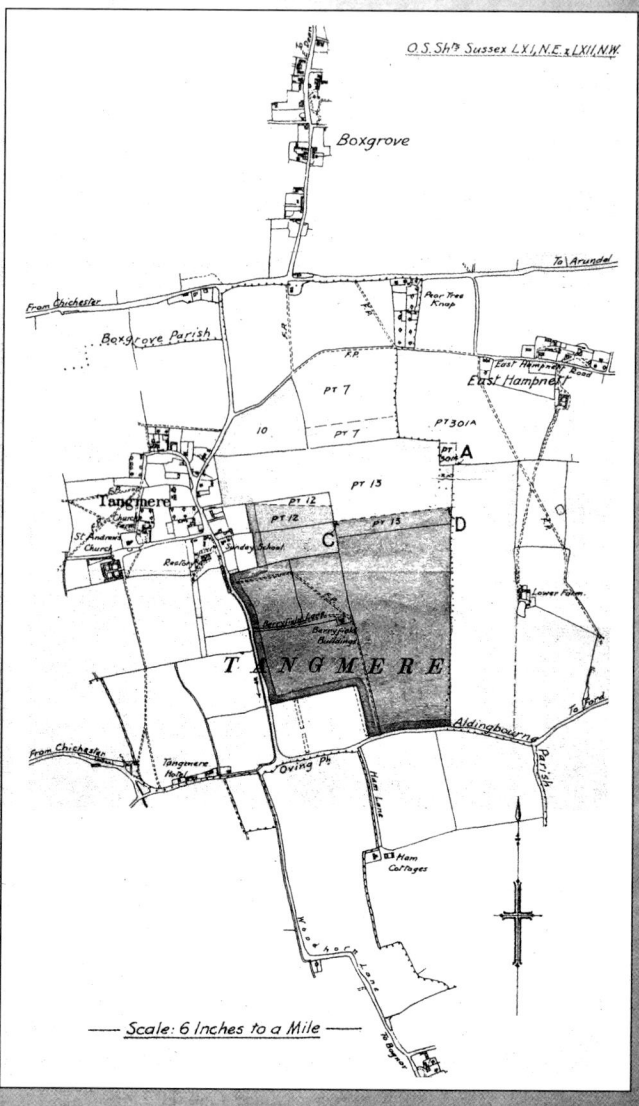

A map showing some of the land purchased from the Duke of Richmond in 1923. (*Tangmere Military Aviation Museum*)

9: LAND ACQUISITION MAPS

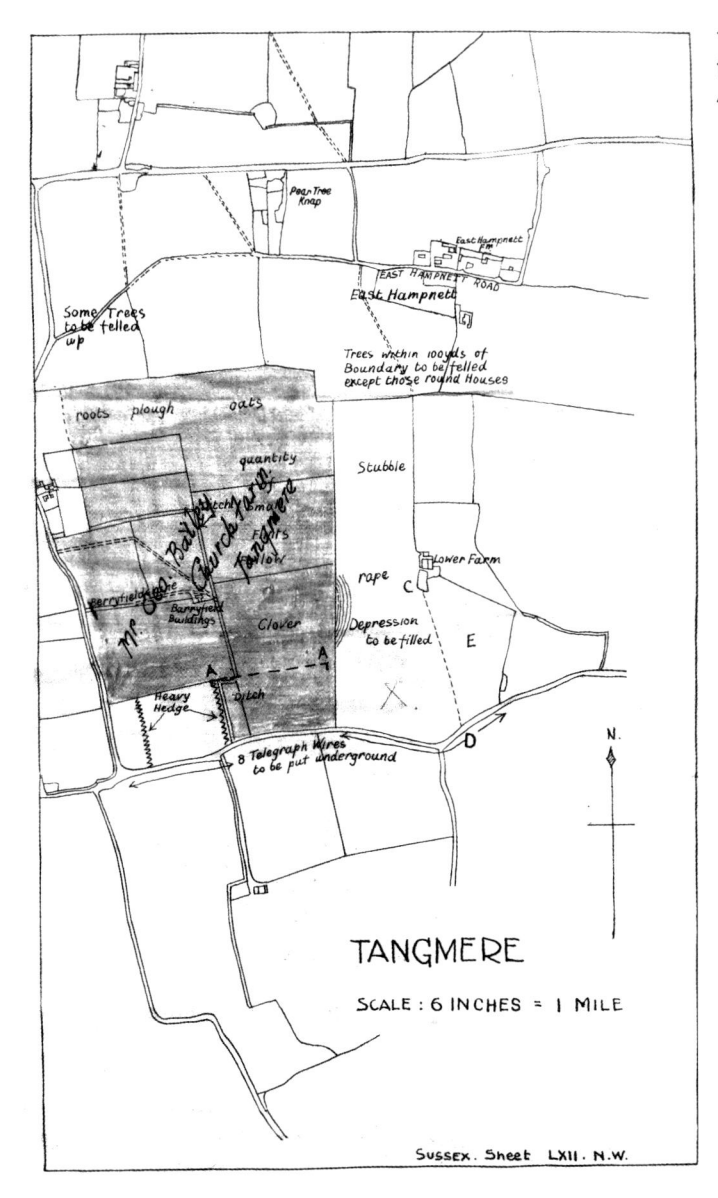

This map shows the land at Church Farm that formed part of the purchase. (*Tangmere Military Aviation Museum*)

One can only imagine what the American response to this offer, and the news of the additional fee, might have been – only a few years earlier they had paid the British Government a total of £256,000 to construct and equip the airfield.

As well as the American-owned land, the British Government sought to purchase the 130¼ acres that had been requisitioned under the Defence of the Realm Regulations (1914), much of which had already been returned to its original agricultural use – it is some of this land that is featured in the maps seen here. Eventually the land was sold by the Duke of Richmond to the Crown for the sum of £7,616 and the tenant farmers compensated for their losses.

With these purchases complete by the end of 1923, work could begin in earnest on turning RAF Station Tangmere in a front line fighter station.

10: Date Stone from Building No.25

Tangmere's Expansion Begins

Work on the development of Tangmere as a front line fighter station for the RAF began almost as soon as the airfield's purchase had been completed in 1923. As already noted, this was part of a national programme of revitalising Britain's aerial defence.

'This expansion of the RAF planned for 1923–4,' notes the author Paul Francis, 'involved designing a completely new range of permanent buildings for the modernization of existing stations … The Lords Commissioners of the Treasury of the New Labour Government allowed £3 million for eight new Home Defence squadrons and granted limited funds for the remodelling of [various airfields].'[15] One the locations listed was Tangmere.'

The redevelopment process at Tangmere was accelerated by the acquisition of further land to the north of the airfield. The various buildings constructed during the 1920s, a time that is often described as Tangmere's 'expansion period', included officer's accommodation, several barrack blocks, various administration buildings, and the Navy, Army and Air Force Institute, or NAAFI – all of which were collectively known as the 'domestic site'.

On display at Tangmere today is the date stone from one of the many buildings constructed during this period. It is stated that the stone was saved from Building No.25 at the time of its demolition. This building, according to a site plan of the airfield dated 1 February 1935, was a Barrack Block Type 'E'. These accommodation blocks were designed to accommodate eighty airmen and three NCOs. At the time the site plan was completed – as can be seen on our section of it – Tangmere had two Type 'E' barrack blocks, and a further two of the Type 'D' design. One of the latter is marked on the map has having been allocated to 'airmen pilots'.

Another building that can be seen on the map, to the left of the arrow and, at the top of the parade square and listed as No.18 (or 'K'), is the former airmen's institute or NAAFI. As can be seen in item 98, this structure, located off Jerrard Road, has survived and is now a Grade II listed building. Its Historic England record states that it was 'constructed of red brick with tiled roofs': 'In plan it resembles a Palladian villa. It has a 5-bay centrepiece of two storeys flanked by projecting single storeyed pavilion wings. This is the remaining administrative building of the former RAF station.' Following Tangmere's closure in 1970, the NAAFI became the 'Spitfire Club'. It was often used for squadron reunions, serving drinks at a bar not unlike a RAFA club or British Legion. It has since been converted into flats, with part of the old parade ground being used as a car park.

The date stone that was salvaged from Building No.25. (*Tangmere Military Aviation Museum*)

10: DATE STONE FROM BUILDING NO.25

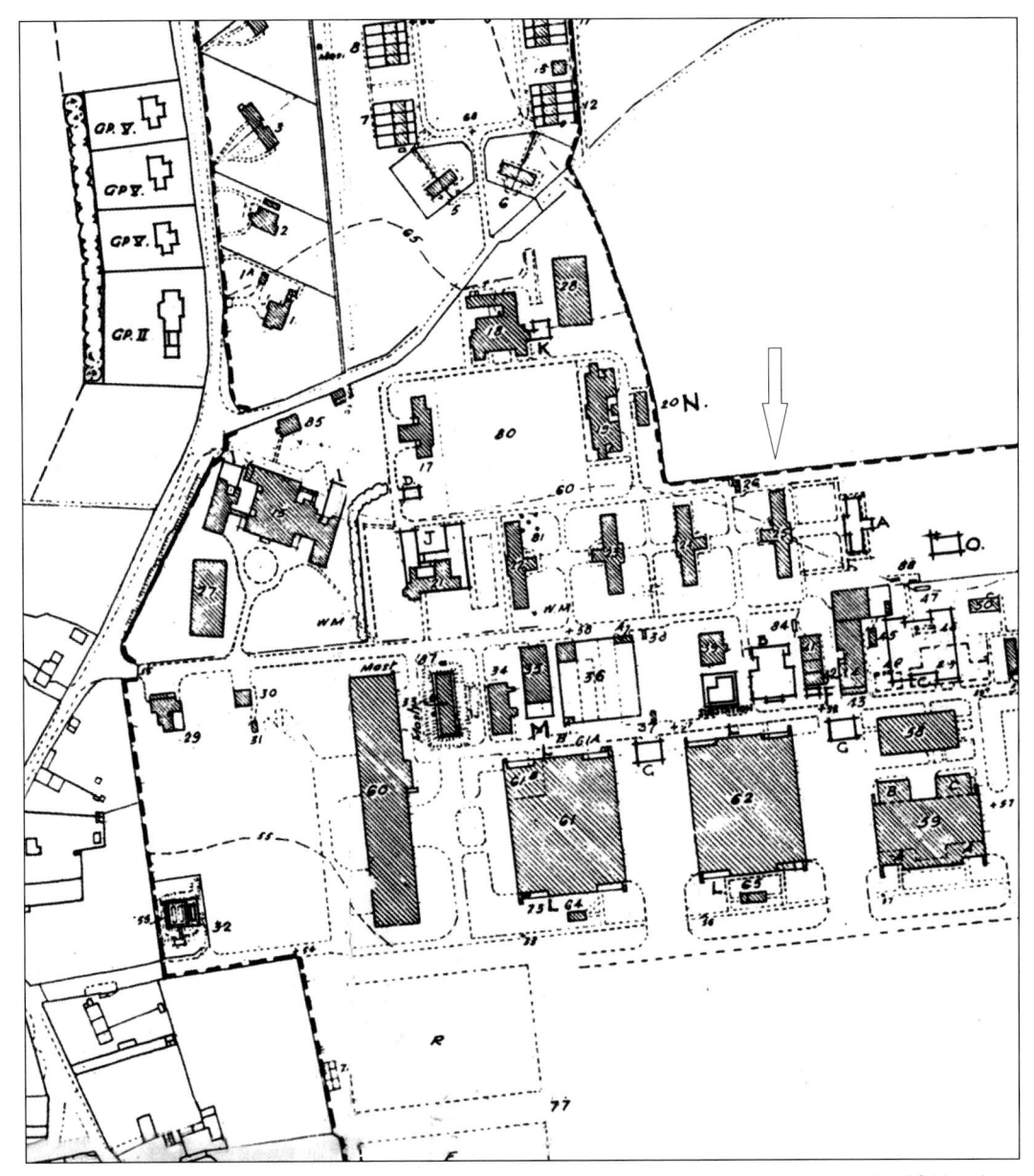

A section from a 1935-dated map of RAF Tangmere, with Building No.25 indicated by the arrow. The main entrance to the airfield can be seen on the far left, with the guardhouse listed as Building No.29. (Historic Military Press)

11: Gloster Gamecock Replica

First Fighters Arrive at RAF Tangmere

On 1 June 1925, Tangmere officially reopened as an RAF airfield, though for the next few months it served no role other than being used for aircraft storage. The next step towards operational service came on 23 November 1926, when the first entry was made in Tangmere's station log, declaring it to be an Air Defence Great Britain station and noting the arrival of its new station commander, Wing Commander John Tyssen MC.[16]

Within weeks RAF Tangmere's first fighter squadron moved in. 'In February 1927,' writes Jimmy Beadle, '43 Squadron moved from Henlow to Tangmere in Sussex. Here it was joined soon afterwards by No 1 Squadron, lately stationed in Iraq, and so began a period of intense but friendly rivalry that lasted for more than thirteen years. Tangmere had been used during the latter part of the war but it was 43 who became its first peacetime permanent inhabitants. Before long the camp had a reputation as a highly desirable posting and its "summer routine", which from May to August compressed the working day into an extended morning session and so allowed every afternoon free, was a perk not available on any other Home Station."[17]

Commanded by Squadron Leader Arthur 'Pongo' Brooke, an Ulsterman and RFC veteran, 43 Squadron's three flights were equipped with the Gloster Gamecock. In July 1924, Gloucestershire Aircraft, which later became the Gloster Aircraft Company, began work on the Gamecock, a biplane fitted with the newly developed and relatively light and simple Bristol Jupiter IV radial engine. The first prototype was delivered to Martlesham Heath on 20 February

The replica of 43 Squadron's Gamecock J7904 that was flown by Squadron Leader Arthur 'Pongo' Brooke from RAF Tangmere.

11: GLOSTER GAMECOCK REPLICA

1925, and, following successful trials by service pilots, an order was placed in September of that year for thirty machines.

One contemporary account of the Gamecock notes that 'as regards outward appearance, [it is] a fairly normal single-bay biplane, fitted with Bristol "Jupiter" engine. As a matter of fact, the Gamecock is a good deal less orthodox than a casual inspection would indicate, partly aerodynamically, and also in the matter of constructional details.'[18]

Other than 43 Squadron, just five other RAF squadrons were equipped with the Gamecock. It had a fairly short service life, with 23 Squadron being the last operational unit to relinquish its machines in July 1931. No complete example of the type has survived, though two fuselage sections are reported to exist in Finland. The aircraft seen here is a replica that is on display in the Jet Age Museum in Gloucestershire. Carrying 43 Squadron's distinctive black and white chequerboard pattern down the fuselage, the serial number J7904 indicates that it represents the aircraft flown by Squadron Leader Brooke during his time at Tangmere.

An early aviator at Tangmere, in this case a member of 604 (County of Middlesex) Squadron pictured at a summer camp at the Sussex airfield between the wars. (*Historic Military Press*)

12: Training for Hendon Air Pageant

The Importance of Aerobatics

'Some hold that formation flying is unnecessary, serves no useful purpose in war, is merely a trick. In fact formation flying is an outward and visible sign of the inward and invisible grace of a squadron. It is like march-discipline in the Army and sloppy formation in the air is first hand evidence that the CO is unfit for his job, or at any rate has just taken over from one that was.'[19] These are the words of C.G. Grey, a renowned aviation author and one-time editor of *The Aeroplane*, who clearly held the view that the prowess of a squadron in its display formations was a mark of its teamwork and discipline.

Armstrong Whitworth Siskins of 43 Squadron practising for the Hendon Air Pageant. (*Tangmere Military Aviation Museum*)

Since their arrival at Tangmere, Nos. 1 and 43 squadrons took this advice to heart – no doubt inspired by their attendance at displays such as the world-famous Hendon Air Pageant. For its part, 43 Squadron first made an appearance at Hendon in 1926, just before it moved to Tangmere. It did so again in 1927, with the result that formation flying and aerobatics became a regular sight in the blue skies over the South Coast.

Air Marshal Sir Anthony Dunkerton 'Mark' Selway, KCB, DFC was one of those pilots who wrote about the 1930s at Tangmere; he joined 'A' Flight of No.1 Squadron in September 1929. At the time the squadron was equipped with Armstrong Whitworth Siskin biplane fighters and commanded by a distinguished First World War veteran, Squadron Leader Eustace Grenfell.

'The spring of 1932 was typical of life on the station in the early 1930s,' Selway recalled. 'Both Tangmere squadrons would be seen working up for the annual Hendon Air Pageant. The RAFs shop window to the British public. No.43 would be found practicing their "roped show" (three squadron Furies performing an air display tied together), and No.1 would be seen practicing combined aerobatics with three Furies.'[20]

During the summer months for the next few years, Tangmere's squadrons were kept busy competing at, or participating in, annual air pageants, air defence exercises and gunnery camps, winning many awards along the way. Tangmere was certainly the posting for honing ones' skill, a sentiment that was echoed by a correspondent from *Flight* magazine who was present at the Hendon Air Pageant in the summer of 1932. Having witnessed the precision of 43 Squadron with its 'tied together' aerobatics, as well as a synchronised display by a pair of No.1 Squadron Furies, he noted: 'In vain did we seek for any sort of flaw in the combined aerobatics by a flight of three Furies of No 1 Squadron. No 1 has not had Furies long, but there seems to be something in the air of Tangmere which makes for a very high class flying'.[21]

13: Royal Visit Press Photo

The Prince of Wales Lands at Tangmere

In its fifty-or so years of operational flying, the RAF Station at Tangmere would experience a number of visits by various members of the Royal Family. One of the earliest of these, involving the Prince of Wales (the future King Edward VIII), occurred on Friday, 26 April 1929 – an event captured in the press photograph seen here.

This flight, however, was not the Prince's first visit to the Sussex airfield, as *The Scotsman* of Thursday, 4 April 1929, pointed out: 'The Prince of Wales flew to Bognor yesterday [3 April] in a Royal Air Force two-seater aeroplane. He left one of the R.A.F. service aerodromes in the neighbourhood of London, not Croydon, and flew to Tangmere Aerodrome, which is about five miles from Craigwell House.[22] The journey occupied just over half an hour, and he landed at ten minutes past noon. Three planes from Tangmere went up to greet the Prince.'

Such was the interest in the Royal flight, *The Scotsman* also detailed the return flight: 'The Prince arrived back at Northolt Aerodrome, Middlesex, shortly before six o'clock last night, the sixty miles from Tangmere Aerodrome, near Bognor, having taken about thirty minutes. The outward journey was accomplished in twenty-two minutes, representing a speed of nearly 180 miles an hour.

'He motored from Craigwell House to the aerodrome in one of the Royal cars, accompanied by Sir Bryan Godfrey Faussett, who saw him off. As soon as the car came into sight, the engines of the RAF Westland Wapiti machine, which had brought him to Bognor, were started, and the Prince's pilot, Flight-Lieutenant Don, climbed into his seat.

'The Prince was wearing a thick fawn coat and a cap, which he exchanged for a brown leather flying helmet. A parachute was strapped on to his back, and he clambered into the rear seat. As the machine rose in the air the Prince leaned over the side and waved his hand in response to the cheering crowd. When the machine was sighted at Northolt, another aeroplane went up to act as escort. The sky was overcast, and a gusty wind did not conduce to a perfect landing, but the pilot landed smoothly and taxied to the sheds, where the prince was met by officers of the aerodrome. After spending a few minutes chatting in the officers' mess, the Prince, still in his flying kit, drove to London.'

It was reported that the flight to Tangmere on 26 April 1929, was also made in a Westland Wapiti with the same pilot, though on this occasion his rank was given as Squadron Leader. The Prince of Wales had taken off from Hendon, to where he also returned.

13: ROYAL VISIT PRESS PHOTO

The Prince of Wales waves to those on the ground as Squadron Leader Don takes off from Tangmere, in a Westland Wapiti, on 26 April 1929. (*Historic Military Press*)

14: Hawker Fury Mk.I K5674

An Early Tangmere Aircraft

Operated by the Historic Aircraft Collection, Hawker Fury Mk.I K5674 is a remarkable survivor of the inter-war period at RAF Tangmere, having been delivered to there, and 43 Squadron in particular, on 2 June 1936.

The Historic Aircraft Collection's own account takes up the story: 'F/O FE Rosier, later to become Air Chief Marshal Sir Frederick Rosier GCB, CBE, DSO, recorded in his log book that the aircraft was his aircraft whilst he was OC "B" Flight between December 1936 and January 1939. It was called *Queen of North and South*. We are lucky to have F/O FE Rosier's log book which records that he first flew her on 7 December 1936.'[23]

Whilst Sir Frederick's first flight in K5674 took place in December, his first in a Fury from Tangmere took place on 13 May 1936. Of his posting to this airfield, he would later write: 'Tangmere is situated three miles from Chichester, close to the south coast, and importantly south of the Downs. As a result it has one of the best weather factors in the country

The Historic Aircraft Collection's stunning Hawker Fury Mk.I, K5674 – one of the earliest aircraft to fly from RAF Tangmere that is still airworthy – landing, not at Tangmere but nearby at Goodwood. (*Tangmere Military Aviation Museum*)

14: HAWKER FURY MK.I K5674

A photograph of a 1 Squadron Hawker Fury, K2899, at Tangmere in 1937. (*Tangmere Military Aviation Museum*)

… I spent the next three years at what was affectionately known as 'Tanglebury' with what was without doubt one of the finest squadrons in the RAF.'[24]

In his memoir, Sir Frederick also reveals some detail on what life was like at Tangmere: 'A little bit about the daily routine: the batman I shared with another officer would awaken me with a cup of tea at 7.00 a.m., the curtains would be drawn, the bath filled, my clothes for the day laid out, and my shoes polished. After breakfast I would go down to the flight office and we would then fly two or three times a day. The summer routine was to rise at 6.00 a.m. and to work until 1.00 p.m., leaving the afternoon free for sports and sailing at West Wittering and Itchenor.'

The Historic Aircraft Collection's account details more of Sir Frederick's links to K5674: 'His last flight was on 21 February 1939 when the comment in his log was "Last fling in Queen of North and South. Perfect". Between those dates his log book records that he flew her on 394 separate sorties spread over 217 days and accumulating 293:35 hours. On 29 March 1937 he recorded reaching a height of 29,000ft! On 9 April 1937 he records visiting Duxford; he also displayed her at the Empire Air Display at Hendon in both 1937 and 1938.'

Interesting, after the Historic Aircraft Collection's stunning restoration of K5674, its first flight was made from Goodwood – 'as close as we could get to Tangmere' – on 30 July 2012.

15: Empire Air Day Programme 1938

Show-casing RAF Tangmere

First held on 24 May 1934, the Empire Air Day, in which K5674 participated, became an annual air show held at various RAF stations throughout the UK. Organized by the Air League of the British Empire and the RAF, the event was intended to allow the public to see the nation's air force in action and to encourage interest in flying. This was confirmed by Lieutenant Colonel Anthony Muirhead who, in his post as Under-Secretary of State for Air, stated the following in the House of Commons: 'The idea of Empire Air Day is that the public should be enabled to see the Royal Air Force at its everyday work. As many stations as possible ... are opened to the public on payment of a small charge for admission. At each station a programme of flying is arranged.'

Needless to say, Tangmere was among the RAF stations that participated in the Empire Air Days from the very beginning, one of forty airfields opened to the public in the first year. The programme seen here was from the 1938 event, which took place on 28 May. Despite somewhat poor weather, the event was undoubtedly a success, as the following account, published in the *Chichester Observer*, reveals:

'A crowd numbering several thousands watch[ed] a programme of aeronautics which eclipsed even the excellence of the dress rehearsal seen the previous Thursday. Thrills came fast

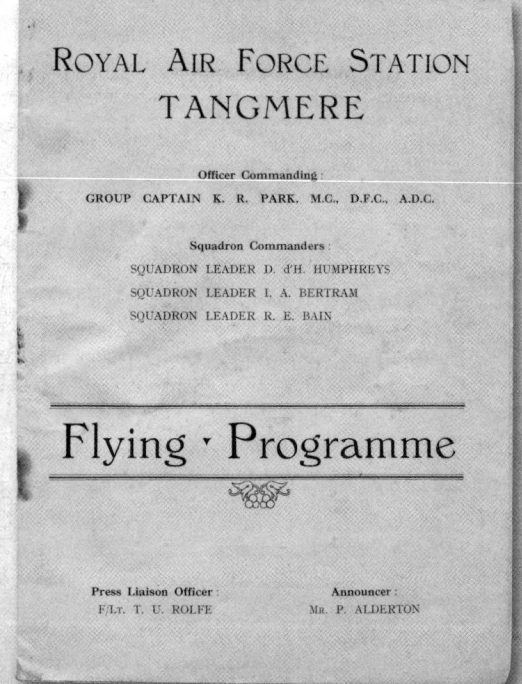

The programme for Tangmere's Empire Air Day held on 28 May 1938. (*Historic Military Press*)

and furious and motorists on the nearby main roads stopped their cars to watch the display. An impressive opening to the spectacle was provided by 18 Furies and nine Ansons which took off in squadron formation to carry out air drill ... After the formations the squadrons broke up, each flight landing independently. Three Furies gave a heart thumping display of aerobatics while a quick get-away and interception and attack by a flight of fighters on a formation of bombers followed. Other items included individual aerobatics by Flying Officer A.C. Douglas; air drill by nine Furies of No.43 Squadron; a demonstration of quick re-fuelling and re-arming; message picking-up and supply dropping by parachute, as carried out by Army cooperation aircraft for communicating with troops when other means of communication are not available; the protection of seaborne trade by nine Ansons of No.217 Squadron; interception of a bomb raid of three bombers by a flight of fighters; flight air drill; and take-off and fly past by various service type of aircraft.'

A variety of ground exhibits were also laid on by the personnel at Tangmere. These included an 'air raid precautions room equipped for demonstrating the method of guarding private dwellings against gas attacks [which was arranged by West Sussex County Council]; a motor transport section, including tenders, petrol tankers, floats, and fire tenders with a demonstration of the use of flame-proof suits; an armament section including various types of guns and equipment; a photographic section showing an air camera fitted up ready for electrical working; [and] the workshops, containing the parts of a Kestrel engine dismantled and laid out for inspection.'

The last Empire Air Day was held, under the war clouds gathering over Europe, on 20 May 1939. Once again Tangmere was one of the many hosts.

At the same time that the Empire Air Days were taking place, Tangmere was still continuing to expand. Taken by Corporal Robert Pearson, a member of groundcrew in 604 (County of Middlesex) Squadron (see the next item), this photograph shows a new building nearing completion at Tangmere in the summer of 1936. (*Historic Military Press*)

16: 'Tangmere Tonic' Cartoon

Memento of a Squadron's Summer Camp

While 43 Squadron was a long-term resident at Tangmere, being based there from December 1926 right through to November 1939, it was not the only fighter squadron to operate from the airfield. Another that used Tangmere throughout much of the inter-war period was 604 (County of Middlesex) Squadron.

No.604 Squadron was formed at Hendon on 17 March 1930, as a day bomber unit of the Auxiliary Air Force. In 1918, Sir Hugh Trenchard decreed that a Reserve Air Force should be set

The copy of the 'Tangmere Tonic' cartoon that Pearson kept as a reminder of one of his summer camps in West Sussex. (*All Historic Military Press*)

16: 'TANGMERE TONIC' CARTOON

Pearson's squadron badge that used to adorn his groundcrew overalls and which he subsequently stuck inside the front of his photograph album.

up on the lines of Britain's Territorial Army. An order in Council, made in the name of the King, was duly signed on 9 October 1924; it was this that established the Auxiliary Air Force, with the first squadron, 602 (City of Glasgow), being formed the following year. To be eligible to join a squadron an early Auxiliary pilot had to hold a private pilot's licence and, in addition, be prepared to make time from his employment and private life to attend courses and flying training to RAF standards to gain his wings.

On 2 April 1930, 604 Squadron received its first DH9As on 2 April 1930, and flew these until the delivery of Westland Wapitis in September 1930. On 23 July 1934, the squadron was redesignated a fighter unit and received Harts as an interim type, pending the delivery of Demon two-seat fighters which arrived in June 1935.

Usually based at Hendon, it was often the case that each year No.604 would travel down to Tangmere for its summer camp. Among the squadron's personnel that would make that journey was Robert Pearson. A motor mechanic in civilian life, Pearson enlisted in the squadron in April 1932, at the age of 19. At this point he held the rank of Aircraftman 2nd Class. Over the years that followed, he would regularly attend the squadron's summer camp at Tangmere, building up a selection of images in his own photograph album. Promotions also followed, so much so that on 4 August 1938, he attained the rank of Corporal. This he held until his discharge the following year.

Among the many documents that Pearson retained was the copy of 'Tangmere Tonic' seen on the previous page. As the cartoonist noted (he is featured, but unfortunately not named), the summer camp at Tangmere was 'to be taken annually, with a broad mind, a pinch of salt and, when they're closed, a glass of water'.

This photograph from Pearson's album shows the personnel of 'A' Flight at Tangmere in the summer of 1936. Some of the pilots seen here would later serve in the Battle of Britain.

17: Jeffrey Quill's Pilot's Logbook

The First Spitfire at Tangmere

It was in 1936 that Mutt Summers, then the chief test pilot at Vickers, first flew the Supermarine Spitfire. Jeffrey Quill, his assistant, was the second person to fly it.

Quill's first time at the controls of the Spitfire prototype, K5054, came on 26 March 1936. Beforehand Summers briefed him on the points to watch: 'He stressed the need to make a careful approach during the landing. The flaps could be lowered only to 57 degrees on the prototype. With the wooden prop ticking over there was very little drag during the landing approach and she came in very flat. If one approached too fast one could use up all of the airfield in no time at all. Then it was my turn, and off I went. Of course, at that time I had no idea of the eventual significance of the aeroplane. To me it was just the firm's latest product ... I made my first flight, getting the feel of the aircraft, and landed normally.'[25]

Over the days and weeks that followed, Jeffrey flew K5054 many times, getting to know both the aircraft and its designer, R.J. Mitchell, well. One of those susbequent flights, that made on

A full-size replica of the Spitfire prototype K5054 can be seen in Tangmere Military Aviation Museum. In 1983, Quill, decided that R.J. Mitchell's contribution to the development of military aviation had never truly been recognised. Accordingly, a group comprising Quill, Dr Gordon Mitchell (R.J.'s son) and members of the original design team joined forces with the Spitfire Society and decided to sponsor a full-size replica. The result of these endeavours was unveiled at the RAF Museum in May 1993, at which point Quill was able to report that the replica was '99% the original prototype'. This is the replica that can be seen at Tangmere today. (*Tangmere Military Aviation Museum*)

The page in Jeffrey Quill's logbook on which he has recorded his flight in K5054 to RAF Tangmere. (*Tangmere Military Aviation Museum*)

4 December 1936, and which he duly recorded in his logbook, saw a Spitfire land at RAF Tangmere for the very first time.

'In the course of a series of level speed runs up and down the south coast at high altitude over cloud,' he later wrote in his memoirs, 'I got further to the east than I had intended and ran short of fuel so I had to land at Tangmere, which was the home of 1 and 43 Squadrons, equipped with Hawker Furies, a lovely little biplane fighter. I taxied in to the tarmac and shut down the engine and a crowd of pilots and airmen immediately gathered round to examine this strange new beast.

'I took off my helmet and began to shed my Sutton harness and parachute straps when a strange crescendo of sound came from the rear fuselage which considerably startled me – a sort of high-frequency hammering noise, rather as sometimes happens in ancient domestic hot water system. I leant out of the cockpit and looked towards the tail in some alarm and there I saw a crowd of airmen all tapping on the metal fuselage with their knuckles. It was the first time they had ever encountered a metal skinned aeroplane!

'There were a number of convivial souls at Tangmere, such as Prosser Hanks and Fred Rosier and I decided that it would be sensible to stay the night and get a Supermarine ground crew over in the morning to look over the aeroplane which had had a hard day's flying. And so, the Spitfire spent its first ever night on a Royal Air Force Fighter station, and where better than Tangmere.'[26]

18: Air Ministry Fuel Depot, Portfield

Keeping Tangmere's Aircraft Flying

The expansion of the RAF in the 1930s created a huge variety of issues that needed to be dealt with – some obvious, others less so. Undoubtedly falling into the latter category was the question of providing an adequate fuel storage and supply system – and one that could be protected from attack. After all, the RAF could base as many fighters as it wished at aerodromes such as Tangmere, but without suitable supplies of their 'life-blood' – fuel – they would be all but impotent.

The sheer scale of the issue was highlighted by Lord Ailwyn during a debate in the House of Lords on 26 July 1939, albeit that the example he gave related to Bomber Command: 'When one considers, for example, that a modern large high-speed bomber uses approximately a gallon of petrol a mile, which means that one of these aircraft in one journey of 300 miles consumes no less than one ton of fuel; when one considers further that it takes approximately three tons of crude oil to produce that one ton of petrol;

A recent view of the Portfield fuel depot, complete with a railway spur off the mainline and the protected storage tanks. The site was last used by a private company until the late 1990s. (*Historic Military Press*)

when one considers, in short, that a bomber uses a gallon of petrol a mile, more than three gallons per minute, and that one ton of crude oil produces only sufficient petrol for one of these aircraft to go fifty miles and back, it will be seen that we very soon arrive at staggering figures.'

As early as 1937, technical sub-committees of the Oil Board had been investigating the design of storage tanks to be used at fuel depots, as well as exploring the means of combating aerial attack or accidental leaks. No doubt encompassing the conclusions reached, a new fuel depot for RAF Tangmere was constructed on open land adjacent to Bognor Road in Portfield, Chichester, between 1938 and 1939. It was built by Esso as part of an Air Ministry contract.

Consisting of four protected rectangular Whessoe Foundry Company D1 steel tanks, each with a capacity of 500-tons, and two smaller 350-ton Whessoe tanks, the Portfield site was not connected to the national fuel supply grid but was restocked by rail via a dedicated siding off the main line at Chichester. The fuel was transported to Tangmere, and, in due course, airfields such as Westhampnett and Merston, by road.

As the historian D.A. Gregory notes, 'Despite being camouflaged, by 1940 the depot appeared on Luftwaffe target maps and was even mentioned in a broadcast by the infamous 'Lord Haw-Haw', William Joyce, with the chilling words, "We know about the petrol dump in Chichester". Air raids were carried out by German bombers on two separate occasions, but luckily for the people of Chichester the bombs fell wide of their mark.'[27]

It is not clear when the depot was decommissioned, though it is known that it was transferred from Air Ministry control to the Ministry of Power in 1959.

One of the earth-covered fuel tanks at the Portfield site. (*Historic Military Press*)

19: Newspaper Cutting of No.1 Squadron Accident

Tangmere's First Hurricane Loss

Despite the fact that the Prime Minister, Neville Chamberlain, had not long returned from Munich to declare 'peace in our time', the RAF's programme of expansion and modernisation continued apace. As part of this, the Hawker Hurricane, which had first flown in November 1935, continued to rolled out into front line fighter squadrons.

For the pilots of 1 Squadron, the Hurricane's arrival could not come soon enough. 'The day of re-equipment could not be far away,' wrote the squadron historian Michael Shaw, 'and the CO intended to get every last ounce of value out of the Fury before the Hurricane arrived. Practice dog fights with No 43 were all part of the routine, while the Ansons of No 217 Squadron, also at Tangmere, were frequently used as interception targets. Even these relatively slow aircraft emphasised the dated performance of the Fury.

'Then, one day in early November 1938, a hump-backed little fighter burst into the Tangmere circuit accompanied by the unforgettable growl of its Rolls-Royce Merlin. The Hurricane had come to No 1. To the obvious envy of the "Chicken Farmers" the squadron began to receive its new aircraft in twos and threes over the winter. With considerable nostalgia, the Furies were lined up, tail to tail in accordance with tradition, for a final photograph …

'By March 1939 all the pilots of No 1 Squadron had been checked out to fly the Hurricane. To their surprise they found that the new aircraft handled very much like the Fury, for its controls were perfectly balanced in the true Hawker tradition … One newspaper ran a story about the new breed of supermen who were being specially developed by the RAF to fly its new fighters. These pilots, it was claimed, were abstemious of all vices. Their biceps bulged and her hands were gnarled with wrestling with the controls of their Hurricanes. This news was received at Tangmere with the hoots of mirth that it deserved. Abstemious indeed! The publican's and fathers of Sussex had good cause to know otherwise.'[28]

Even before all of its pilots had converted to the Hurricane, 1 Squadron had suffered its initial losses with the type. The first of these occurred on Thursday, 24 November 1938.

That day, one of the squadron's pilots had taken off in Mk.I L1677. The flight was uneventful until the return to the airfield. 'Britain's got the fastest 'planes in the world today …,' reported *The Daily Mirror* the following day, 'but yesterday it went a little too fast. It just couldn't stop in time, went past the aerodrome boundary, through a hedge, across the road, and finished up in a ditch with its tail in the air.'

A report in the *Chichester Observer* the next day later provided a little detail on the aircraft's fate after it had skidded on wet grass: 'A Tangmere pilot had a narrow escape from injury on Thursday, when the Hurricane plane he was flying overshot the aerodrome in landing. The nose of the machine finished up in a ditch in the Tangmere Road, leaving the rest of the fuselage slanting diagonally across the roadway. The machine was subsequently dismantled and returned to the hangars.'

Though it had been recovered from the crash site, L1677 was deemed to have been too badly damaged to repair to full airworthiness. Written off, it was reclassified as an instructional airframe.

19: NEWSPAPER CUTTING OF NO.1 SQUADRON ACCIDENT

Friday, November 25, 1938 — THE DAILY MIRROR

THE 'PLANE THAT WENT TOO FAST

BRITAIN'S GOT THE FASTEST 'PLANES IN THE WORLD TO-DAY. THE ONE IN THE PICTURE, FOR INSTANCE, DOES A NICE 330 M.P.H. WHEN IN FULL FLIGHT. BUT YESTERDAY IT WENT A LITTLE TOO FAST. IT JUST COULDN'T STOP IN TIME, WENT PAST THE AERODROME BOUNDARY, THROUGH A HEDGE, ACROSS THE ROAD, AND FINISHED UP IN A DITCH WITH ITS TAIL IN THE AIR, AS YOU SEE IN THIS PICTURE AT TANGMERE AERODROME (SUSSEX).

P.S.: NOBODY IN IT SUSTAINED EVEN A SCRATCH.

A cutting from *The Daily Mirror* revealing the fate of Hawker Hurricane Mk.I L1677 on 24 November 1938.

Section Three

A Second World War

20: 'Fighter Pilot'

War Comes to Tangmere

Chamberlain's promise of 'peace in our time' was short-lived. For the pilots of Nos. 1, 43, 92, and 605 (County of Warwick) squadrons, all of which were based at Tangmere on 3 September 1939, it appeared that their training was about to be put to the test.

One of the pilots at Tangmere on that fateful Sunday was Flying Officer Paul Richey. Serving with No.1 Squadron, he recalled the atmosphere on the airfield at the time in his memoir, *Fighter Pilot*, which was first published in 1941: 'The standard of flying in 1 Squadron was red hot. Johnny Walker and Prosser Hanks, members of the 1937 aerobatic team, were still with the Squadron … On Sunday morning, 3 September, all our officers gathered in the mess at eleven-fifteen to hear Mr Chamberlain's broadcast to the nation. It was with heavy hearts and grave faces that we heard the sad voice of that man of peace say: "This country is at war with Germany."'

As Richey went on to write, he was one of the first pilots to be scrambled from an RAF fighter station in the Second World War, and almost certainly one of the first from Tangmere: 'No.1 Squadron was called to Readiness at dusk on the first night of war. At stand-by in our blacked-out crewroom we sat around talking fitfully or just drowsed. I thoughtfully considered two of the Squadron's World War I trophies hanging in the gloom near the ceiling: the fins of a Pfalz and a Fokker, both bearing the sinister German black cross.

'An intelligence report came in: "Heavy concentration of German bombers crossing the Dutch frontier." A few minutes later Johnny, Sergeant Soper and I were scrambled and we roared off one by one down the flare path.'

The three Hurricanes quickly climbed to their patrol height of 20,000 feet. 'As we droned up and down between Brighton and Portsmouth,' Richey continued, 'we could see the coastline clearly below us under the bright full moon. But the whole country was in darkness. Not a single light showed, in sharp contrast to our previous night flights … After an hour on patrol without sighting a German aircraft we were recalled by radio and returned.'[29]

As it turned out, No.1's time at Tangmere was short-lived. Within a few days, Richey and his colleagues were ordered to France as the vanguard of the RAF's Advanced Air Striking Force. They did not return until June 1940 – by which time the Phoney War had come to an end.

A first edition of Paul Richey's excellent *Fighter Pilot*, which was initially published anonymously in 1941. (*Mark Hillier Collection*)

A pair of Hawker Hurricane Mk.IIs of 43 Squadron make a low-level pass over other aircraft of the squadron, the latter lined up at Tangmere.

21: New Spitfires at Tangmere

No.238 Squadron Re-formed

Throughout the Phoney War, the process of expanding and fortifying the RAF continued apace. As part of this, squadrons that had been disbanded after the First World War were being reformed. This included 238 Squadron, which was reborn at Tangmere at the same time that Hitler was unleashing his Blitzkrieg on France and the Low Countries.

First formed in August 1918 at the seaplane station at Cattewater, Plymouth, 238 Squadron flew anti-submarine patrols until the Armistice in November that year. It was reduced to a cadre on 15 May 1919, prior to being completely disbanded on 20 March 1922.

The first three personnel posted to the 'new' 238 Squadron arrived at Tangmere on 12 May. This trio included at least one pilot – Pilot Officer John Spencer Wigglesworth. Over the days that followed, further personnel for the squadron appeared at Tangmere. They included, on the 13th, Pilot Officer Charles Davis, on what was almost certainly his first posting after training, and Flying Officer Derek MacCaw, who had previously served in 2 (Army Co-operation) Squadron and had just recovered from a period of sickness. The following day saw two more pilots arrive, one of whom was Pilot Officer Brian Bertram Considine. An Irishman, Considine had attended 3 FTS Grantham in November, completing his training there on 10 May 1940. Shown as having been posted to 6 OTU Sutton Bridge to convert to Hurricanes, he arrived at Tangmere on the 14th.

By 15 May, some thirty-seven members of 238 Squadron had gathered at Tangmere. This was also the day on which its first three aircraft

A member of 238 Squadron's groundcrew working on one of its freshly delivered Spitfires at Tangmere in May or June 1940. As the squadron soon converted back to Hurricanes, photographs such as this one are hard to find. (*Chris Goss Collection*)

One of 238 Squadron's Spitfires, coded VK-N, in a blast pen at Tangmere in May or June 1940. Note the Armstrong Whitworth Ensign landing in the background. (*Chris Goss Collection*)

were received – a trio of Hurricanes that arrived by air. It was the next day that, according to its Operations Record Book, 238 Squadron 'is considered to have come into being'.

In keeping with the frantic and often confused nature of events at this period of the war, on the 17th an official 'postagram' was received, informing those present that three squadrons, namely 257 at Hendon, 249 at Leconfield and, of course, 238 at Tangmere, were officially formed. At the same time, 238 was instructed that its 'equipment [was] changed from Hurricane to Spitfire' – despite the fact that it had been noted only twenty-four hours earlier that only one of the arrivals at Tangmere had ever flown the latter!

The first Spitfires for 238 Squadron were duly delivered to Tangmere, by air, on 18 May. This was the same day that its new CO arrived – Squadron Leader Cyril Baines. A pre-war regular, who entered RAF College Cranwell as a Cadet in September 1928, Baines served in a variety of squadrons before joining the Administrative Staff at HQ Fighter Command on 7 March 1938. He remained there until his arrival at Tangmere in May 1940.

Baines promptly set about turning his new command into an effective fighting force. In the process, the Hurricanes were moved on, and the remaining Spitfires received. This included twelve that arrived by air from 9 M.U. at Cosford on the 19th, and a further sixteen that were collected the next day.

The Spitfires were short-lived, for the squadron converted back to Hurricanes in June. Its time at Tangmere ended on 20 June 1940, when it was ordered to move to Middle Wallop. No.238 Squadron was finally declared operational on 2 July and, apart from four weeks in Cornwall, went on to spend the period of the Battle of Britain in the Middle Wallop sector.

22: The World's Oldest Surviving Hurricane

Flown from Tangmere; Damaged Over Dunkirk

Hanging in one of the halls at the Science Museum in London is the world's oldest surviving Hawker Hurricane. With the serial number L1592, this Mk.I was the forty-sixth aircraft off the Hawker production line from the initial batch ordered for the RAF.

Initially issued to 56 Squadron, L1592 passed through the hands of a number of units before finally being allocated to 43 Squadron in the spring of 1940. As Operation *Dynamo* gathered pace, 43 Squadron, which had been based at Wick, was sent south to assist in covering the evacuation beaches, returning to its pre-war home at Tangmere on 31 May. Within hours of their arrival in Sussex, 43 Squadron's pilots were airborne and heading out over the Channel, as the Operations Record Book reveals:

'No.43 Squadron were ordered to carry out an offensive patrol over Dunkirk in company with No.145 Squadron, No.245 Squadron and a Squadron of French fighters; the last two to rendezvous over Hawkinge. The Squadron took off at 0530 hours with the following pilots, Squadron Leader C.G. Lott (in command), Flight Lieutenant J.W.C. Simpson, Flying Officer J.D. Edmonds, Flying Officer W.C. Wilkinson, Sergeant Hallowes, Pilot Officer C.A. Woods-Scawen, Flying Officer M.K. Carswell, Sergeant Ottewill and Sergeant

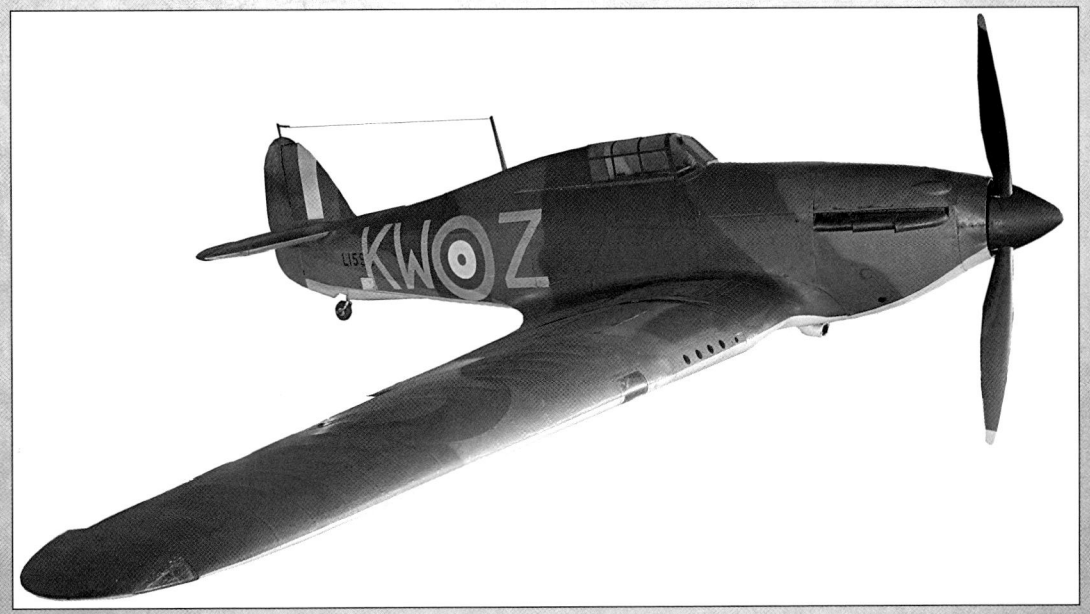

Hawker Hurricane Mk.I L1592 on display in the Science Museum, London. In the spring of 1944, plans were put in place to preserve a selection of historically important aircraft for future generations. L1592 was one of them. It was refurbished by Hawker in the early 1960s and first placed on display in the Science Museum in 1963.

Gough. No enemy aircraft were sighted on this patrol and all returned to Manston to refuel. The French fighters were not seen.'[30]

It was Pilot Officer Charles Anthony Woods-Scawen who was at the controls of L1592 during this patrol, as he was during the one that followed: 'A similar patrol was ordered later and the same formations took part; on this occasion heavy enemy opposition was encountered in the shape of about 60 ME.109 and ME.110. A general melee ensued and pilots returned individually to Tangmere. Flying Officer M.K. Carswell and Sergeant Gough were missing and reported as such, but news was later received that Flying Officer M.K. Carswell had been landed at Dover from a destroyer, suffering from superficial burns and sent to hospital.'

During the dogfight over the Channel near Dunkirk, Woods-Scawen, who was flying as Yellow 2 in 'A' Flight, tangled with a Messerschmitt Bf 109. In his combat report he recorded that the combat occurred at 11.35 hours at an altitude of 7,000ft: 'While on offensive patrol over Dunkirk with 145 & 245 Squadrons, we were attacked by several ME.109s. I engaged one in a dogfight and put two bursts into him [of four and five seconds respectively and from a range of 100–200 yards], which knocked pieces off his trailing edge, port wing. I was then shot at from below & a hit was registered in my radiator compelling me to retire. The resultant deluge of Glycol inside the cockpit prevented my seeing what had happened to my opponent. I returned immediately to Tangmere alone, having left earlier than the rest of our pilots.'[31] Because of L1592's rapidly overheating engine, Woods-Scawen was forced to make a wheels-up landing at Tangmere.[32] For his part in the engagement, Woods-Scawen was credited with a 'probable'.

The damage meant that L1592 was no longer serviceable. On 4 June it was collected from Tangmere and transferred to No.10 Maintenance Unit at Hullavington on the 27th of the same month. L1592 remained there, almost certainly under repair, until 23 July when it was allocated to 615 (County of Surrey) Squadron.

23: RAF Westhampnett

Tangmere's First Satellite Airfield

RAF Goodwood, or RAF Woodcote as it was described in an account by a member of 610 (County of Chester) Squadron's groundcrew in 1941, later became known by all as RAF Westhampnett.

Frederick Charles Gordon Lennox, the 9th Duke of Richmond, Lennox, Gordon and Aubigny (1904–1989), had been a keen aviator. He not only designed and flew his own aircraft but developed his own flying field to the south of Goodwood House, complete with a thatched hangar to house his aircraft. The land that the current Goodwood airfield was constructed on was once a collection of fields belonging to Goodwood Estate located to the south-west of the Duke's own airfield. As the threat of war grew, this area of flat land was requisitioned by the Air Ministry. The intention at the time had not been to construct a fully operational airfield, but an emergency landing ground for nearby RAF Tangmere.

In 1940, the site was literally a field with no purpose-built facilities other than a windsock. However, the status of the airfield changed just prior to the Battle of Britain when it was upgraded to serve as a full satellite airfield of Tangmere and grass runways were laid out. Only then did some basic facilities start to appear, among which was a Watch Office. Early aerial photographs show that the RAF went to some

A recent aerial photograph of the airfield and racetrack at Goodwood. (*Historic Military Press*)

Taken in June 1940, this is one of the earliest known photographs of RAF personnel at Westhampnett. Known as the Headquarters Flight, these men were posted in from Tangmere to help establish the airfield. The building behind went on to serve as the station armoury and survived until recently. (*Mark Hillier Collection*)

lengths to camouflage the airfield by trying to create fake hedges and field boundaries using tar on the ground to break up the shape and confuse prying Luftwaffe eyes.

The entry in Tangmere's Operations Record Book for 8 August 1940, records that the 'Satellite aerodrome at Westhampnett brought into operation and 145 Squadron transferred from Tangmere'. It goes on to note that 'HRH the Duke of Gloucester visited the station [Tangmere] and inspected the Operations Room, squadron dispersal points, also made a visit to Westhampnett'.

So primitive was the airfield in the early months that aircraft were serviced in the open and airmen were required to sleep in tented accommodation – although the officers were soon accommodated in relatively luxurious surroundings, initially at Woodcote Farm then Shopwyke House. The two cottages that stood within the airfield boundary were quickly put to good use, as were many surrounding buildings, accommodating, for example, the NCO pilots and cooking/messing facilities.

By the time 145 Squadron left Westhampnett mid-way through the Battle of Britain, at least two flight huts had been constructed. That for 'A' Flight was located by the northernmost cottage on the airfield opposite Woodcote Farm and along the Lavant Straight of the racecourse. 'B' Flight, on the other hand, was situated by the old control tower, along the eastern boundary following the road back to Chichester.

In the winter of 1940–1941 the airfield was badly waterlogged, so the decision was made to put in a perimeter track as well as erect blister hangars. In 1941, two squadrons of the Tangmere Wing, which was commanded by Wing Commander Douglas Bader, flew from the airfield. Indeed, it was from Westhampnett that Bader took off on his last sortie on 9 August 1941 – which we will examine in due course.

By the end of the war, RAF Westhampnett had been extensively developed and the site encompassed many of the surrounding villages. It had been home to at least forty-six squadrons and sub-units, some of the squadrons being based at the airfield more than once, as well as many thousands of service personnel.

24: Tangmere's Battle Headquarters

A 'Lost' Part of the Airfield's Infrastructure

The threat of a German invasion in the summer of 1940, along with the Luftwaffe's onslaught, led to an urgent review of the defence of the RAF's airfields. Among the steps taken was the introduction of underground Battle Headquarters. The purpose of these structures was simple – to provide the Station Commander with a hardened and secure location from which he could direct the defence of the airfield in the event of an attack by enemy forces.

The first Battle HQs were introduced on fighter airfields in 1940. With the Air Ministry building design number MS 2279, these early structures were more correctly known as the 'Battle Headquarters and Station Control'. The airfield archaeologist and historian Paul Francis notes that 'these were only built at the fighter stations protecting London, although now none are thought to survive. At ground level they look like a 6-sided pillbox, but below this was a room with another larger one adjacent to it (but at a slightly lower level).'[33]

As Paul Francis points out, the MS 2279 design comprises two main underground chambers. The one situated below the observation cupola,

The hexagonal chamber of Tangmere's Battle HQ pictured having been uncovered during excavation work in the late 1970s or early 1980s. Note the emergency exit shaft with an iron ladder on the far side. (*via Historic Military Press*)

Water and sludge being pumped out of the Battle HQ. (*via Historic Military Press*)

Another view of the Battle HQs hexagonal chamber, with the entrance to the control room also visible. (*via Historic Military Press*)

which was at ground level and offered good all-round visibility of the airfield, was hexagonal in shape. From the middle of this chamber an iron ladder provided access to the cupola above, whilst to one side was an emergency exit shaft, again with an iron ladder. Steps from the hexagonal chamber led down into the adjacent control room, which was nine-foot square. This chamber could also be reached by a separate set of steps leading down from the surface.

Whilst the MS 2279 Battle HQs served their purpose, the design was soon superseded by others, no doubt drawing on lessons learnt from the use of the early structures. It was in 1941 that the standard pattern of Battle HQ was drawn up – the Type 11008/41. Though originally intended for use on bomber stations, so successful was this design that it would go on to be used, sometimes with local variations, on all types of RAF airfield.

Rectangular in shape, the Type 11008/41, constructed almost entirely below ground for concealment and protection, had four main chambers: a messengers' and runners' room; the Defence Officer's room; a communication, or PBX (Private Branch), room; and the observation room with its thick concrete cupola on top, once again usually at ground level. A small WC cubicle, equipped with an Elsan chemical toilet, was positioned off the main passageway, which had steps to the surface at one end and an emergency exit at the other.

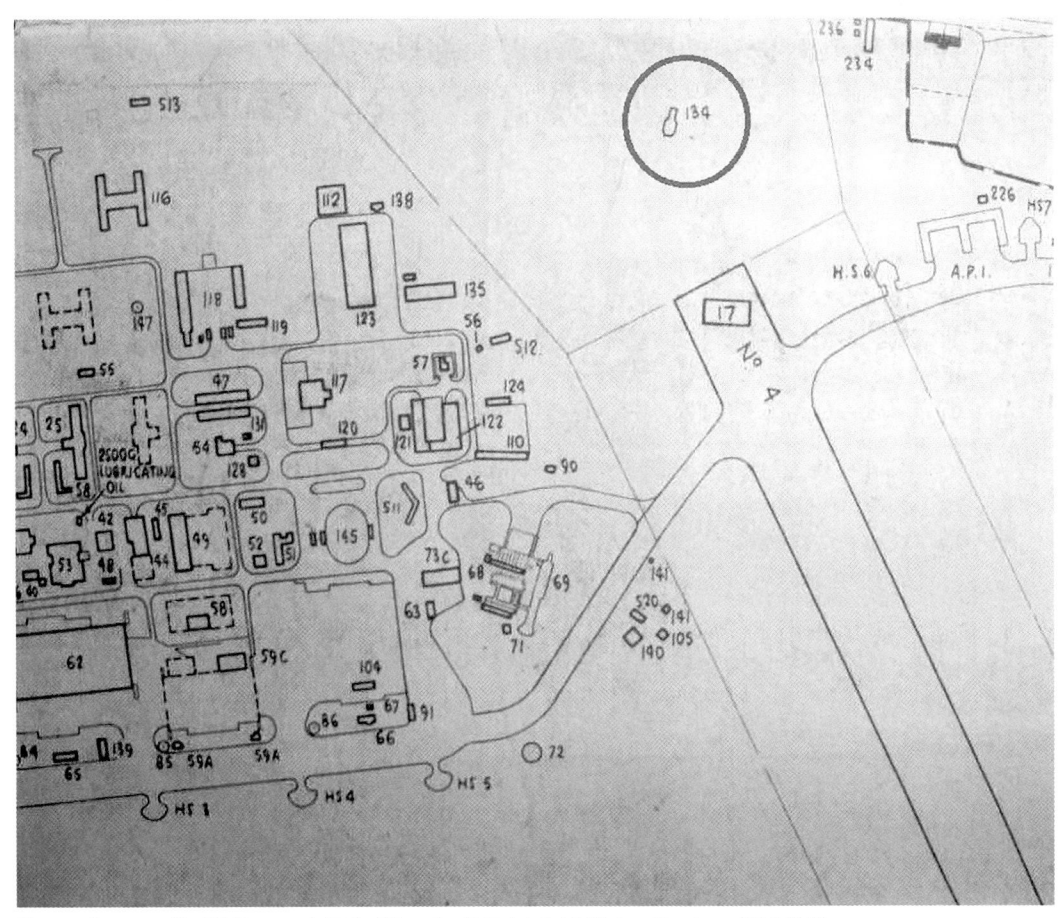

The site of structure No.134, Tangmere's Battle HQ, on the 1946-dated airfield plan. (*Courtesy of Matt Field*)

The control room of the Battle HQ, with the doorway to the steps leading to the surface beyond. (*via Historic Military Press*)

The fact that a Battle HQ was constructed at Tangmere is beyond doubt. Indeed, an official airfield plan dated July 1946 clearly shows that one had been built to the north of the north-south runway. The key to the plan, which lists the Battle HQ as structure No.134, states that it was of the Type 11008/41 design, suggesting that it was not constructed until the second half of 1941 at the earliest.

However, the images seen here pose an interesting question. They were taken during demolition work at Tangmere during the late 1970s or early 1980s. The position of this underground structure was exactly that of the Battle HQ marked on the airfield plan – i.e. structure No.134. The photographs suggest a two-chamber construction, one half being hexagonal with an emergency exit shaft, again with an iron ladder, to one side – exactly as per the MS 2279 design.

It would seem, therefore, that Tangmere was in fact a recipient of one of the first Battle HQs in 1940. But was a later Type 11008/41 also constructed on the airfield, presumably close to its predecessor at site No.134? Sadly, with much of Tangmere's infrastructure having long since gone, the physical evidence that would solve the conundrum no longer remains. In fact, the site of Tangmere's Battle HQ, or HQs, has disappeared under the modern buildings of Chichester Business Park, which in turn is located off City Fields Way.

25: The Medals of Air Vice-Marshal Lott

Prelude to the Battle of Britain

Among the many emotive medal groups in the care of Tangmere Military Aviation Museum is that of Air Vice-Marshal C. George Lott. Having been rejected by the Royal Navy, he joined the RAF as a Halton Apprentice in 1922. Lott soon rose through the ranks; he trained as a pilot in 1927 and was granted a commission in 1933.

In October 1939, Lott was appointed Officer Commanding 43 Squadron, which, as we have already seen, was based at Tangmere. Over the eight months that followed, the squadron, under Lott's command, distinguished itself by claiming more enemy aircraft than any other unit based in the British Isles. For his part, Lott opened his account on 10 April 1940, when he attacked a Heinkel He 111. He was awarded the Distinguished Flying Cross at the end of May 1940.

At 11.40 hours on 9 July 1940, Lott, leading Red Section, which also included Pilot Officer Frank Carey and Sergeant Jack Mills, was ordered to intercept six enemy aircraft near Selsey Bill, though they were subsequently redirected to St Catherine's Point. Sighting the enemy, Lott later recalled what happened next: 'Giving a Tally Ho I gave chase at 16½ lbs. boost climbing slightly. When about 20 miles South of the Isle of Wight the two leading formations, believed to be Ju.87's, dived down through the

Air Vice-Marshal Charles George Lott's medal group – which is on display in the museum at Tangmere. From left to right can be seen the Distinguished Service Order, Distinguished Flying Cross, 1939–45 Star, Aircrew Europe Star, Defence Medal, War Medal, with a bronze oak leaf denoting that he was Mentioned in Despatches, and the 1953 Coronation Medal. (*Mark Hillier Collection*)

clouds and the rear two sections of Me.110 went into line astern and turned about. They spread out and attacked head on, and I turned into No.2 of the enemy who opened fire at about 800 yds. His fire did not appear to me to be well directed and I held my own fire until about 300 yds range, after a ½ sec burst I received some hits in my A/C and a piece of glass, or Perspex, entered my right eye.'

Badly wounded, Lott turned to head back to Tangmere, 'but glycol fumes were increasing and engine failing, so I released my harness and prepared to abandon A/C. The engine finally stopped about 4 miles from base, and as the windscreen was obscured and I had the use of only one eye, I decided to take to parachute. I removed the side panel and abandoned ship at what must have been about 700 ft. and landed successfully, though with rather a bump, on my back in the middle of the road.' Lott's Hurricane crashed on Fontwell racecourse and was completely burnt out with only the tail wheel recognisable.

It was announced on 3 August 1940, that Lott had been awarded the Distinguished Service Order. The citation for the latter, published in *The London Gazette* on 6 August 1940, states: 'Since June 1 this officer has led his squadron on operational patrols over Dunkirk, Amiens and Abbeville, and other parts of enemy occupied territory. In July, as leader of a section of Hurricanes, he pressed home an attack in adverse weather against six Messerschmitt 110s.

A portrait of Squadron Leader George Lott. (*Tangmere Military Aviation Museum*)

During the combat Squadron Leader Lott's aircraft was badly hit but despite an injury which eventually necessitated the removal of an eye, he brought his aircraft to within three miles of the base before he was compelled to abandon it. He has personally destroyed two enemy aircraft and possibly another. This officer has displayed outstanding leadership and an intense desire to engage the enemy.'

Lott missed out on qualification for the Battle of Britain Clasp by just a few hours.

Section Four

The Battle of Britain

26: Squadron Leader Max Aitken's Flying Boots

Based at Tangmere on the First Day of the Battle of Britain

The aerial engagments that had already been taking place over the Channel and Southern England officialy morphed into the Battle of Britain on the morning of Wednesday, 10 July 1940. One of the squadrons based at Tangmere that day, alongside Squadron Leader George Lott's 43 Squadron, was 601 (County of London) Squadron. An Auxiliary Air Force unit, 601 was unofficially known as the 'Millionaires' Squadron'. Its members had taken to embellishing their service uniforms by having bright red silk linings stitched inside their tunics and wearing blue ties rather than the regulation black examples.

On the day that the Battle of Britain began, 601 was commanded by Squadron Leader The Honourable Sir John William 'Max' Aitken. The son of the Canadian newspaper magnate and businessman William Aitken, the 1st Baron Beaverbrook, Churchill's Minister of Aircraft Production, Aitken had joined the Auxiliary Air Force in 1935. Having taken command of the Hurricane-equipped 601 Squadron in early June 1940, Aitken had actually been based at Tangmere since February that year, though his section had been deployed to France for a time in May. It was on his return to Tangmere that he was promoted to Acting Squadron Leader and given command of 601. In June 1940, he shot down a Heinkel He 111 over Brighton; for this and his earlier victories in France he was awarded the DFC, this being gazetted on 9 July 1940.

For Aitken and his fellow pilots, the first day of the Battle of Britain may well have seemed

Squadron Leader Max Aitken's flying boots that are on display in the museum at Tangmere.

little different from those that had preceded it. The squadron's ORB, for example, simply states: 'A Ju.88 was damaged during a combat on this day. There were two interception flights, and 12 hrs. 10 mins. flying was carried out by day.' Aitken was not one of the pilots scrambled on that Wednesday.

Aitken was posted to non-operational duties on 20 July 1940, and departed from 601 Squadron. A reminder of the time he spent at Tangmere can be found in the form of a pair

26: SQUADRON LEADER MAX AITKEN'S FLYING BOOTS

A picture of a relazed Max Aitken. He survived the war and was released from the RAF in 1946 with the rank of Group Captain. (*Courtesy of the Battle of Britain London Monument*)

of flying boots he wore whilst stationed at the Sussex airfield. A private purchase, having been acquired from 'The Man's Shop at Harrods', the boots are said to have been donated to the museum by a former landlord of the White Horse public house in Bognor Regis. Legend has it that on one occasion when Aitken was off duty and frequenting the pub, he found himself unable to pay his bill and left his boots behind as payment!

27: Tangmere's 'Scramble' Bell

A Signal to Go Into Action

It was the news reels in the long hot summer of 1940 that firmly established the 'Scramble Bell' in the historiography of the Battle of Britain. The reality was that these bells were simply official Station Bells that had, in some cases, been repurposed as a means of warning groundcrew and pilots waiting at dispersal that the latter had been ordered to take-off, more often than not to intercept an incoming Luftwaffe raid – as may well have been the case for Squadron Leader Max Aitken's 601 Squadron on the first day of the Battle of Britain.

From about 1936 onwards the Air Ministry purchased official ceremonial, or Station bells, for use at its multitude of locations, not just airfields. Research offers up a multitude of accounts that reveal that were not only used at dispersals, but could also be found in guardrooms, hanging outside headquarters buildings, at fire stations and even in sick quarters. Many stations, therefore, had more than one Station Bell.

Produced in two sizes, Station Bells from the Second World War era are all engraved with the letters 'AM' and the year of manufacture on the side, both beneath a King George VI crown. They appear to have been mostly made in a silver colour, nickel-plated bronze until around 1942, from when they seem to be more of a brass colour.

Pilot Officer Kenneth Wilkinson, a Spitfire pilot with 616 (South Yorkshire) Squadron in the Battle of the Britain, once recalled the following: 'The pilots themselves could be scattered quite widely, some reading, some listening to the radio, some playing football; engineers could be running engines & a means becomes necessary that reaches through all this & tells everybody

One of Tangmere's former Station, or 'Scramble', bells which can be seen on display in the museum. (*Historic Military Press*)

to scramble. I guess at first this was done by mouth once the ready hut phone went, but not everybody heard the call; then some bright spark thought we need something loud & the loudest thing on the airfield would have been the big bell outside the Guard room or the base commander's office.' As Kenneth concluded, 'I can tell you that I scrambled to the sound of the Bell many a time.'[34]

The museum at Tangmere is fortunate to have one of its former bells on display: 'Following the [airfield's] closure, the bell engraved "Air

27: TANGMERE'S 'SCRAMBLE' BELL

A still from a 1940-dated news reel showing an airman about to ring a 'Scramble Bell', an action that would send the pilots racing for their aircraft. As someone has chalked on the bell, 'Don't come and tell – ring this like "Hell"'. (*Critical Past*)

Ministry 1939" was amongst many items that quickly disappeared as "souvenirs". However, in 1998 a young Royal Naval Cadet returned it to the Museum having found the bell hidden away in a naval paint store underneath some sacks.'

28: German Bomb Fragment

Luftwaffe Attack on 16 August 1940

An important Sector Station in 11 Group, it was inevitable that as the Battle of Britain raged on Tangmere would eventually receive the full attention of Göring's bombers. They finally struck early on the afternoon of 16 August 1940 – a vivid reminder of which is the fragment of a German bomb seen here.

The airfield's Operations Record Book provides a brief summary of what happened: 'Tangmere bombed between 13.00 hours and 13.30 hours by approximately seventeen Junkers Ju 87s and Messerschmitt Bf 110s. Following casualties were sustained: Ten service personnel, three civilians and twenty personnel injured … The following aircraft were destroyed or damaged: three Blenheims (written-off), three Blenheims, seven Hurricanes, and one Magister (repairable at contractor's works). Six Merlin engines damaged but repairable. Seven MT and thirty private cars damaged beyond repair. A large amount of equipment etc. was buried under debris and salvage work was put in hand immediately and ninety per cent recovered.

'The discipline at this station, and after, the attack was exceptionally good. During the attack, twenty-five enemy aircraft were brought down between this station and the coast. The depressing situation was dealt with in an orderly manner, and it is considered that the traditions of the RAF were upheld by all ranks. In conclusion, it must be considered that the major attack launched on this station by the enemy, was a victory for the RAF.'[35]

Anne Turley-George was a member of the Women's Auxiliary Air Force who had been posted to Tangmere following the outbreak of war in 1939. On the basis that she had once 'made mint sauce when I was a girl guide', and that she 'couldn't type and couldn't drive', Anne found herself posted to the airfield's kitchens. 'I was so awful,' she recalled, 'that the pilots christened me Hitler's secret weapon!'.

Anne was on duty at Tangmere when the bombers struck on 16 August: 'You could hear this awful howling noise and we looked up into the air and there was this thing which seemed to be coming straight down upon us … We rushed like mad and managed to push into the air raid shelter. Then all hell let loose.

The bomb fragment recovered after the attack on Tangmere on 16 August 1940. (*Tangmere Military Aviation Museum*)

28: GERMAN BOMB FRAGMENT

The airfield at Tangmere under attack on 16 August 1940. (*Courtesy of the Andy Saunders Collection*)

'There were bombs falling everywhere, rubble falling on us everybody was rocking as if they were in a ship at sea. The whole dugout was moving, mess and dust everywhere, and there was our hurricane lamp flickering round and everybody was sort of crouched over … One girl who was an avowed atheist kept calling on God which rather cheered me up. Eventually this died away, and the shocks and rumbles and bangings died away into the distance and we at last emerged into the air to find absolute devastation. Tangmere as we had known it seemed to have disappeared.'[36]

29: Bomb-Damaged Centre Punch

Target Tangmere

Leading Aircraftman Maurice Haffenden was an engine fitter serving with 43 Squadron in the summer of 1940. A dedicated letter writer, he frequently committed to paper his experiences of serving on a front line Fighter Command station. On 13 August 1940, for example, he noted how the Luftwaffe was gradually closing in: 'Loudspeakers blared forth usual "Take cover" warning. The sky was alive with aircraft. Three of our flight had gone up some time ago. The machine guns make a hell of a din. A few bombs fall ¼ mile away. A "Schmitt" crashed just outside the Aerodrome grounds. 5 'bale-outs' from various Kytes landed on the drome & were taken to the guard-room.'

Regarding the events on the 16th, he duly recorded the following: 'Lunchtime at 1pm the loudspeakers with a greater urgency than before suddenly appealed "Take cover, Take cover." Within 3 minutes of that warning I saw the first formations of Junkers coming straight down on the 'drome in a vertical line. The leader was within 2,000 ft of the ground – long wing span – fixed undercarriage – twin engines & then wheeeee …

'I went head first down a manhole as the first bomb landed on the cookhouse. For 7 mins their 1,000 pounders were scoring direct hits, and everything was swept by machine gun bullets. I have never believed such desolation & destruction to be possible. Everything is wrecked – the hangars, the stores, the hospital, the armoury, the cookhouse, the canteen … well everything!

'By special permission a Lions [sic] ice cream fellow is allowed in the 'drome. He always stands just outside the cookhouse on the square. He was last seen standing there guarding his tricycle but now at that same spot is a bomb crater 30 ft deep. But there were quite a few casualties. In the early evening they still sorted out the bloody remnants of flesh & bones & tied them in sheets.'

The next day Haffenden noted how he had spent the hours after the attack: 'Last night we slept in adjacent fields & woods, after invading the local Waafs quarters for food. – I found a decent spot between 2 haystacks. This morning hundreds of men & loads of machinery are still being brought in to clean up some of the debris & to fill in craters on the field. The fire engines are leaving.'[37]

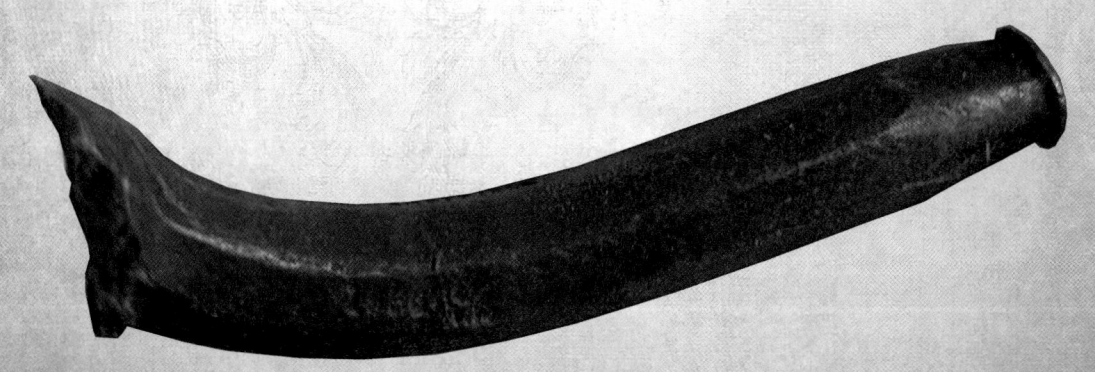

A small, but intriguing relic of the raid on 16 August 1940 – half of Ronald London's bomb-damaged centre punch. (*Tangmere Military Aviation Museum*)

29: BOMB-DAMAGED CENTRE PUNCH

A despatch rider's motorcycle pictured in a bomb-damaged building at Tangmere after the events of Friday, 16 August 1940. (*Courtesy of the Andy Saunders Collection*)

Another of the fitters at work in the hangars at Tangmere on the 16th was Ronald London. Like Haffenden, Ron, as he was known, took his cue from the station tannoy and sought shelter, abandoning his equipment in the process – including a centre punch which he left on his work bench. At some point in the raid, a bomb splinter ploughed across the bench and sliced the punch in two, leaving the part seen here almost unmoved on the bench.[38]

Damaged vehicles lie among the wreckage of some of Tangmere's buildings after the passing of the German bombers. (*Courtesy of the Andy Saunders Collection*)

30: A Tangmere Military Cross

Flight Lieutenant Courtney Willey MBE, MC

The Military Cross was instituted in 1914 to recognise 'the distinguished services in time of War of Officers of certain ranks in our Army'. It is, therefore, unusual for a member of the RAF to be a recipient. Just how unusual is revealed by the research of Michael Maton who notes that of the 10,000 or more MCs awarded in the Second World War, just sixty-nine (including one Bar) were to RAF personnel.[39] The German assault on Tangmere on 16 August 1940, led to one of these awards – that to Flying Officer Dr Courtney Beresford Ingor Willey.

Born into a medical family in Hendon, Middlesex, in 1912, Willey was educated at Balliol College, Oxford. He volunteered for service in the RAF in March 1940 and, having been granted a commission, was posted to RAF Tangmere, to take up the role of medical officer for 601 (County of London) Squadron, a few weeks later in May.

Willey was on duty when the station's tannoy system announced the impending arrival of the Luftwaffe bombers. One of his first actions was to move ten of his patients from the sick quarters to a nearby air raid shelter. As the bombs rained

A specimen example of the G V R issue of the Military Cross and Bar. (*Historic Military Press*)

A portrait of Flying Officer Dr Courtney Beresford Ingor Willey. Though this is not the image in question, Willey was unusual in that, despite being non-aircrew, he still had his portrait drawn by Cuthbert Orde. (*Tangmere Military Aviation Museum*)

down, the sick quarters took a direct hit. The citation for Willey's award of the MC reveals a little of his subsequent actions: 'Flying Officer Willey was buried in the debris of a building which received a direct hit during an intensive air raid on an aerodrome. In spite of slight injuries and shock, this medical officer extricated himself and immediately rendered first aid to other injured personnel. He displayed a fine example of calm behaviour and efficiency.'[40]

It is said that many of Willey's injuries were caused when the building's chimney breast collapsed on him – interviewed in 2013 he declared that he had been saved by his tin helmet. That he had narrowly escaped a worse fate was revealed by Air Vice-Marshal Sandy Johnstone, then a squadron leader in command of 602 (City of Glasgow) Squadron. 'I drove over to Tangmere in the evening,' he wrote, '… Already stories are going around of how the fellows reacted during the aerial onslaught – some patently numbed by the force of it, whilst others seem to have become spurred to greater action by the terrifying enormity of the moment. And the heroes were often those whom one would least expect to stand out among their fellow men. Such a man has been our medical officer, Doc Willey, who apparently was doing great deeds throughout the blitz.'[41]

During the months following the raid Willey served at a number of other Fighter Command stations before being posted, in April 1941, to the Far East. As the Japanese moved to capture Singapore, Willey was evacuated to Sumatra and Java. It was there that he was eventually captured, marking the start of more than three years' incarceration as a prisoner of war, during which time he was one of the many forced to labour on the infamous Death Railway in Burma and Thailand.

Having survived, on his return to the UK Willey was made a Member of the Most Excellent Order of the British Empire for his work in the PoW camps. Post-war he was to become a consultant physician at West Cumberland Hospital and live at Woodend, near Egremont. He passed away in December 2004 aged 90.

Like so many of the items in this book, Willey's Military Cross is on display at Tangmere Military Aviation Museum.

31: Military Medal Gallantry

For 'Calm courage and devotion to duty'

Despite its brevity, so intense was the attack on 16 August that Doc Willey's Military Cross was not the only gallantry award made to ground personnel that day. For their actions, both Corporal George Jones and Aircraftman 2nd Class Cyril George Faulkner were to receive the Military Medal.

Along with their civilian driver, who is only referred to as Bill, Jones and Faulkner had been instructed to take their Albion ambulance and attend to a pilot who had made an emergency landing and required urgent medical attention. Faulkner later recalled these events in more detail: 'Corporal Jones and I had been called to attend by ambulance to a crashed Hurricane and proceeding along the [southern] perimeter we suddenly saw a cloud of dust some 25 yards ahead of us. We stopped and realised that we were being bombed, the first salvo [falling] on to parked aircraft causing the dust.'[42]

The front and reverse of a specimen Military Medal and Bar. Some 15,000 MMs were awarded during the Second World War, along with 177 first Bars and one second Bar. (*Historic Military Press*)

Groundcrew pose in front of Fiske's Hurricane Mk.I, P3358. Note the code letter shown on the leading edge of the wing on the left. (*Courtesy of the Battle of Britain London Monument*)

In a different account, Faulkner went on to state: 'A bit shaken, we pulled up for a few moments, but then decided to carry on anyway to the Hurricane that was up against the western boundary. When we got there the pilot was still in the cockpit. It was Billy Fiske. For the life of me I cannot recall if the aeroplane was on its wheels or its belly, but the airfield was still under attack and we got on to the wing and managed to lift the pilot out on to the grass. The aeroplane was not burning, but the cockpit had been badly damaged by fire and the pilot was very seriously burned. We managed to get his flying helmet and jacket off and covered him over. I can recall that he was conscious and talking to us, but not terribly coherently.'[43]

Having loaded Fiske into their ambulance, Jones and Faulkner set off for Tangmere's sick quarters. Willey remembered how 'he emerged from the ruins [of the sick quarters] to be confronted by Jones and Faulkner bringing the stretcher bearing Fiske to him': 'The ambulance arrived with Billy Fiske. I got in the back of the ambulance and lifted off the blanket and found he was charred black from the waist down. He was conscious and talking, but I gave him a shot of morphine, although I realised we had to get him to hospital. In any case, the sick bay was no longer there! Unfortunately, because of the bombing, all the roads on the airfield were blocked and covered with debris so we couldn't get him away for at least 20min or so.'[44]

With both of his eardrums punctured by the blast, Willey had to communicate with Jones and Faulkner by sign language. Having administered a dose of morphine and ordered that the terribly injured pilot be transported to hospital in Chichester, speaking in 2003, Willey recalled that he had been 'very pessimistic about Fiske's chances of survival due to the severe burns to his lower body'.[45]

Jones' and Faulkner's joint citation for the Military Cross was published in the same issue of *The London Gazette* as Willey's MC. It reads: 'During a heavy attack on an aerodrome a burning British fighter aircraft landed. Despite heavy bombs which were falling and enemy machine gunning, Corporal Jones and Aircraftman 2nd Class Faulkner took their ambulance across to the burning aircraft, assisted the pilot from it, extinguished his burning clothing and rendered first aid treatment. Both airmen displayed calm courage and devotion to duty.'

32: Stained Glass Window, Boxgrove Church

Commemorating Pilot Officer William Meade Lindsley 'Billy' Fiske III

Despite the best efforts of the staff at the Royal West Sussex Hospital in Chichester, Pilot Officer Fiske did not survive. As Willey had feared might happen, Fiske succumbed to his wounds the following day. He was 29 years old.

Pilot Officer William Meade Lindsley Fiske III was one of only two Americans who died in the Battle of Britain. Having won gold medals with the US Olympic bobsleigh teams in the 1928 and 1932 Olympics, Fiske was no ordinary American. He was also an exceptional driver and had taken part in the Le Mans 24-hour races. Having learnt to fly pre-war, he took the decision to risk losing his American citizenship to enlist in the RAF. After completing his flying training, Fiske was posted to 601 (County of London) Squadron, otherwise known as 'The Millionaires Squadron'.

On the morning of 16 August, twenty-nine Stukas of 1/StG2 targeted RAF Tangmere. Already airborne, 601 Squadron was ordered

The beautiful stained-glass window commemorating Pilot Officer William Meade Lindsley Fiske III that can be seen in the Priory Church of St Mary and St Blaise at Boxgrove. (*Historic Military Press*)

A portrait of Pilot Officer William Meade Lindsley Fiske III. (*Courtesy of the Battle of Britain London Monument*)

to patrol base at 20,000 feet and soon saw the incoming Ju 87s which they dived on to engage. It was during this dogfight that Fiske is believed to have been hit by return fire, forcing him, badly burned, to make the emergency landing back at Tangmere.

One member of 601 Squadron who had fond recollections of Fiske was Squadron Leader Hugh 'Jack' Riddle: 'My memories of Billy as a pilot was that he was quite exceptional. His Flight Commander, Sir Archibald Hope, having assessed Billy's flying ability on arrival with the squadron, said "In all my flying experience I have never come across a pilot with such completely natural flying ability, and quick reactions. He made his aircraft become part of him." Archie was definitely impressed!

'Billy liked to talk with everyone around him, particularly the ground crews. He wanted to know them and all about their jobs, aircraft maintenance and where difficulties lay – always helpful. Very soon he managed to endear himself to the whole squadron – not just the officers, but the other ranks too.

'There was club a few miles away from the airfield at Tangmere and this was made our unofficial Squadron Headquarters. It was somewhere pleasant, overlooking the waters of Chichester Harbour, where our wives and friends could meet and be with each other, and wait together until we could be free from Tangmere. Billy always seemed to get there before I did – maybe his motor car was faster than mine – I'm sure it was! ... Billy was aware and caring, a very nice aspect of his character.'[46]

Fiske was laid to rest a short distance from RAF Tangmere, in the grounds of the Priory Church of St Mary and St Blaise at Boxgrove, on 20 August 1940. His coffin was draped with both the Union Flag and the Stars and Stripes.

The 601 Squadron Old Comrades Association had originally considered commemorating Fiske with a memorial table, but in conjunction with the Priory, who wanted to enhance the aesthetics during a restoration of the Church, the suggestion of a stained-glass window was made and adopted. Designed by Mel Howse, it was unveiled on 17 September 2008.

Pilot Officer Fiske's headstone in in the grounds of the Priory Church of St Mary and St Blaise at Boxgrove. (*Courtesy of Robert Mitchell*)

33: 'The Glorious 16th' Cartoon

Defending Tangmere From the Ground

The defence of Tangmere had not just come from the air – and men such as Pilot Officer Fiske – but also from the ground. Lieutenant E.P. Griffin, for example, was serving with 717 Artizan Works Company Royal Engineers at the time.

The Royal Engineers' Artizan Works Companies were made up of skilled men from a variety of trades and were employed on a wide range of tasks, from hut construction and road making through to preparing an airfield's defences and camouflage schemes. As the attackers appeared over Tangmere on the 16th, Griffin manned his allotted post and, when the moment was right, opened fire with a Lewis gun. It is stated that he shot down a Messerschmitt Bf 110, the aircraft crashing three quarters of a mile from the aerodrome. To mark his exploits, his colleagues subsequently presented him with a cartoon entitled 'The Glorious 16th Aug 1940' – that seen here.

The attack undoubtedly left its mark on everyone who had been on the airfield at the time, as Air Vice-Marshal Sandy Johnstone recalled: 'I drove over to Tangmere … wisps of smoke [were] still rising from shattered buildings. Little knots of people were wandering about with dazed looks on their

The cartoon presented to Lieutenant E.P. Griffin for his part in the defence of Tangmere on 16 August 1940. (*Tangmere Military Aviation Museum*)

Lieutenant E.P. Griffin's RAF identity card which was issued for his time at Tangmere. (*Tangmere Military Aviation Museum*)

faces, obviously deeply affected by the events of the day. I eventually tracked down the Station Commander standing on the lawn in front of the Officers' Mess with a parrot sitting on his shoulder. Jack was covered in grime and the wretched bird was screeching its imitation of a Stuka at the height of the attack!'[47]

Still convalescing after being badly wounded when he was shot down on 19 July 1940, Flight Lieutenant John Simpson DFC had decided to head to RAF Tangmere where his unit, 43 Squadron, was based to collect his car and a few personal belongings. He arrived at the airfield almost at the same time as the bombers: 'The noise was terrific. I could hear it, although had my hands tightly over my ears and my head well down in the ditch. The bombs dropped all around me and I was terrified. I looked up now and then, but not very often. I saw black smoke. The smell of cordite and dust was horrible …

'When the three minutes had passed, there was sudden silence. All I could hear was the crackling of a burning building, and a fire-tender that drove past me at a hellish speed. I got up slowly. Two airmen got out of a slit trench a few yards away and asked me if I was all right. They were as dazed as I was. I was all right, but I realized that with my ankle and arm I would not be of much use. The smoke and flames and dust forced me into my car, which was dented where a piece of shrapnel had struck it.'

Leaving the airfield behind him, Simpson later mulled over the fact that 'the aerodrome was serviceable again in about eight hours. That is what really makes me wonder if these raids are worth the enemy's while.'[48]

34: Fontwell House

Tangmere's Dispersed Sick Quarters

Tangmere's Station Log records the scale of the damage that resulted from the attack on 16 August 1940. 'The following buildings were destroyed: all hangars, workshops, stores, sick quarters, pumping station, Y-hut Officers' Mess, and Salvation Army hut. Many buildings damaged, but promptly made fit for habitation. The following services were temporarily out of action: tannoy broadcasting system, all lighting, power, water and sanitation.'[49]

Though this indicates that many buildings were soon back in use, that was not always the case. Serving in the WAAF, Janet Pieters (née Hind) was posted to Tangmere in 1941. She later recalled being housed in temporary accommodation at Fontwell: 'Our first few nights were spent under the spectators' seats at a racing course called Fontwell. Things were a bit confused at Tangmere at that time … and the WAAFs had been moved off, not only as a safety precaution, but their accommodation had also been destroyed.

'We were then moved to the "new" accommodation – four huts in a field, one for each Watch. There was a fifth hut which contained Elsan toilets! From this field, there was a gap in the hedge, [we walked] across a lane, another field and we reached the Administration area where there was a dining hall, ablutions (I love that word) which consisted of three or four showers, ditto baths, in a very draughty area with a concrete floor.'

Fontwell, like so many leisure facilities across the country, had been badly affected by the outbreak of war, as the following account notes: 'Due to the Second World War, racing was suspended at Fontwell from March, 1940. As Fontwell was a few miles from Tangmere, the course saw its own action. After one bombing raid on the RAF station, in which living quarters were hit, some officers of the Women's Auxiliary Air Force (WAAF) spent several nights in the racecourse stands. Fontwell was also used as a holding station for wounded personnel … The

Fontwell House, which was used as Tangmere's temporary, dispersed sick quarters.

34: FONTWELL HOUSE

An aerial photograph of Tangmere taken on 17 June 1941. Much of the damage from the various Luftwaffe attacks of 1940 and early 1941, particularly that of 16 August, can still be seen. The station Sick Quarters were on the western side of the Parade Ground, at the rear of the Officers' Mess and NAAFI, roughly in the area indicated by the arrow. The last Belfast Truss hangars are visible; the rest had been destroyed on 16 August 1940. The No.1 hangar was very badly damaged. Whilst half of it had been dismantled, the rest of the structure had been re-purposed and turned into a camp theatre. This last surviving hangar roof then collapsed during a storm on 17 November 1944. (*Tangmere Military Aviation Museum*)

centre of the racecourse was also used for grazing cattle due to food rationing.'[50]

Tangmere's sick quarters were indeed relocated to Fontwell, and, more specifically, Fontwell House, after the building on the airfield had been destroyed on 16 August.

The racecourse at Fontwell owes its existence to Alfred Day. The son of a horse trainer, Day had been lured into the world of horse racing despite having begun a career in medicine. In 1887, he bought a property known as The Hermitage, a few miles from Arundel. Fontwell House was originally the farmhouse that stood on the land prior to the racecourse's development, which Day began in 1924.

One pilot who recalled the use of Fontwell House as Tangmere's dispersed, temporary sick quarters is Sergeant Jeff West of 616 (South Yorkshire) Squadron. Based at Westhampnett, West made the following entry in his diary for Friday, 8 August 1941, when he visited Sergeant Alan Smith, Douglas Bader's wingman: 'Rained heavily all morning. Eggs for breakfast. Went to Woodfield to see Gp Capt re commission. Recommended OK. Went to Chi with Mardon after lunch. Left shoes & film in Chi. Went to sick bay at Fontwell to see Smithy. OK. McWatt also there.'[51]

35: 'Tangmere Hurricanes'

Into Battle in the Summer of 1940

By the renowned aviation artist Nicolas Trudgian, the painting *Tangmere Hurricanes* depicts four Hurricane Mk.Is of 601 (County of London) Squadron as, refuelled and rearmed, they 'climb to re-join the battle during the summer of 1940'. The aircraft are readily identifiable by their 'UF' squadron codes and the famous Winged Sword emblem on the tail – the latter reflects the 601's connection with the City of London which has the sword in its Arms.

As the pilots climb up to engage the enemy, below them life is depicted as carrying on as normal – at least as much as it could in wartime Britain. A Southern Railway train can be seen pulling out of a local village station, a backdrop that, whilst fictional, could represent many locations in East or West Sussex. With rolling hills so typical of the South Downs, it represents a countryside over which much of the Battle of Britain was fought.

As with the other Tangmere units, 601 Squadron was heavily engaged throughout July and August. Having led 601 until posted away from Tangmere towards the end of July 1940, Max Aitken would later recall the deadly nature the Battle: 'You could tell if a fellow was going to get killed – yes you could. He sort of lost it you know, my greatest friend was killed; he was shooting at a Messerschmitt and another Messerschmitt hit him from behind. I was shouting at him and you couldn't do anything,

Nicolas Trudgian's painting *Tangmere Hurricanes*. (With the kind permission of Nicolas Trudgian; www.nicolastrudgian.com)

and you saw him go in. That affected you but you had to get on with it. Your friends affected you deeply, terrible, but you couldn't help it ... I say there was no chivalry at all between the German Air Force and the British. I'd say absolutely none, not as far as I was concerned. I hated them. They were trying to do something to us; they were trying to enslave us ...

'Radar really won the Battle of Britain, because without it we would have been doing standing patrols, and with a limited number of aircraft and limited number of pilots you couldn't have done it. As it was, we could wait on the ground and then radar would watch and through the various controls we would be told to take off at a time when the Germans were massing over Calais or Abbeville and so, therefore, we wasted no petrol, no time, no energy. In fact, we could sleep in between patrols and we would take off and be directed towards the German formation, given height distance and numbers which was very important.'

On 19 August, by which time some eight of its pilots had been killed in action (including Billy Fiske who we have already mentioned), 601 Squadron was posted to RAF Debden in Essex.

A Hurricane pictured at Tangmere. This is No.1 Squadron's CO, Squadron Leader James MacLachlan, pictured by his Mk.IIC at Tangmere on 20 November 1941. MacLachlan flew bombers in France in 1940, but transferred to fighters in June 1940 and shot down six enemy aircraft during the Battle of Britain. He joined 261 Squadron RAF in Malta, as a flight commander, and was shot down in February 1941, as a result of which his left arm was amputated. He quickly returned to operations after being fitted with an artificial limb, and in July 1941 returned to the United Kingdom to take command of No. 1 Squadron. The Hurricane is sporting his personal emblem showing his amputated arm waving a 'V' sign. He was again shot down in 1943 and became a prisoner-of-war, by which time his score had risen to 16.5 victories.

36: Last Letter Home

Sergeant Dennis Noble RAFVR

On the same day that 601 (County of London) Squadron took off from Tangmere bound for Debden, one of the pilots left behind, Sergeant Dennis Noble of 43 Squadron, wrote a letter home to his sister, Phyl. Originally from Retford in Nottinghamshire, Noble had joined the RAFVR, aged 18, in 1938. He learnt to fly at weekends and during his holidays. Having moved to London for work, he continued his flying training at Redhill aerodrome.

Called up on the outbreak of war in September 1939, Dennis duly completed his pilot's training before being posted to 43 Squadron at Tangmere on 3 August 1940. As he highlighted in his letter, he was soon found himself in the thick of the action: 'I am with a fighter squadron on the South Coast and what a hot spot it is too. We are the busiest sector in the Group at the moment. For five days a week we have to stay on the camp all day and every day, and the sixth is free for us to go out where we please. Even so, we never get away on time, for the Hun has a bad habit of having raids about a quarter to one, which means a couple of hours' hard work and a late dinner.

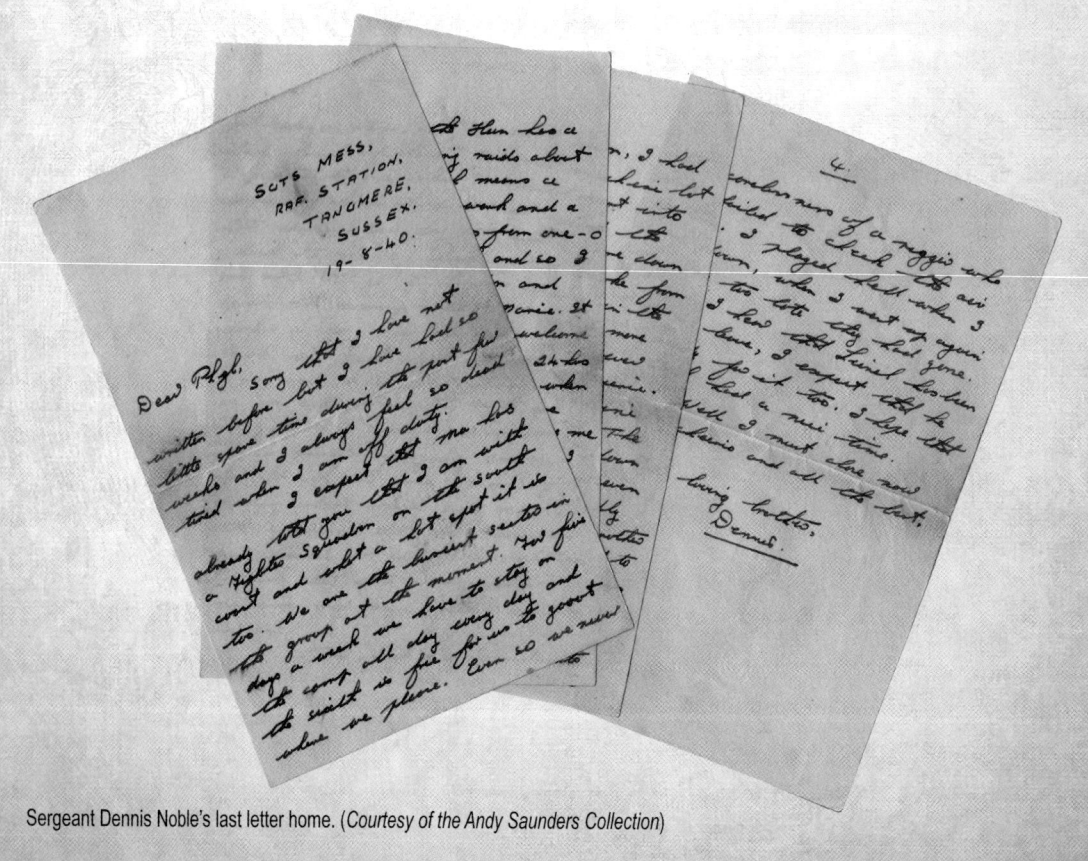

Sergeant Dennis Noble's last letter home. (*Courtesy of the Andy Saunders Collection*)

36: LAST LETTER HOME

A portrait of Sergeant Dennis Noble. (*Courtesy of the Andy Saunders Collection*)

The damaged control column and grip of Hurricane P3179, with its gun button still turned to fire. Recovered during the dig in 1996, it serves as a poignant reminder of the man whose hands were the last to hold it.

'Our day is from one o'clock to one o'clock … We work more or less 24 hours a day and its pretty tiring. When we are not intercepting raids we are patrolling convoys and believe me its hard going. Anyway, I like it all the same. Plenty of larking about which suits me to the ground.

'I still fly Hurricanes and would not change for anything. I think that they are marvellous machines and would tackle anything in one.'

Dennis would not send any more letters home. Late on the morning of 30 August 1940, 43 Squadron was airborne and engaged enemy aircraft over East Sussex. At 11.50 hours, one of its Hurricanes, with Noble at the controls, was seen to dive away from the battle. Dennis had been shot and killed in his aircraft and was, therefore, unable to pull out of the dive. His Hurricane, P3179, crashed vertically into the pavement of Woodhouse Road in Hove near Brighton.

Dennis was buried in East Retford Cemetery in August 1940.

The crash site was excavated once again in November 1996, when substantial remains of P3179 were recovered. These now form the basis of a reconstruction of the Hurricane's cockpit area in the museum at Tangmere. As a result of the dig in Hove, a second funeral service was held in Retford, with full military honours, on 22 January 1997.

37: Hawker Hurricane Mk.I, P2617

A Tangmere Battle of Britain Survivor

One of the many aircraft in the care of the RAF Museum is Hawker Hurricane P2617. A Mk.I, it is a rare survivor not only of the Battle of France, but also of the Battle of Britain. One of a batch of 500 Hurricanes ordered in 1938, P2617 was built by Gloster Aircraft Co. Ltd at Brockworth near Gloucester. It was taken on charge by the Air Ministry on 19 January 1940. Although originally allocated to 615 (County of Surrey) Squadron in France, within a few days of arrival P2617 was taken on charge by 607 (County of Durham) Squadron.

As the fall of France seemed increasingly likely, 607 reassembled at Croydon in late May. P2617 was still on the squadron's strength when it was posted in to Tangmere on 1 September 1940, replacing a battle weary 43 Squadron.

Little is known of P2617's sorties at Tangmere, though the RAF Museum's records do note that it was flown by Flight Lieutenant James Michael Bazin on 11 September. It was, according to Bazin's own logbooks, the only occasion when he flew this particular Hurricane. The squadron's ORB notes that Bazin was in its third sortie of the day. Having taken off at 16.00 hours, he landed back at Tangmere at 16.50 hours, with 'nothing seen'.

As might be expected, 607 Squadron endured a tough time at Tangmere and was withdrawn on 10 October 1940. During the few weeks it had

Hurricane P2617 being exhibited in the RAF Museum. (*Courtesy of Alan Wilson*)

37: HAWKER HURRICANE MK.I, P2617

Hurricane P2617 on display in Horse Guards Parade, Whitehall, London, on Battle of Britain Day in 1961. It was likely that she was carrying the codes AF-T at the time. (*Historic Military Press*)

been based there, the squadron lost eight pilots and eighteen Hurricanes. As for P2617, it was re-allocated to No.1 (Canadian) Squadron at Prestwick on the 26th of the month.

Having survived at least two subsequent accidents, P2617 was one of several Battle of Britain-era aircraft selected for preservation by the Air Historical Branch on 3 April 1944. Packed and crated, it arrived at RAF Wroughton, marked up 'For Museum Purposes', in December 1944.

In an interesting post-operational career, P2617 'starred' in at least three films. The first, filmed at Kenley in 1951, was *Angels One Five* – which we will encounter later – in which P2617 can be seen taxiing on the ground. It is stated by some sources that she was also flown in the film, though this role was chiefly undertaken by Portuguese Air Force Hurricanes. Again, shot at Kenley, P2617 was loaned by the RAF for the making of *Reach for the Sky*, before, in early 1968, she was used for various taxiing scenes in the filming of the blockbuster *Battle of Britain*. P2716 was finally handed over to the RAF Museum's care in May 1972.

38: Plaque to Squadron Leader Caesar Hull DFC

Battle of Britain Casualty

Though he was born in Shangani, Southern Rhodesia, Caesar Barrand Hull was brought up in South Africa. He was accepted for an RAF commission in 1935 and, after pilot training, joined 43 Squadron at RAF Tangmere in August 1936. In early 1940, following the outbreak of war, he destroyed a He 111 and shared in the destruction of two others before being posted, in May 1940, to 263 Squadron flying Gladiators.

Hull returned to Tangmere to take command of 43 Squadron on 31 August 1940. During the following week he claimed three aircraft destroyed. His time as 43 Squadron's CO was, however, short-lived for he was killed in action on 7 September. One of the squadron's pilots, Frank Carey, recalled that fateful day: 'Caesar Hull and a number of us were sitting outside the mess at Tangmere, including George Lott [see item 25], a patch over his missing right eye, just discharged from hospital, and Jack Boret, the station commander. That afternoon the squadron took off.'[52]

Having taken-off from Tangmere at 16.26 hours, 43 Squadron intercepted a large force of Dornier Do 17s escorted by Messerschmitt Bf 109s over the Thames Estuary. Hull, at the controls of Hurricane V6641, was last heard speaking to the leader of the squadron's rear section, Flight Lieutenant John Kilmartin, before diving to attack the bombers. Hull's Hurricane crashed in the grounds of Purley High School at 16.45 hours, probably a victim of a JG 54 pilot. Hull was later buried in St Andrew's Church, Tangmere. He was 27 years old.

After his death, the citizens of Shangani erected a memorial to his honour. This consisted of a granite plinth into which was affixed a brass plaque. Many years later the road system in Shangani changed and the monument to Caesar Hull became isolated, overgrown and largely forgotten.

In January 2004, Alistair Hull, a second cousin to Caesar, visited the area and found it intact. In order to thwart any attempt at stealing the plaque for its brass value, he tried to recover it but, on being shot at by nearby squatters, withdrew hastily from the scene. It was at this time that the Hull family, including Caesar's sister in England, Mrs Wendy Bryan, decided that the Tangmere Military Aviation Museum should be the plaque's ideal 'resting place'. Sometime later, two patriotic Zimbabweans delivered it to Alistair in Harare. It was then air freighted to the UK and presented to the Museum by Wendy Bryan on 17 April 2004.

The memorial plaque to Hull that is now in the care of the Tangmere Military Aviation Museum.

39: Memorial to Pilot Officer Własnowolski

One of Tangmere's International Airmen

Standing at the edge of a field in the remote Sussex village of Stoughton, within the South Downs National Park, is a memorial to one Polish member of 'The Few' who never returned home.

A veteran of the Polish Air Force who had participated in the defence of his country following the German invasion in 1939, Boleslaw Andrzej Własnowolski arrived in the United Kingdom towards the end of 1939. An experienced pilot, he was commissioned into the RAF in January 1940 and promptly posted to 6 OTU at RAF Sutton Bridge to begin his conversion to Hurricanes. His first posting was to 32 Squadron at Biggin Hill on 3 August 1940.

Własnowolski was soon in the thick of the action and he claimed a Bf 109 destroyed on 15 August, along with a second, and a Do 17, on the 18th. On 13 September, he was posted to 213 Squadron at Tangmere – just one of the many international aircrew who flew from the airfield during the war.

On 15 October 1940, Własnowolski claimed a Bf 109 damaged, but his luck was soon to run out. His last flight from Tangmere took place the day after the Battle of Britain had officially

The memorial to Pilot Officer Boleslaw Własnowolski that can be seen by the crash site in Stoughton. (*Historic Military Press*)

The field in which Pilot Officer Własnowolski's Hurricane crashed. (*Historic Military Press*)

ended. At the controls of Hurricane Mk.I V7221, coded AK-V, he scrambled at 15.10 hours on 1 November 1940; it was his second sortie of the day.

Along with the rest of the squadron, Własnowolski was directed towards Portsmouth to intercept an incoming raid. It was following the subsequent combats with Bf 109s that his Hurricane came down in a field at Liphook Game Farm, Stoughton, in West Sussex. Barely an hour had passed since Własnowolski had taken-off.

Aged just 23, Własnowolski was buried in Chichester Cemetery. At the time of his death, he had claimed five aircraft, with a sixth shared. His awards and decorations include the Virtuti Militari 5th Class and the Polish Cross of Valour. As well as being commemorated by the memorial at the crash site, he is also named on the Polish War Memorial at Northolt.

A close-up on the panel on Pilot Officer Własnowolski's memorial. (*Historic Military Press*)

Section Five

The Road to Victory

40: Presentation Biscuit Barrel

The Tangmere Wing

With the Battle of Britain won, Fighter Command began to switch from a defensive role and adopt a more offensive stance. As Marshal of the Royal Air Force Sir Sholto Douglas, Dowding's successor as the head of Fighter Command, noted, 'In the middle of December the German fighter force, which had suffered heavy losses since the Summer, virtually abandoned the offensive for the time being. Clearly, the moment had come to put our plans into effect and wrest the initiative from the enemy.'

The code-names chosen for these new operations were respectively *Mosquito* (later changed to *Rhubarb*, to avoid confusion with the aircraft of that name) and *Circus* – others, on a similar theme, soon followed. Providing valuable experience, the *Rhubarb* patrols began on 20 December 1940. It was not until 10 January 1941, that *Circus* No.1, was undertaken. On this occasion, no less than nine squadrons of fighters escorted six Bristol Blenheims of Bomber Command's 114 Squadron to attack dispersal pens and ammunition dumps on the edge of the Forêt de Guînes, to the south of Calais.

Needless to say, the pilots of the Tangmere Sector, in this case Nos. 302 and 610 (County of Chester) squadrons, were involved in this important development. For the first time since Hitler's Blitzkrieg the previous year, an escorted RAF bomber force penetrated German-held airspace.

In due course, 302 Squadron moved out, and was replaced by both 145 and 616 (South Yorkshire) squadrons, forming, along with 610 Squadron, the fledging Tangmere Wing under the famous, and legless, Wing Commander Douglas Bader. Never one to waste time, Bader,

The biscuit barrel presented by the men of 616 (South Yorkshire) Squadron.

who reported to Tangmere's Station Commander on 18 March 1941, flew his first sortie with the Wing that same day.

Following their arrival on 26 February 1941, initially being housed at Tangmere before moving the short distance to Westhampnett in May, 616 Squadron set about exploring the local amenities. The object seen here suggests that one of the pilots' favourite haunts was the Royal Oak in East Lavant, a 19th Century inn that is still a hostelry today. This biscuit barrel was presented by them to the pub's landlady, Mrs Violet Elcock, during their time at Tangmere in 1941, a period when they helped take the battle to the skies over France, no doubt in recognition of the many enjoyable occasions they enjoyed in her establishment, located as it was, within staggering distance of the airfield's boundary.

41: Spitfire Mk.IIa P7350

The BBMF's Tangmere Veteran

For many years the oldest flying Spitfire, as well as being only the fourteenth of 11,939 aircraft that rolled off the production lines at the Castle Bromwich shadow factory, the Battle of Britain Memorial Flight's Mk.IIa P7350 is another of the few surviving aircraft that flew from Tangmere during the Second World War.

Originally test flown by Alex Henshaw in August 1940, P7350 was taken on charge by the RAF on the 13th of the same month. It was duly delivered, again by Henshaw, to No.6 Maintenance Unit (MU) at Brize Norton. With the Battle of Britain still raging, P7350 immediately entered squadron service, with 266 (Rhodesia) Squadron at RAF Wittering, on 6 September. She was allocated the code letters 'UO-T'.

A change of unit followed on 17 October 1940, when P7350 was transferred to 603 (City of Edinburgh) Squadron at RAF Hornchurch. She was once more thrown into the fray. On 25 October, P7350 was hit during combat with a Messerschmitt Bf 109 while being flown by Polish pilot Ludwik Martel. A cannon shell punched a large hole in the port wing and Martel himself was wounded by shrapnel in the left side of his body and legs. Despite his injuries, Martel, in pain and fighting to remain conscious, managed to nurse P7350 down through 16,000 feet of thick cloud to force land in a field near Hastings.

An air-to-air shot of the BBMF's P7350. (© *MoD/Crown Copyright, 2021*)

P7350 was dispatched to No.1 Civilian Repair Unit at Cowley on 31 October. Fully repaired, it was ready for collection on 7 December. She was then allocated to 616 Squadron at Tangmere, where it landed on 18 March 1941 – the same day as Bader arrived to take charge as Wing Leader. Though P7350 only remained at Tangmere for a few weeks, being transferred to 64 Squadron at Hornchurch on 10 April, it played its part in some of the first of the RAF's new offensive operations.

Having survived all its wartime adventures, P7350 was declared surplus to requirements by the Air Ministry in 1947. It was sold as scrap in 1948, but the management of John Dale & Sons Ltd recognised the airframe's historical importance and subsequently donated it to the RAF Colerne Museum.

The making of the *Battle of Britain* saw P7350 emerge from twenty years of retirement, having been selected for a return to flying condition to star in the film. It was flown to Duxford for its starring role on 20 May 1968. After filming was completed, it was donated to the Battle of Britain Memorial Flight, or BBMF as it is better known, which continues to operate it to this day.

Another view of the Battle of Britain Memorial Flight's Spitfire P7350, this time in company with Hurricane PZ865. (© *Crown/MoD Copyright 2025*)

42: Night Fighter Crew at Tangmere

Recording Details of a Victory

The main photograph seen here depicts the scene in a dispersal hut at Tangmere one morning in May 1941. The individual sat at the desk, writing in what appears to be a logbook, is Flight Sergeant Trevor Williams, while on the right, on the telephone, is Flight Lieutenant Anthony Dottridge. The pair formed the crew of a Beaufighter night fighter of 'B' Flight, 219 Squadron; being the navigator/radar operator and pilot respectively.

Dottridge had two claims in May – on the 3rd and 10th respectively. It is possible, therefore, that this scene shows the two men in the immediate aftermath of one of those victories – a scenario that would have been played out at Tangmere many times during the course of the war. The black-out screen covering the window behind Williams would suggest that it was still dark outside.

The first interception the pair was involved in occurred in the area of Selsey Bill at 22.30 hours on the 3rd. Dottridge's combat report reveals a little of the work done by night fighters operating from Tangmere. When one 'blip was lost', he wrote, 'Flintlock [Control] told me that he had another E/A for me'. He was given vectors that eventually placed him astern of the raider, a Heinkel He 111 'coming in south of Selsey Bill': 'Was told to flash weapon & my operator [Williams] obtained a blip and brought

The scene in the dispersal hut used by 'B' Flight, 219 Squadron at Tangmere in May 1941. (*Chris Goss Collection*)

An informal group photograph of members of 219 Squadron, at their dispersal at RAF Tangmere in June 1941. Those whose identity is known are, in the back row, left to right, Sergeant Clandillon, ?, Sergeant Wilson, ?, Flying Officer Sinclair, Sergeant C. Berridge, and ?. Meanwhile, in the front row, are Flight Sergeant Billy Stringer (a member of groundcrew), Flight Lieutenant J.G. Topham, Flying Officer D.O. Hobbis, and Wing Commander Ivins. Note the Beaufighters in the background. (*Chris Goss Collection*)

me up astern of E/A. E/A was about 800 yards in front and about 1000' above when a visual was obtained.

'He appeared, according to my A.S.I. [air speed indicator] & altimeter to be climbing very slowly as I was overtaking him when my A.S.I. was showing only 140 m.p.h. I then noticed that E/A was showing a small white light on his tail & by this time I was level & about 500 yds on his starb'd beam.'

Dottridge and Williams then prepared to make their move. 'I commenced a turn to through 360° to prevent overtaking E/A,' continued Dottridge, '& then came up astern again by A.I. directions from my operator. I recognised E/A as He 111 & closed to 75 to 100 yards astern & then opened fore with 4 second burst closing to about 25 yds astern when I had to break off attack to avoid colliding with E/A. From time of opening fire until attack was broken off shells were seen to burst in engines & fuselage which emitted smoke & sparks, and pieces of E/A flew back touching my own A/C. As attack was broken off E/A caught on fire and circled slowly, then dived vertically towards the ground in the vicinity of Selsey Bill.'

The Heinkel He 111 H-5, werke 4064 and coded 1H+DS, of 8 Staffel, III/KG 26, broke up in the air. The wreckage fell to ground at Keynor Farm, Sidlesham. Unteroffizier G. Macher and Gefreiter B. Winterscheid baled out and were captured. The rest of the crew, Unteroffizier O. Kaminski and Gefreiter B. Möllers, were killed.

43: RAF Merston

Tangmere's Last Satellite Airfield

Often incorrectly termed as Advanced Landing Ground, RAF Merston was actually built on land which was requisitioned in July 1939. It was originally intended to be developed as a grass airfield, with a thirty-foot perimeter track around the edge, that would serve as a satellite to RAF Tangmere.

The site was completed in early 1941, ready for the first operational unit to arrive in the form of 145 Squadron flying the Spitfire Mk.II. The first landing by one of the squadron's aircraft occurred on 6 May 1941; this was made by Flight Lieutenant Stephens at the controls of Spitfire P7975. Stephens had made the short five or six mile hop from Tangmere. Further aircraft arrived the following day, these being led by Flight Lieutenant Michael Newling.[53]

Despite having no fixed runways until 1943, between May 1941 and August 1942, aside from 145 Squadron, Merston was occupied by a number of fighter units, including Nos. 41, 131, 232 and 412 (RCAF) squadrons. In June 1942, Merston was allocated to the USAAF's Eighth Air Force alongside RAF Westhampnett. At this point it became home to the 307th Fighter

An aerial view of what was RAF Merston looking to the south. The outline of the perimeter track can still be seen. (*Historic Military Press*)

91

Squadron of the 31st Fighter Group, equipped with Spitfire Mk.Vs.

Merston's occupation by the Americans was short lived, for it was closed at the end of 1942 so that improvement work could be undertaken. In this period, which lasted through into 1943, the airfield had Sommerfeld track runways, twenty hard-standings, with blast pens, and a number of blister hangars installed.

Merston duly reopened for operational flying in May 1943 with its first unit being 485 (NZ) Squadron, then operating the Spitfire Mk.Vb. A whole host of Hurricane and Typhoon squadrons rotated through the airfield during the following year, being engaged on *Roadsteads*, *Ramrods*, *Rodeos* and *Circus* operations. In this period, Merston was home to a multi-national mix of pilots including, as well as the New Zealanders, Polish, Canadian and Free French airmen.

The airfield at Merston ceased to be used as an operational fighter base in August 1944, when the last Spitfire Mk.IX of 402 (City of Winnipeg) Squadron departed. Having briefly housed Air Disarmament Units of SHAEF between March and May 1945, and then used by the Royal Navy for storage of war surplus equipment, Merston was completely closed in November 1945. The process of returning it to its pre-war agricultural past then began.

Squadron Leader M.G.F. Pedley, Commanding Officer of 131 Squadron, is assisted by his ground crew as he prepares to set out on a sweep in his Spitfire Mk.Vb, BM420 and coded NX-A, from RAF Merston in June 1942.

44: Tangmere Defence Map

Guarding an Airfield

With Tangmere located only a few miles from the beaches of the South Coast, the question of its defence, from both aerial and ground attack, was an important consideration by the beginning of the summer of 1940, following the fall of France.

The section seen here of a wartime map of Tangmere's defences dated 16 January 1941 focuses on the immediate defences in and around the airfield perimeter; the wider map also includes broader defence lines in the area.

The red annotations indicate positions manned by the Home Guard.

As we can see, the defences included twin Browning machine-guns, single Lewis guns, twin Lewis guns, searchlight positions, Hispano 20mm cannon, Bofors guns and pillboxes. Interestingly, the map also shows the location of at least five Parachute and Cable, or PAC, units. As the excellent Kenley Revival website notes, the PAC system for airfield defence was 'originally developed in the early twentieth century as a land based means of sending a rescue

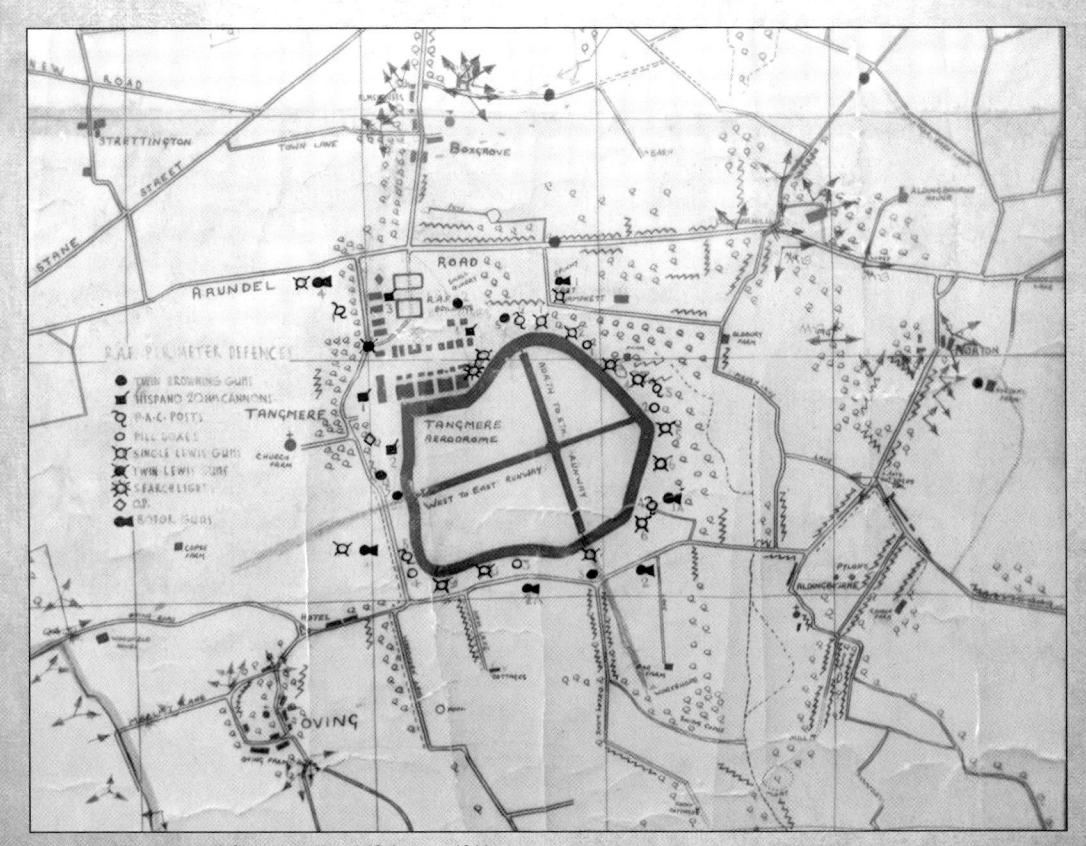

A section of Tangmere's defence map dated 16 January 1941.

line to stranded ships on the coast … It was then further developed by the Royal Aeronautical Establishment (RAE) at Farnborough as a defence for low level bombing attacks.'

The device consisted of a rocket with parachute fitted on the top that was fired electrically, by means of a cartridge, out of a tube vertically into the air. The rocket climbed to a height of 600 feet, unwinding a length of 1-ton cable as it went. With the parachute opening at the top, and another at the bottom end, the whole assembly floated to earth at a rate of forty feet per second. The intention was that the cables would literally hang as a vertical barrage in front of low-flying attackers, hopefully snaring them as they passed.

By the beginning of the Battle of Britain, a total of twenty-six airfields and similar sites had been equipped with the PAC system.

One of Tangmere's defenders – an RAF anti-aircraft gunner mans a 20mm Hispano cannon in a revetment on the airfield, 8 June 1941.

45: Gumber Decoy Site

Tangmere's Diversion 'Airfield'

In October 1939 the Air Ministry originated a special branch of the Air Staff to organize a system of decoys for the protection of RAF airfields and stations against air attack. The two main forms of decoy for airfields were 'K' sites, for daytime decoy work, and 'Q' sites, which were for night deception.

The first to be introduced were the 'K' sites. The locations for these were generally two to six miles from the RAF base to be protected, and, wherever possible, on the anticipated line of approach of hostile aircraft. The site selected for Tangmere's decoy was on the South Downs, at Gumber Farm near Slindon.

The work to create the 'K' site consisted of levelling and modelling hedges to resemble the dummy hedges painted on Tangmere itself, which also created the wide open spaces that were the most marked feature of RAF airfields. In addition, dummy Hawker Hurricanes were arranged around the site, as well as simulated roads and dumps, dummy tracks on the fake airfield, real and bogus machine-gun posts, and the all-important shelters and trenches for the operating crew.

In due course, Gumber also became a 'Q' site. In this way, lights were arranged on the ridge along the path of Stane Street in such a way as to resemble those at Tangmere. The power for these was provided by a generator housed in an underground bunker – this can still be seen today. In order to reduce the risk that friendly pilots might mistake Gumber for the real Tangmere (which sadly did happen), certain lights were omitted and others deliberately introduced which identified it as a decoy to routinely briefed Allied pilots and aircrew.

Leading Aircraftman Tom Merritt was one of those stationed at Gumber: 'The dummy Hurricanes were arranged in such a way as to look like operational aircraft ready for action, and so draw the fire of the attacking Germans. Both the flarepath lights and the Hurricanes were on the same field at Gumber. To start with, the only structures at Gumber were the tents and the trenches we dug. The concrete control room came later.

'Whilst at Gumber I remember that we often had to dig further extensions to the flarepath lights, which went for about half-a-mile towards

One of the control buildings that can still be seen at the Gumber Farm decoy site near Slindon. (*Historic Military Press*)

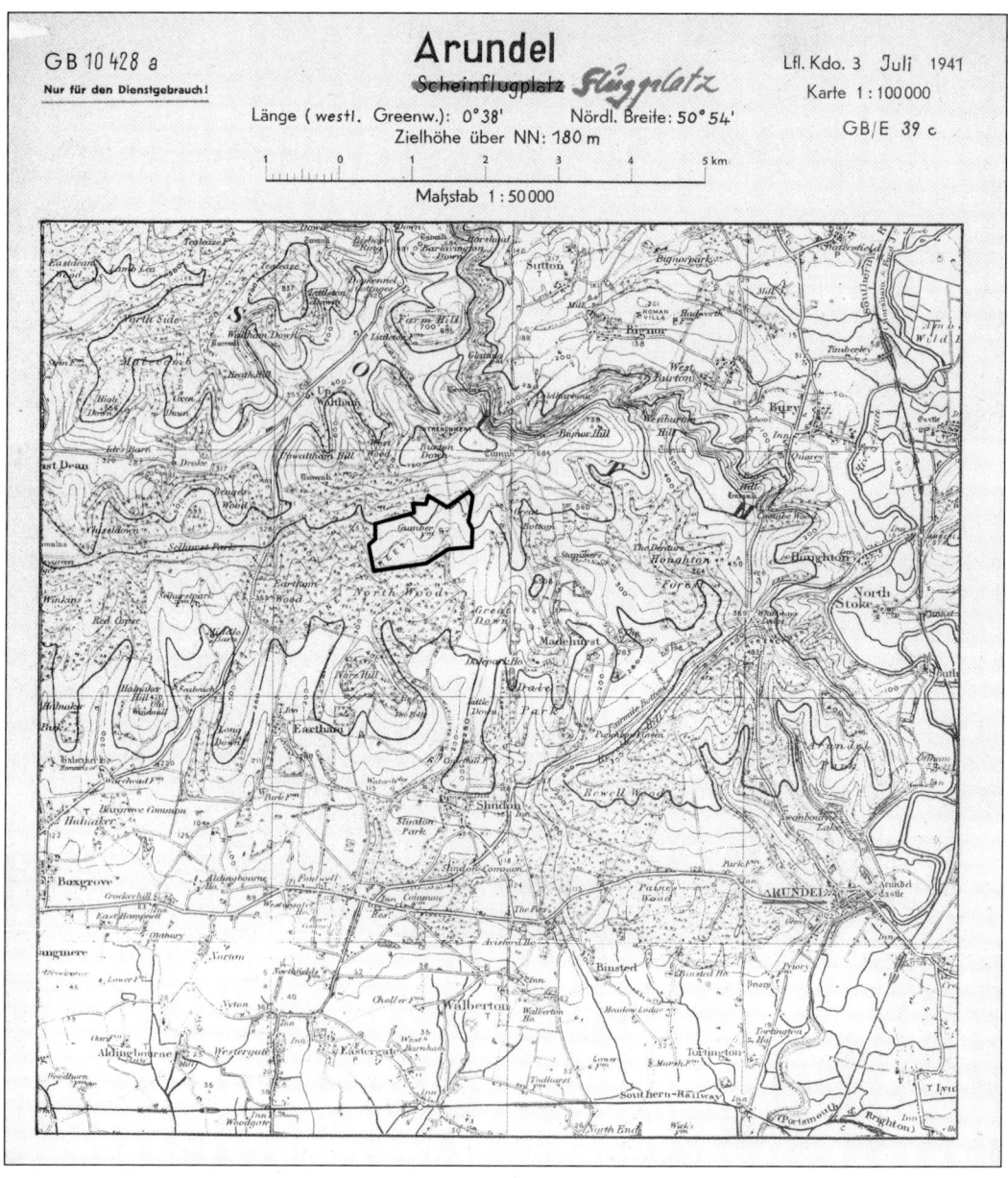

It would appear that the Luftwaffe was indeed taken in by the presence of the decoy site, as indicated by this target map for 'Arundel Flugplatz', or 'Arundel Aerodrome', dated 3 July 1941. (*Historic Military Press*)

Eartham. My main task at Gumber was that of gunnery crew – operating and maintaining the anti-aircraft guns – though we were expected to help in the maintenance and operation of the site. We had between two and four men working in shifts looking after the engines that powered the decoy lights. Our orders at the Gumber site came from Tangmere. If a raid was developing or German aircraft were expected, orders would be given to turn on the dummy airfield lights, while the real lights at Tangmere would be extinguished.'[54]

46: Douglas Bader's PoW Photograph

The Tangmere Wing Losses its Famous Leader

An early casualty of the RAF's increasingly offensive stance in 1941 was also one of the most famous pilots to be associated with RAF Tangmere – Douglas Bader.

On 9 August 1941, Bader led the Tangmere Wing which had been tasked with providing an escort for *Circus* 68, a bombing raid on Gosnay, near St Omer. Sergeant Geoff West was flying in place of Bader's normal wingman, Sergeant Alan Smith. As two of the Wing's three squadrons crossed the French coast, they soon became embroiled in combat with numerous Bf 109s. In the ensuing melee Bader was 'downed', though exactly what happened cannot be said with complete certainty; some say he was shot down, others that it was the result of a mid-air collision, with a friendly aircraft or otherwise. Regardless of the circumstances, the Tangmere Wing's leader was forced to abandon his Spitfire.

Back at Tangmere, the indomitable pilot was duly posted as missing. Then, on 14 August the German authorities notified the British, via the Red Cross, that Bader had in fact survived, albeit that he was now a prisoner of war. Group Captain Woodhall broadcast the welcome news over Tangmere's tannoy system.

It transpired that in abandoning his aircraft, Bader had lost one of his false legs. The Germans took the unusual step of guaranteeing free passage for an RAF aircraft to deliver a replacement to Oberst Adolf Galland's JG 26 airfield at Audembert. The British declined the offer, but, instead, dropped a spare leg by parachute from a Blenheim during a *Circus* operation to Longuenesse on 19 August.

Smith, who had just been commissioned, was one of the pilots who escorted the bombers

A copy of one of Bader's PoW registration photographs. This was taken at Oflag X-C, a camp for officers (Offizierlager) located in Lübeck in northern Germany. (*Andy Saunders Collection*)

that day: 'I can still remember seeing the box dropping under the parachute; it was one hell of a day, low broken cloud and rain. We had six Blenheims, the weather was appalling, and the bombers could not drop their bombs on the target at Lille, but the leg was dropped over St Omer.'[55]

Following his capture, Bader was initially taken to hospital in St Omer. His missing right leg was then found near the Spitfire's crash site. Repaired, it was returned to him by his captors. Seizing the moment, Bader made his first attempt to escape using a rope made of bed sheets to climb down from a window. His liberty,

A German airman holding the box in which Douglas Bader's replacement leg was flown to, and dropped over, France, by a Blenheim of 18 Squadron. (*Mark Hillier Collection*)

though, was short lived. Eventually incarnated in the infamous Colditz Castle, Oflag IVC, it would be years before Bader would see Tangmere again – see item 71.

Sir Alan Smith later recalled the effect that Bader's loss had: 'Morale was affected; we thought we would get our revenge as they had taken Bader away. A real loss to the Wing. He had such a strong personality and was a good leader. I can't say that had I been flying that day things would have been different, but I often wonder if I had been there, if I could have made a difference at all. Maybe I would not have come back?'

47: Tangmere's Role in Operation *Anthropoid*

The Assassination of Reinhard Heydrich

At 22.00 hours on the evening of 28 December 1941, a Handley Page Halifax of 138 (Special Duties) Squadron lifted off from Tangmere. The bomber's sortie that night was an early illustration of the part that the airfield played in supporting clandestine operations in Occupied Europe – a role that, as subsequent objects will reveal, grew in importance as the war continued.

As well as the crew, on board the Halifax that night were a number of members of the Czech resistance. Two of the men, Jozef Gabčík and Jan Kubiš, were assigned to Operation *Anthropoid*, the others to two missions given the codenames *Silver A* and *Silver B*. It was in 1941 that the Czechoslovak government-in-exile, led by Edvard Beneš, devised Operation *Anthropoid*, the aim of which was the assassination of

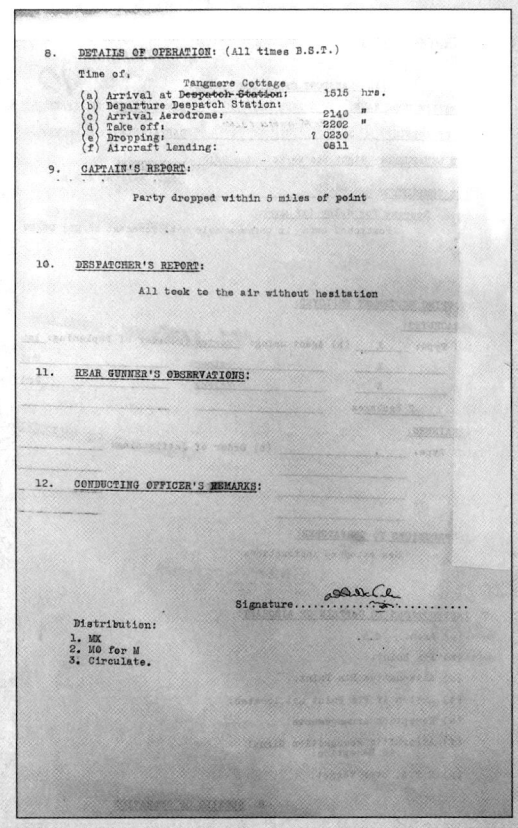

The air transport operation report regarding the despatch of the Czech agents on the night of 28/29 December 1941. As can be seen, the drop had previously been delayed due to bad weather. The rear of the form, seen here on the right, is interesting as it gives times for the moment of the agents to, and through, Tangmere.

A depiction of the attack on SS-Obergruppenführer Reinhard Heydrich in Prague on 27 May 1942, that was produced for the Ministry of Information circa 1942. (*The National Archives, INF/3*)

SS-Obergruppenführer Reinhard Heydrich, the acting governor of the Protectorate of Bohemia and Moravia.

Once airborne, the Halifax, L9613 and coded NF-V, set course for the French coast, which it crossed at Le Crotoy. The squadron's Operations Record Book takes up the story: 'Course [was] then set for Darmstadt and shortly after an enemy fighter sighted on the port quarter. Two flares dropped by this aircraft, but no attack made on the Halifax and, owing the heavy loading, the Halifax took no punitive action and after twenty minutes contact was lost. Visibility good and several pinpoints obtained despite snow on the ground.

'Darmstadt reached at 00:42 hrs and although another aircraft was seen, it was lost shortly after. Course set for target, eventually pinpointing became impossible owing to heavy snow which blotted out all roads, railways, rivers, and small towns. Owing to cloud, height was lost and at 02:12 hrs flak was seen ahead and identified to be from Pilsen, course altered to south of town and then to target area.'[56]

Once in the target area, the *Anthropoid* team was the first to jump at 02.24 hours. They were followed shortly after by the other agents. Over the weeks that followed, Gabčík and Kubiš remained in hiding whilst they prepared to carry their mission.

The pair eventually carried out their SOE-backed attack in Prague on 27 May 1942; Heydrich, mortally wounded, died on 4 June. Heydrich was the highest-ranking Nazi to be killed by any resistance group during the war.

Gabčík and Kubiš did not live much longer than Heydrich. Both men lost their lives on 18 June having been cornered in a church in Prague.

As for the Halifax, it returned safely to Tangmere, although not without incident. Having dropped the last of the agents, Flight Lieutenant Ronald C. Hockey turned for home: 'No other pinpoint recognised until more flak met at Brussels. Course changed to Westward at 05:40 hrs. French Coast crossed at 07:20 hrs and shortly after the cockpit hood blew up and jammed. The second pilot held the hood to prevent it being jettisoned and fouling the controls, speed was reduced to 140 mph. English Coast crossed 08.07 hrs near Selsey Bill and a landing effected at Tangmere at 08.19 hrs.'[57]

48: Caterpillar Club Pin

Tangmere Wing Pilot Shot Down in the Channel Dash

February 1942 saw the Tangmere Wing involved in another major event of the war in Europe – Operation *Cerberus*, otherwise known as the Channel Dash. This was the breakout by a Kriegsmarine armada comprising two German battleships, *Scharnhorst* and *Gneisenau*, the heavy cruiser *Prinz Eugen*, and a number of escorts, from Brest in Brittany. Putting to sea late on 11 February, the plan was for these warships to race up the English Channel to the relative safety of home ports in Germany.

Predictably, the Royal Navy and RAF did all it could to prevent the enemy warships getting through. As part of this response, Spitfires of Nos. 41 and 129 Squadrons, based at Westhampnett, and Hurricanes of No.1 Squadron from Tangmere were scrambled in appalling weather. Escorted by the cannon-armed Spitfire Vbs of 129 (Mysore) Squadron, the Hurricanes arrived on the scene on the afternoon of 12 February in very poor visibility, promptly being thrown into the thick of the action.

Sergeant Raymond 'Mick' Wilson's Caterpillar Club badge. (*Mark Hillier Collection*)

One of the Spitfire pilots, Canadian Pilot Officer Ray Sherk, vividly recalled events that day: 'We were called to readiness at noon (without dinner) and took off at 1:15 p.m. to escort some cannon armed Hurricanes of No.1 Squadron to shoot up some shipping of Calais that turned out to be the *Scharnhorst* and *Gneisenau* with some destroyers. Several aircraft missing. Dixie Davis was shot down and killed in action. McPhie got a bullet in his shoe which grazed his heel and had several bullet holes in his aircraft. Sergeant Mick Wilson baled out over Ipswich after losing part of his starboard wing. Bowman got two 109s damaged. It was a pretty shaky do – I recall avoiding ship masts. I was involved in the melee but was not hit although a shell from a destroyer just missed me!'

As Sherk noted, Sergeant Raymond 'Mick' Wilson had lost a third of his wing to the accurate anti-aircraft fire put up by the German warships. Somehow he managed to limp back to the safety of home shores before baling out. In the process he qualified for membership of the Caterpillar Club.

Formed in 1922, the Club was for those individuals whose lives had been saved through the use of a parachute manufactured or designed by the Irvin Air Chute Company. On enrolment, new members were presented with a membership certificate or card, and the now famous caterpillar badge. It is Sergeant Wilson's that is seen here.

A portrait of Wilson that was taken prior to his involvement in the Channel Dash. (*Mark Hillier Collection*)

49: Lysander Replica

The First Special Duties Lysander Sortie from Tangmere

Though relatively few in number, one aircraft that has an enduring association with RAF Tangmere is the Westland Lysander Mk.III (SD). In 1941, the RAF issued a contract which resulted in some forty Westland Lysander Mk.IIIs and Mk.IIIAs being modified for Special Duties work – though standard Lysanders had been used in such roles as early as 1940. The conversion work was carried out by Fairfield Aviation, a sub-contractor of Westland, with the resulting aircraft redesignated as the Mk.III (SD).

The work on these aircraft 'involved removing all the armament and replacing the variable pitch propeller with a constant speed version. A 150 gallon fuel tank was added under the fuselage which increased the aircraft's range from 600 miles to about 1000 miles along with a larger internal oil tank to allow for the longer engine running.

Tangmere Military Aviation Museum's replica Special Duties Lysander. It is seen here displayed as V9875, MA-J, the Lysander flown by Squadron Leader Hugh Verity, flight commander of 161 Squadron's 'A' Flight in 1943.

'The rear gunner's compartment was modified by replacing the canopy with a one-piece unit that slid rearwards on rails, lengthening and strengthening the rear floor and fitting a fixed metal ladder to the port side allowing quick entry and exit. A rearward facing bench for two passengers was installed with a locker underneath and a shelf was built at the rear of the compartment which could also serve as a seat for a third passenger.'[58]

The first Lysander Special Duties sortie to take-off from RAF Tangmere is believed to be that undertaken by Flight Lieutenant Alan Michael 'Sticky' Murphy on the night of 27/28 February 1942. Murphy was at the controls of 161 (Special Duties) Squadron's Lysander V9428 – the converted Lysanders were also used by Nos. 138 and 357 squadrons. The flight that night marked 161's first pick-up operation.

Under Operation *Baccarat*, Murphy took off from Tangmere at 21.45 hours with one passenger, a female agent known only as *Anatole*. Passing over Beachy Head, Murphy set course for Abbeville. Over the Channel, however, he encountered 10/10ths cloud. Struggling to locate his position, Murphy took the unusual step of requesting a fix from Tangmere on his R/T. This, though, enabled him to finally locate his landing field near the village of Saint-Saens, despite the weather still closing in.

Once on the ground, Murphy hastily handed *Anatole* over to the reception committee before loading a number of bags of courier mail and two passengers. The latter were the BCRA agent Pierre Julitte, code-name *Julie*, and Gilbert Renault-Roulier, better-known by his code-name *Remy*. He was airborne again at 00.06 hours and soon re-crossed the French coast to the east of Dieppe.

Murphy duly returned his precious cargo back to Tangmere at 01.20 hours, successfully concluding the first of many such flights to be made from there. These are flights which are commemorated through Tangmere Military Aviation Museum's full-size replica Lysander. It was originally constructed in 2015 by Gate Guards UK for use in the film *Allied*, before being acquired with the help of a contribution from the Museum's Society of Friends.

Westland Lysander R9125 in the markings of a Special Duties Squadron. This aircraft is known to have been taken on charge by 161 (Special Duties) Squadron in October 1944. R9125 survives in the care of the RAF Museum at Hendon. (*Historic Military Press*)

50: Squadron Leader H.E. Bates' Tunic

Famous Pre-war Author Posted to Tangmere

Already a renowned author by the time that war broke out in 1939, Herbert Ernest Bates was commissioned in the RAF in October 1941. Following training, his first posting was to RAF Oakington in Cambridgeshire. His role was to mix with personnel at the base with the intention of gathering material for future books and short stories.

To continue this process, Bates was posted to RAF Tangmere in March 1942, and would remain there for a total of five months. Though he was based at Shopwyke House, Tangmere's Officers' Mess, Bates was not billeted there, but accommodated in an otherwise empty house a short distance away.

His time with the RAF eventually led to creation of a series of stories published under the pseudonym 'Flying Officer X'. These accounts were widely read and captured the spirit, struggles, and heroism of Allied pilots and crew members. They were also packed full of links to Tangmere and the many men he encountered there.

Take, for example, Bates' chapter entitled 'Free Choice: Free World', which is based around the story of Pilot Officer Romualdas Marcinkus. Born in Jurbarkas, Lithuania, on 22 July 1907, Marcinkus was a gifted athlete and passionate about aviation. He joined the Lithuanian Air Force in the 1930s, where he became a distinguished pilot and was involved in competitive sports, including football. After Lithuania was annexed by the Soviet Union in 1940, Marcinkus managed to flee to the West, eventually, via a circuitous route, reaching the UK, where he enlisted in the RAF.

Squadron Leader H.E. Bates' tunic on display at Tangmere.

Serving with No.1 Squadron, Marcinkus, the only Lithuanian to serve in the RAF in the war, was at the controls of one of the Hurricanes from No.1 Squadron that took off from Tangmere on 12 February 1942, to participate in the various actions surrounding the Channel Dash. While pressing home an attack on the escorting German destroyers, Marcinkus' cannon-armed Hurricane was shot down by cannon fire. He was duly posted as 'missing'.

Just a matter of weeks later Bates was posted to Tangmere, and was, it would seem, soon hearing

The cover of H.E Bates' book *The Stories of Flying Officer 'X'*, a collection of stories packed full with Tangmere links.

accounts of Marcinkus' actions. What Bates did not know to start with, is that the Lithuanian had survived the events on 12 February, and, though badly wounded, been rescued by the Germans to become a prisoner of war.

In 'Free Choice: Free World' Bates recounts how he came to frequent a Russian restaurant near Tangmere that was run by Mr and Mrs Koussevitsky. It was 'a little eating place,' as he described it, 'with marble-top tables and huge silver hand-stand cruets and yellow cane chairs and a smell of fried fish that is the shadow of Russia'. Over time, Bates came to know the Koussevitskys well – and they him.

During one visit, Mrs Koussevitsky asked Bates if he knew 'Mr Markus', this being Marcinkus. It transpired that Romualdas had been a regular visitor to the restaurant, but had not been seen for some time. The hosts were devastated to learn from Bates that he had been shot down during the attacks on the German warships. Mrs Koussevitsky, for her part, refused to believe he was dead.

In time, the news that Marcinkus was a prisoner of war filtered through to Tangmere – information that Bates, as he revealed in his short story, immediately passed on to the couple. 'Now it was Mrs. Koussevitsky who could not speak,' he wrote. 'She stood crying quietly, slowly clasping and unclasping her hands.' The story ends with hopes of a post-war reunion, or more properly a celebration, with the missing Lithuanian airman.

Tragically, that peacetime gathering never happened. Incarcerated in Stalag Luft III, Marcinkus was one of the first ten men out of the tunnel during the Great Escape in March 1944. Recaptured, he was one the fifty men subsequently executed by the Gestapo, in his case on 29 March 1944.

51: Flight Lieutenant Ball's Album

Dieppe Raid Participant

Another important event for the Tangmere-based squadrons in 1942 was Operation *Jubilee*, the attack on Dieppe that was carried out on 19 August 1942. One of the pilots involved that day was Flight Sergeant Godfrey Massey Ball RAAF.

At the time of the raid Ball was serving in 43 Squadron, which, notes the squadron ORB, 'took an energetic part' in the events that day. Having been brought to readiness at 04.00 hours, just twenty-five minutes later twelve of the squadron's Hurricanes took off and headed out over the Channel. Led by Squadron Leader Danny Le Roy du Vivier (a Belgian), their task was to attack gun positions on the beaches and buildings immediately to the west of Dieppe Harbour. In this attack, which was undertaken through intense flak, two of the Hurricanes were shot down, though both pilots survived. The remainder of the squadron landed back at Tangmere just after 06.00 hours; only five aircraft were undamaged.

Flight Lieutenant Ball pictured with his Hurricane at the time of the Dieppe Raid. (*Tangmere Military Aviation Museum*)

Having been quickly rearmed and refuelled, 43 Squadron was back in the fray at 07.50 hours, when twelve Hurricanes, including that flown by Ball, took off on the second sortie of the day. Their mission on this occasion was to locate and attack a force of E-boats reported to be heading down from Boulogne towards Dieppe. Despite a long search, none were found and the squadron was back at Tangmere by 09.20 hours.

The third sortie began at 11.15 hours – though on this occasion Ball remained at Tangmere. Having attacked various German gun positions on the eastern headland, everyone returned safely having encountered less flak than on the previous visits.

The fourth and final sortie was airborne at 13.45 hours, with the same task as the previous one. Despite the frantic nature of the day's action, twelve Hurricanes were still available, though Ball was, once again, not on the roster. The strain was undoubtedly felt throughout the squadron. Indeed the ORB noted that 'special mention should be made of the efforts of the ground crews who worked splendidly to keep 12 aircraft serviceable all the time and also to refuel and re-arm them between sorties'.

Born in Dublin on 23 September 1912, the son of Major George Joseph Ball CBE, Godfrey spent his childhood in Ireland, before being educated in England and emigrating to Australia in 1932. He enlisted in the RAAF in July 1940, and promptly began his pilot training. Having spent time at 61 OTU Heston, he was posted to 43 Squadron on 30 October 1941. The museum at Tangmere is the proud custodian of Ball's logbook, medals, various bits of uniform, and, of course, his photograph album as seen here.

52: The Night Hawk

Squadron Leader Karel Kuttelwascher DFC & Bar

One of the many remarkable individuals who operated from Tangmere during the Second World War was Karel Miloslav Kuttelwascher. Known as 'Kut', Kuttelwascher had enlisted in the Czech Air Force in 1934. Following the German occupation, he escaped through Poland to France where he flew for the Armée de l'Air in the Battle of France. After the French surrender, Kuttelwascher's unit was withdrawn to Algiers, at which point he travelled to the UK by sea.

With the rank of sergeant, Kuttelwascher was posted to No.1 Squadron on 3 October 1940. On 8 April 1941, Kuttelwascher achieved his first confirmed kill – a Messerschmitt Bf 109. In February 1942, Kuttelwascher was involved in the air operations surrounding the Channel Dash before the squadron began night intruder

Flight Lieutenant K.M. 'Kut' Kuttelwascher of No.1 Squadron RAF, sitting in the cockpit of his Hurricane at Tangmere, shortly after shooting down his seventh and eighth enemy aircraft during a night intruder mission over France on 30 April/1 May 1942. At the conclusion of night intruder operations, No.1 Squadron moved north to Acklington to convert to Hawker Typhoons. Kuttelwascher, however, stayed in the south and moved down the road from Tangmere to Ford. There he joined 23 Squadron.

missions. During these he had considerable success whilst flying from Tangmere – usually at the controls Hawker Hurricane Mk.IIc BE581, which, coded JX-E, carried nose art depicting a scythe and the legend 'Night Reaper'. He later described these flights:

'A full moon is always a good time to fly. We can follow the canals of Holland and the gleaming railway lines across northern Europe. Like the cats-eyes on the roads, moonlight reflects from the railway lines and we follow them. I become like a night hawk searching for my target. I want to destroy the 'planes not the people. When we have done our work, we head home as fast as lighting.'[59]

During one sortie from Tangmere, Kuttelwascher achieved a 'triple kill', as his biographer, Roger Darlington, reveals: 'Just 40 minutes before midnight [on 4 May 1942], the Czech took off from Tangmere and headed south across the Channel ... Reaching St André at 00.50 hours, he circled the blacked-out base for ten minutes. Then the airfield lit up with a double flare path east to west and there, ready to land, was a gaggle of no less than six enemy aircraft ...

'For two minutes he circled outside the Heinkels, cautiously stalking his prey, carefully positioning himself for a kill. He closed the Hurricane in behind one of the Germans and took a precise aim. He fired a two-second burst from about 100 yards dead astern but slightly below. Four streams of cannon fire converged into a cone of destruction and at its apex the starboard engine of the Heinkel caught fire. The German aircraft twisted grotesquely and dived to the ground north-east of the airfield. Immediately, he was able to repeat the same tactics on a second machine. A one-second burst of uncompromising accuracy caused the hit Heinkel to plunge downwards ...

'Quickly pressing on the attack, Kut lined up behind yet a third Heinkel. Ruthlessly he fired a two-second burst of ammunition from dead astern and saw his shells slam into the target. The enemy aircraft dived down steeply from 1,500 feet ... 30 seconds later, sweeping round on orbit, he saw three separate fires burning on the ground ... At 2.05 am – almost three hours after leaving base – he touched down at Tangmere to report his astonishing achievement to his ecstatic colleagues.'

The RAF's most effective night intruder, sixth highest-ranked night fighter Ace, and the highest-scoring Czech RAF pilot, Kuttelwascher ended the war with eighteen confirmed victories. He died of a heart attack in August 1959.

53: C-Type Flying Helmet

Worn by a Special Duties Lysander Pilot

As the war progressed, the work of the Special Duties squadrons, such as 161 equipped with the specially-adapted Westland Lysanders, grew in importance. As the same time, the increasing demands placed on such units led to a regular influx of new aircrew. One of the latter was Peter Vaughan-Fowler.

An outstanding pilot, Vaughan-Fowler was only 19 years old when he was selected for Special Duties training. He was duly posted to 161 Squadron, joining 'A' Flight, in April 1942. Through a lack of experience in such night-time operations, it was not until the night of 26/27 October 1942, during the October moon period, that he undertook his first flight to Occupied Europe.

One of his contemporaries, Flight Lieutenant James McCairns DFC & Two Bars, MM, would record his first impressions of his squadron's new arrival: 'I found myself becoming firm friends with another pilot, a young, impetuous flyer named Peter Vaughan-Fowler. Peter was born to fly. His father was a RAF officer and flew in the last war. His brother, after becoming a Cranwell overall sports champion, had been killed in an aircraft in 1932, and one could see that Peter took to the air like a duck to water. His first ops were rather erratic ... Then he settled down and produced the most brilliant flying and the best results that we could wish for. No field was too difficult, no target too far, and weather never defeated him.'

Returning to Vaughan-Fowler's first operation, he took off that night at the controls of Lysander V9367. Airborne at 19.55 hours, he crossed the French coast at 20.45 hours. His load on the outward leg consisted of a pair of radios and five packages. The target landing strip must have been some way into France, for he did not reach it until 00.35 hours. He found that an 'exceptionally good' flarepath awaited him.

After just five minutes on the ground, during which he handed over his cargo and boarded two passengers in return, he was airborne again. He landed back at Tangmere at 02.35 hours.

This operation was the first of twenty-one successful operations out of twenty-seven he attempted from Tangmere between October 1942 and September of the following year. For his work during a highly successful tour with 161 Squadron, Vaughan-Fowler was awarded the DFC and a Bar. The leather C-Type flying helmet seen here was one that he used during one or more of these flights.

Peter Vaughan-Fowler remained in the RAF after the war, retiring in 1975 with the rank of Group Captain. He passed away in Oxford on 24 April 1994.

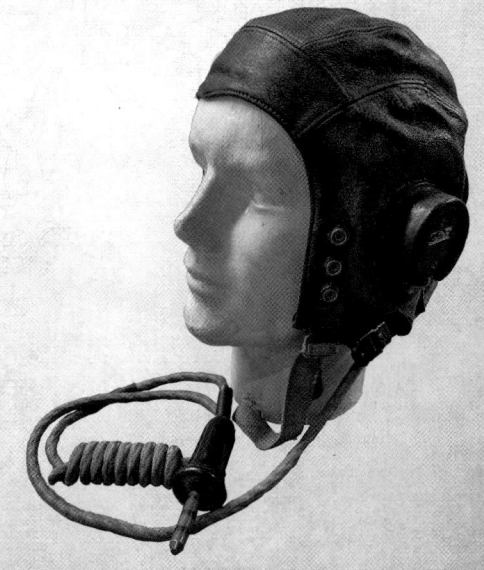

The C-Type flying helmet that Peter Vaughan-Fowler wore during Special Duties sorties from Tangmere.

54: Tangmere Cottage

A Secret Special Duties Base

Hidden from view by a brick wall, Tangmere Cottage lies off the main road running south from the A27 towards Tangmere Military Aviation Museum. Its tranquil and somewhat inconspicuous setting belies its wartime purpose, for it served as an operations and accommodation centre for the Special Duties flights undertaken from the airfield – not only by the RAF personnel, but also SOE staff and agents alike.

One of the pilots in 161 (Special Duties) Squadron, Hugh Verity, DSO & Bar, DFC, would recall the following: 'The Cottage at Tangmere was just opposite the main gates of the Royal Air Force station. It was partly hidden by tall hedges and the car park was hidden behind overlapping screens of woven laths. There was little that the passer-by could see by looking through the gate … The walls were thick, the ceilings low and the windows small. On the ground floor there was the kitchen (which also served as an informal guardroom) and two living rooms. One went in through the door at the back and through the kitchen.'[60]

Verity went on to describe the two living rooms in greater detail. 'Having got past the kitchen' he noted, 'on the right [was] the operations room/crew room and on the left the dining room with two long trestle tables … The ops room had a big map of France with the flak defended areas marked in red. There was a table and a map chest. There were a mixed collection of chairs, some of them very comfortable and arranged around the coal fire … There was a normal black telephone

Tangmere Cottage as it appears today. Built around the late 18th or early 19th century, it has been a Grade II listed building since January 1986. (*Historic Military Press*)

54: TANGMERE COTTAGE

A view of the rear of 'The Cottage' with the Nissen hut that was added in the war clearly visible. (via Historic Military Press)

and, later on, a green "scrambler" telephone for confidential conversations …Upstairs there were five or six bedrooms with as many beds in each as could be fitted in, rather like a cheap Turkish hotel.'

In all, Verity recalled that Tangmere Cottage was his home for some thirteen moon periods. 'We – the Lysander Flight pilots – were normally there for about a week before and a week after each full moon. We walked across to the normal RAF officers' mess for meals at the usual times when we had no secret visitors.'

Flight Lieutenant James McCairns also provided an insight into a typical day at The Cottage prior to operations: 'We would breakfast about 10 am, proceed to do air tests on our individual aircraft and then, if ops were on, the fun would really start. A scrambler telephone was linked to the Air Ministry so that any secret information could be discussed outright. The afternoon was spent on telephone calls, map-cutting, the study of photographs, flight plans, and, most important, the almost hourly consideration of the meteorological information … Towards evening the tension would increase. Just before dinner, staff cars would arrive from London bringing members of the intelligence service as escorts to the passengers to-be.'

For a number of the 'passengers', the few hours they spent at Tangmere Cottage before take-off would represent the last time they ever saw British soil.

The ante-room at 'The Cottage' which was used by agents en route to or from their missions to the Continent. The original caption points out the 'remains of presents [champagne bottles] brought by agents to the pilots may be seen on the mantelpiece'. Note also the model of the Lysander on the right. (via Historic Military Press)

55: Tangmere's Main Gate

A Hidden Relic of the Airfield's Past

Tangmere Cottage was ideally placed for its role, for, as Hugh Verity pointed out, if you stand in the road facing its wall, immediately behind you was where the airfield's main gate was located, though it has long since been built over.

As would be expected, the main gate welcomed almost all of the visitors to Tangmere during the airfield's existence – from royalty to senior commanders, from politicians to entertainers, and famous pilots to, of course, the secret agents. The latter only to cross the road to reach the main gate from their temporary refuge in The Cottage.

A local civilian, Barbara Bertram served as a hostess for SOE and French Resistance agents passing through Tangmere, many of whom stayed at her family home, the nearby Bignor Manor, before or after having been at The Cottage. In her memoirs, Barbara described one occasion she passed through the main gate at Tangmere: 'One car-load [of agents] was late because neither the Conducting Officer nor the driver knew the way. It was not one of our regular drivers but a strange man. I fed and saw off the two car-loads that arrived punctually and then cut sandwiches for the late ones so that they could go on to Tangmere the moment they arrived.

'When at last they turned up the Conducting Officer asked me to go with them to show them the way. When we approached the guard at the entrance to the aerodrome I was told to crouch down at the back under the legs of the French, as they had no pass for me. This was the only time I saw off a Lysander.'[61]

Directly facing the main gate at Tangmere, in the wall of Tangmere Cottage, is a small white gate. Monica MacKinnon, who moved into

The small stretch of brick wall seen here on the left is all that remains of the main entrance to RAF Tangmere.

The Cottage in 2004, recalls how she was once approached by an elderly passer-by, who, stopping to chat, asked them never to remove the gate, but that if they did, would they contact him first as he would like it. Monica takes up the story: 'We got into conversation and asked why the gate meant so much to him. He replied, "Whenever I walked back through that gate, I knew I was safe". So we have kept the gate in place. It always reminds me of just what Tangmere Cottage has meant to so many brave people.'[62]

A plaque on the wall that gives a clue to its previous importance. (Historic Military Press)

56: Luftwaffe Reconnaissance Photograph

Target Plan for 'Tangmere Flugplatz'

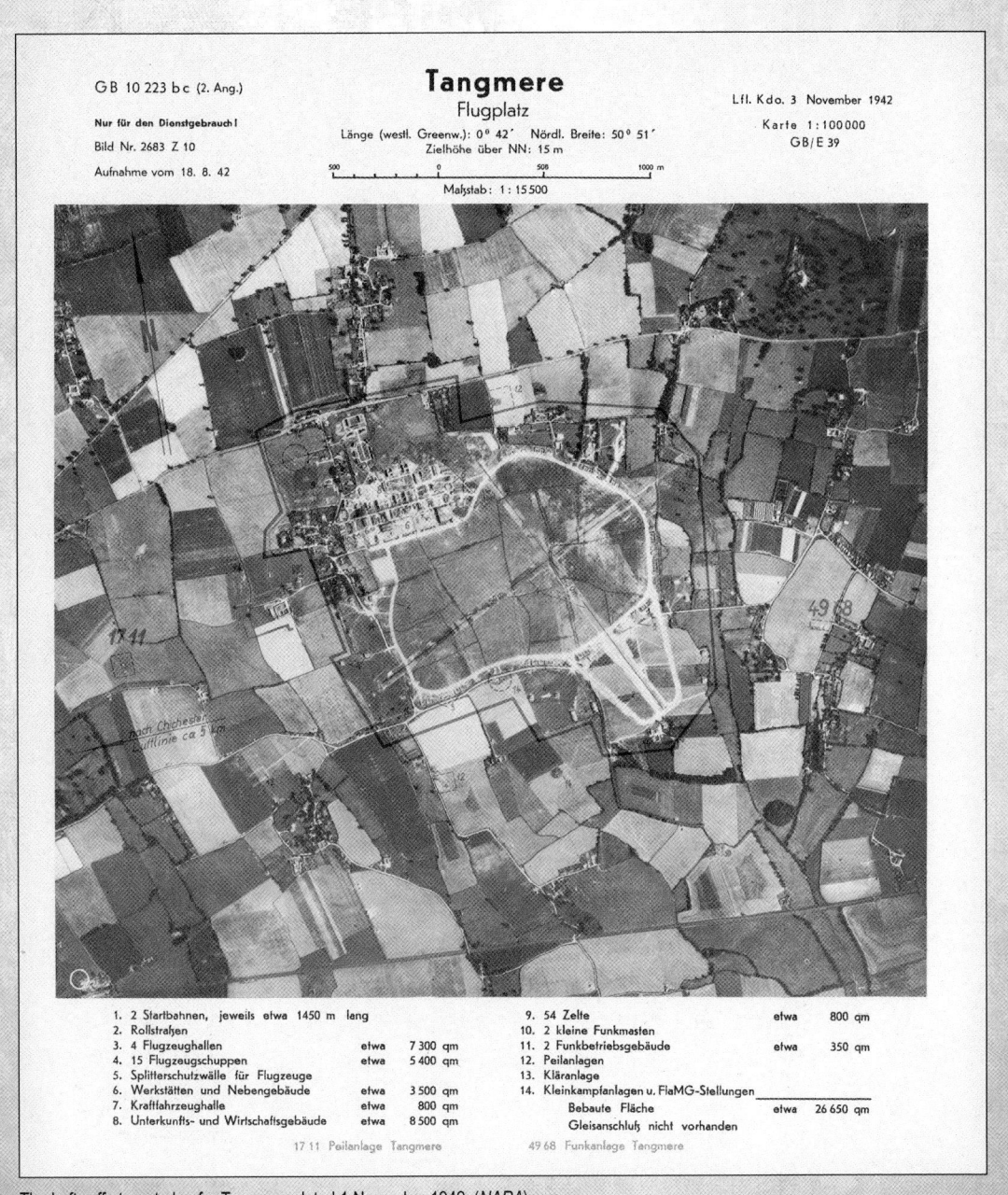

The Luftwaffe target plan for Tangmere dated 1 November 1942. (*NARA*)

As they advanced through the heart of the Third Reich in the last days of the fighting in Europe in 1945, British and American troops discovered huge collections of Luftwaffe aerial reconnaissance photographs, maps, target dossiers and photomosaics hidden at a variety of locations.

The capture and subsequent processing of this information was no small task. Project *Turban* was the code-name for the overall handling of all the material recovered, while each stash was, in turn, given its own title. *Dick Tracy*, for example, related to the material which came from Hitler's mountain retreat at Berchtesgaden. In June 1945, the material was packaged up in crates and flown back to the Allied Central Interpretation Unit at RAF Medmenham, where a joint UK-US sorting and exploitation project soon began.

As the assessment process continued, all the imagery became known as 'GX'. GX was such a large quantity of material that the preliminary sorting work alone continued until 1949. Today, some 2.1 million images and documents from this collection are held in the US National Archives.

Among this impressive collection is the target briefing for RAF Tangmere shown here. The actual photo-reconnaissance image used was taken high over the airfield on 18 August 1942, though the actual target briefing was not published until 3 November the same year. The camouflaging of the runways and facilities did little to deceive the German interpreters, for many of the airfield's hangars, radio installations, electrical substations and key structures are clearly marked. Evidence of previous Luftwaffe visits, such as the raids in the summer of 1940 through into 1941, can also be seen.

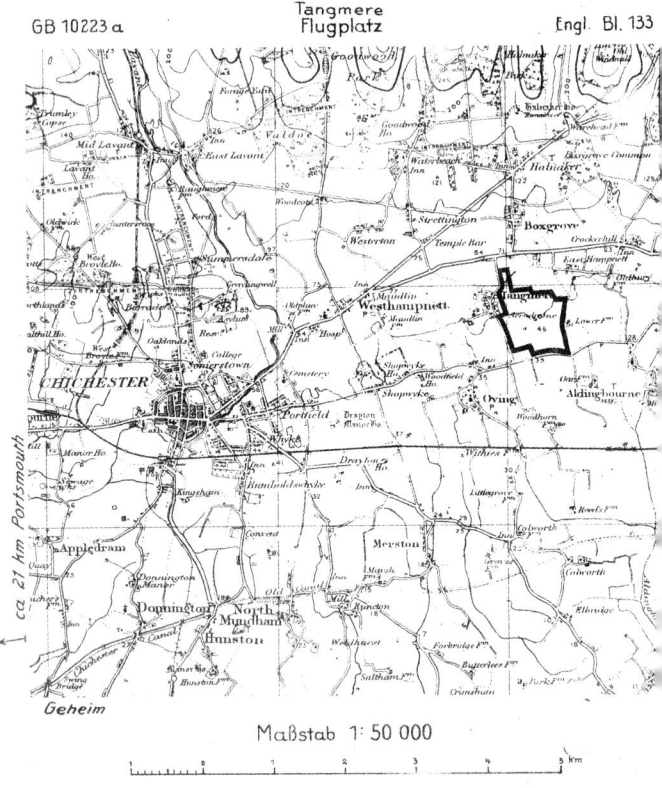

Two additional documents relating to the Luftwaffe's target maps for Tangmere. (*NARA*)

57: Typhoon Squadron First Day Cover

New Zealanders at Tangmere

This first day cover, featuring a Hawker Typhoon of 486 (New Zealand) Squadron and signed by Group Captain Desmond J. Scott DSO, OBE, DFC, RNZAF (Retd.), was issued to mark the 40th anniversary of the squadron's formation at Kirton-in-Lindsay on 7 March 1942. Originally equipped with Hurricanes, later in the year it re-equipped with Hawker Typhoons Mk.IBs.

The conversion to Typhoons was completed in time for 486 Squadron's arrival at Tangmere on 30 October 1942. It was the first Typhoon squadron to operate from Tangmere, and it remained there until the end of January 1944 – the longest period any Typhoon-equipped unit spent at the Sussex airfield. Interestingly, its sister squadron, 485 (New Zealand) Squadron, also served in the Tangmere Wing, albeit flying Spitfires from Westhampnett.

Scott, who went on to be one of the RNZAF's most decorated fighter pilots, had made his name on 3 Squadron, racking up a number of claims before converting to the Typhoon. He took command of 486 Squadron on 1 April 1943, and remained in that role until September that year, at which point he took over as Wing Commander Flying at Tangmere.

The first day cover, featuring a Hawker Typhoon of 486 (New Zealand) Squadron, signed by Desmond Scott. (*Historic Military Press*)

Groundcrew refuelling Squadron Leader Desmond Scott's 486 Squadron Typhoon at Tangmere. (*Air Force Museum of New Zealand*)

Of his time at Tangmere, Scott later recalled the following: 'Much is made of Biggin Hill, due I think to the fact that it was a straight-out fighter station, very close to London and the eager attention of the press, but it could never be compared with such stations as Manston or Tangmere and their round the clock performance. I was no stranger to Tangmere. I had landed there often when shut out by the weather from Manston or on staff visits to its squadrons. A pre-war station, its living accommodation was like that of a first-class hotel.

'Unfortunately, this was in direct contrast to the squadron dispersal areas. Whereas the officers mess and the ground staff accommodation were built in good solid English brick, the squadron dispersal huts appeared to be very much an afterthought – and a hurried one at that. Flimsy wooden buildings, each heated by a pot-bellied stove and furnished with a table and a few old tattered armchairs. If this wasn't primitive enough, behind each hut stood a single lavatory, a tall thin contraption that had obviously borne the weight of many a squadron briefing.'[63]

Squadron Leader Desmond Scott in the cockpit of his 486 Squadron Typhoon at Tangmere. (*Air Force Museum of New Zealand*)

58: Tangmere's Watch Office

An Iconic Survivor from the Airfield's Wartime History

Standing stark and bleak against the soft rolling backdrop of the South Downs is one of the most recognisable reminders of Tangmere's wartime service – its surviving Watch Office. Though a shadow of its former self, this building was once a vital hub in the airfield's operations through into the Cold War and witnessed many of the historic events that took place there.

Tangmere's original watch office, a much smaller structure than the one that can be seen today, was destroyed by enemy action in 1940. A replacement, which largely conforms to a standard Air Ministry design, namely the Type 12096/41, was intended for use on night fighter stations. On the ground floor, a small extension was added to the right of the building as you stand on the airfield and look north; this is a feature unique to Tangmere's Watch Office. The tower was originally constructed with a brick finish; the rendering was added at a later date.

There is some degree of debate around exactly when this Watch Office was constructed and became operational; some sources states 1943, others that it was completed in 1944. Its listing in Historic England's records provides the following information: 'The control tower at Tangmere was built in 1944 as a replacement

Tangmere's Grade II listed Watch Office which stands to the north of what was the main runway. (*Courtesy of Robert Mitchell*)

to earlier facilities. Initially the active squadrons had locker and rest rooms within annexes to the aircraft sheds. But, as this proved unsatisfactory, an old flight office building near the sheds was converted into a small but detached watch office, providing heated accommodation in two rooms: the watch office itself and a rest room. This building, along with the aircraft sheds, was destroyed in German raids on the base in 1940. The watch office facilities were moved to the fire tender house on a temporary basis while the present building was completed. The present building saw active service in the latter part of World War II and also has associations with the later occupation of the base by Meteor jet squadrons.'[64]

Unsurprisingly, the building is now Grade II listed. Awarded in 2011, this status was given on the basis of the Watch Office's 'form and intactness' – it is, notes Historic England, 'a good survival of the Fighter Station watch office type' with 'iconic status' that 'is a visual reminder of the significance of the former RAF Tangmere airfield'. Likewise, the listing record notes, it has a great deal of historical interest, both in the war and during 'the airfield's later history such as the breaking of the world air speed record on two occasions'.

The view of part of the airfield at Tangmere as seen from the control tower in the immediate aftermath of the station's closure. (*Courtesy of the Andy Saunders Collection*)

59: Avro Lancaster 'S' For 'Sugar'

Diverted to Tangmere

While it would be fair to say that the majority of surviving Second World War aircraft with Tangmere links are fighters, there is at least one bomber which has such a claim to fame – and that is Avro Lancaster B.Mk.1 R5868. More frequently known as 'S' for 'Sugar', today this B.Mk.1 has pride of place in Hangar Five at the RAF Museum in Hendon.

Having entered RAF service in June 1942, R5868, as 'Q' for 'Queenie', flew sixty-eight sorties with 83 Squadron before it was transferred to 467 Squadron RAAF in September 1943, at which point it became 'S' for 'Sugar'. While on average a Lancaster's life expectancy was twenty-one operational sorties, R5868 successfully completed a total of 137 – the second-highest number of any RAF bomber.

Though both 83 and 467 squadrons were stationed at Bomber Command bases further north in England, two of R5868's operations ended at RAF Tangmere, when, like so many Allied aircraft during the war, its pilot was forced to divert to the Sussex airfield. With its long runways, proximity to the South Coast, and excellent lighting and associated facilities, Tangmere was a regular choice for such alterations in flight plans.

With Flying Officer Jack Colpus at the controls, according to the RAF Museum's records R5868's first visit to Tangmere occurred

Avro Lancaster B.Mk.1 R5868 on display at the RAF Museum in Hendon. (*Courtesy of Alan Wilson*)

on the night of 7/8 October 1943. The target that evening was the city of Stuttgart, for which 467 Squadron provided seventeen Lancasters – 'which was quite a good effort considering the number of "kites" we have available', notes the Operations Record Book. Such were the conditions that night that all seventeen of 467 Squadron's Lancasters were forced to divert; fifteen landed at Tangmere, the remaining two at nearby RAF Ford.

The second occasion was on the night of 25/26 March 1944. In what was 'considered a quiet trip', 467 Squadron provided just five aircraft as part of a force of 192 bombers despatched to attack the railway yards in the French town of Aulnoye. With Pilot Officer R.E. Llewelyn at the controls, 'S' for 'Sugar' bombed the target from 7,000ft at 22.02 hours. However, during the run in, the port outer engine failed, causing the Lancaster to swing to port.

With one of his engines unserviceable, Llewelyn was forced to make the return leg at just 5,000ft, 'resulting in [the aircraft] just making Tangmere' at 00.35 hours, thankfully having avoided the attention of any prowling German night fighters. Once safely down, Llewelyn and his crew, like so many others before and after him, no doubt gratefully accepted the temporary hospitality and sanctuary that Tangmere offered them.

This graffiti-covered Boeing B-17, serial number 42-30088 and nicknamed *Squawkin' Hawk* I, of the 100th Bomb Group, is pictured at Thorpe Abbott on 17 May 1944. It has been signed by the unit's personnel prior to returning to the United States. This was one of many aircraft that diverted to Tangmere in the Second World War. Badly damaged during a mission to Gelsenkirchen on 5 November 1943, it made an emergency landing at RAF Tangmere. (*Historic Military Press*)

60: Handley Page Halifax Crash Memorial

Tragedy at Tangmere

On Friday, 16 August 2019, a memorial to the crew of Handley Page Halifax HX181, coded ZA-K of 10 Squadron, was unveiled at Tangmere. It commemorates the tragic events of 19 November 1943.

As we have already seen with the case of Lancaster R5868, RAF Tangmere was frequently a place of refuge for aircraft returning from operations badly shot-up or suffering from mechanical problems. Consequently, emergency landings, or, worse, crash landings, were a relatively common occurrence. One such casualty was Halifax HX181. It had taken off from RAF Melbourne at 16.22 hours that fateful day. The summary of events in the Operations Record Book for 10 Squadron states: 'Eleven crews detailed to attack Leverkuson [*sic*]. Seven crews bombed primary target, experiencing thick cloud. FS Wilson returned early due to failure of wireless receiver and GEE. PO Dixon also returned early owing to failure of port inner engine. PO Baxter bombed alternative target owing to engine trouble. The aircraft captained by FS Holdsworth crashed at Tangmere on return from mission and all crew were killed. PO Lucas also crash-landed at Ford on return and himself, his Navigator, Air Bomber and Tail Gunner were injured.'[65]

The Operations Record Book for Tangmere contains the following entry: 'At 21.35 hrs, a

The memorial to the crew of Handley Page Halifax HX181 that was unveiled on 16 August 2019. (Courtesy of Robert Mitchell)

The aftermath of another accident involving a Halifax at Tangmere. Pictured by a pilot of 165 Squadron while he was based at Tangmere, this is the wreckage is of Halifax Mk.V DG271 of 138 Squadron, which crashed on take-off from Tangmere on 4 February 1943. The Operations Record Book for Tangmere notes that, 'A Halifax bomber of 138 Squadron that had been on the aerodrome for repairs, crashed when taking off.' The aircraft swung on take-off, causing the wing to strike the ground and the undercarriage to collapse. (*Chris Goss Collection*)

Halifax returning from a bombing raid over Germany, crashed into the Servicing Hangar at Tangmere, all 7 members of the crew being killed. The Hangar and 6 Typhoons and 1 Spitfire in it were completely wrecked. Later all Station personnel were warned to take cover as ammo. was exploding. A large fire resulted, and, as enemy aircraft were approaching the coast, all personnel not on duty were ordered to evacuate the aerodrome. All aircraft were diverted to Ford.'

An information panel at the Tangmere Military Aviation Museum includes the following eyewitness account: 'The Halifax made four or five attempts to land on Runway 33 (north-westerly heading). Each time the approach was off, too high or off track, suggesting that either the pilot was badly injured or had been killed and someone else was trying to land the aircraft. On the last attempt, the approach was much better aligned but still a little too high and it drifted left off track towards the control tower and was coming straight at me. I thought it was going to hit us when it drifted further to the left side of the control tower and passed us at low height until it crashed into the east side of the most easterly hangar, the one nearest the control tower. Despite valiant efforts by the station personnel, aboard were killed.'

The hangar that HX181 hit was all but demolished. The structure was the last of Tangmere's pre-war Belfast Truss hangars.

61: Flowers Picked by Resistance

Delivered by Tangmere-based Lysander

The dangers and risks faced by the Special Duties pilots and aircrew faced while operating from Tangmere were many and varied. The clandestine flights that they undertook could well end in a pilot or member of aircrew making the ultimate sacrifice. This is what happened on the night of 3/4 May 1944.

That night two Lysanders were tasked with making flights from Tangmere to Occupied France. The first of these was flown by Flight Lieutenant Leslie Whitaker DFC at the controls of V9664. Assigned to Operation *Forsythia*, Whitaker was to deliver two passengers to a landing ground near Châteauroux. It was, though, an objective that they never reached for the Lysander was shot down over Étampes-Mondésir airfield, with all three on board being killed.

For the personnel of the Special Duties aircraft there were also lighter moments to their work. The other pilot flying to France around the same time as Whitaker, Lieutenant Per Hysing-Dahl, a Norwegian, would soon discover this. Having completed a tour of thirty sorties on 161 Squadron's 'B' Flight, which operated the Halifaxes converted for drop operations, he had been posted to 'A' Flight to fly the Lysander.

Having taken off from Tangmere at 22.30 hours, carrying two passengers and two packages, Hysing-Dahl set course for the destination of his mission, Operation *Pipe*, which was the landing ground set up by the Resistance near the village of Segry. Everything went according to plan, the Lysander touching down on French soil at 00.50 hours. The hand-over was quickly made, with two new passengers and two packages replacing those that were off-loaded.

Among the items handed into the care of Hysing-Dahl was an envelope addressed to Mrs Barbara Bertram, the wife of Major Anthony Bertram who was a liaison officer for the agents arriving and departing via the night-time flights operating by RAF Tangmere. As previously mentioned, the pair lived at Bignor Manor, where Barbara acted as a host to many of the agents as they passed through on their way to or from Occupied Europe.

The letter duly reached Barbara upon Hysing-Dahl's return to Tangmere – he landed back at 03.30 hours. In the letter was the dried flower seen here, which was accompanied by the following note: 'Dear Mrs Bertram. These few flowers were picked by moonlight a few hours ago by the faithful friends you have in France. Hoping you will receive them in good condition. We remain yours devoted, Roddy & Armand.'

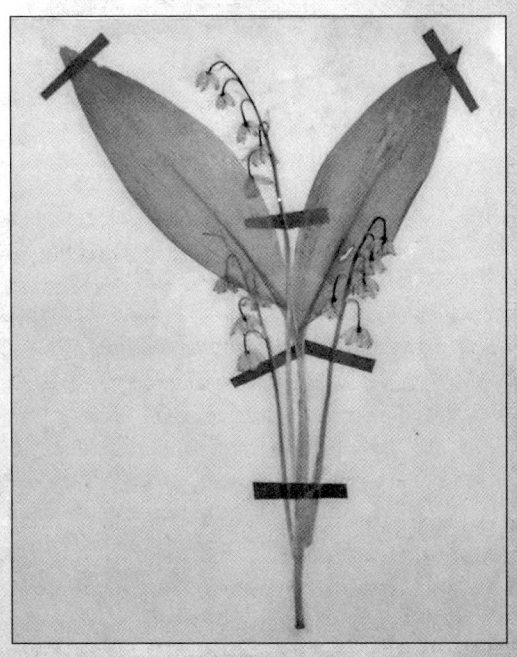

The flowers delivered to Mrs Barbara Bertram via a Tangmere-based Lysander.

62: D-Day Order of Battle

Tangmere's Part in Operation *Overlord*

In the days and hours leading up to 6 June 1944, it was evident to everyone stationed at Tangmere that the invasion was imminent. That this was the case was noted in Tangmere's Operations Record Book, and more specifically its entry for 5 June: 'Rumours were flying round the Station, and the tempo of work increased in the Intelligence Section culminating in the arrival of high ranking officers who proceeded to open large sealed envelopes.' Briefings for the pilots began at 23.30 hours that night and continued until 01.00 hours the next morning, by which time some of the first Allied airborne soldiers had already landed in France.

As the Order of Battle shown here testifies, Tangmere was at the centre of the Second Tactical Air Force's involvement in the invasion. Ready to play their part from this airfield were two Wings, Nos. 126 and 127, with three squadrons apiece – all of which were Canadian Spitfire units.

'The night had been filled with the roar of heavy aircraft going out,' continued the ORB, this time in the entry for 6 June itself, 'and some were so low that it had been possible to pick out gliders and troop carrying planes.'[66] Despite this being 'the day for which everyone has waited so long', to use the words of the Station Adjutant, 'in some ways it seemed rather an anti climax. Everything seemed rather quiet and there was little noticeable excitement, probably due in this case to a desire not to be unduly optimistic. Everyone tried to be near a radio for the hourly News Bulletin but apart from that it might almost have been a normal day.'

A page from a report issued by No.11 Group detailing its administrative instructions for Operation *Overlord*. (Mark Hillier Collection)

Nevertheless, both of the Tangmere Wings were kept busy: 'The operations for the day consisted almost entirely of cover patrol over the assault beaches and the pilots brought back many interesting reports. Nos. 126 and 127 Wings did 4 beach cover patrols each during the day and met no enemy opposition. They reported that Allied troops set foot on the beaches at 06.30 hours between Cherbourg and Le Havre and that the operation continued all the morning. 126 Wing did the last patrol of the day from Tangmere and reported that a tremendous number of airborne troops had landed and that they were heavily engaged soon after landing.'

The Typhoon of Squadron Leader Denis Crowley-Milling of 181 Squadron being bombed up for the cameras during a press visit to Tangmere in the months leading up to D-Day.

63: THE Ale Runs

Tangmere's Unusual D-Day Delivery Service

Fighting was thirsty work – and that was certainly the case for those Allied soldiers and airmen involved in the Battle for Normandy in the days and weeks following the D-Day landings. To help quench that thirst, a couple of ingenious airmen and squadrons put their aircraft to work on a few unofficial, and unusual, sorties – the so-called 'Ale Runs'.

It was soon after D-Day that a Reuter's special correspondent, writing for a number of British newspapers, claimed that only watery cider and poisoned water 'was available to our boys on the front'. Sadly, no spare transport aircraft were available to bring non-essential items to the forward landing grounds in France. As a result of this, several squadrons, including a number of the Spitfire units operating out of Tangmere, rose to the challenge. Groundcrew would, for example, take 45-gallon jettison tanks normally used for fuel, steam clean them and then re-purpose them for carrying ale. One of the breweries that stepped up to offer their beer was Henty & Constable Ltd of Westgate, Chichester, just down the road from RAF Tangmere.

One of the first squadrons to take part in the beer runs was 412 Squadron RCAF, which, part

Wing Commander Rolf Arne Berg of No.132 Norwegian Wing photographed on the wing of a Spitfire watching proceedings as pale ale is decanted from kegs into a drop tank, which was then fitted to the aircraft for the flight to Normandy. It is believed that the picture was taken at RAF Tangmere. (*Public Domain*)

63: THE ALE RUNS

of 126 Wing, Second Tactical Air Force, was locally based at RAF Merston and then latterly at RAF Tangmere during the invasion period. One of the first landings occurred on the strip known as 'B4' at Bény-sur-Mer – which at the time was still within range of German snipers. It may well have been 412 Squadron that carried out what one source states was the 'first known landing of beer', which took place on 13 June. On that occasion some 270 gallons of beer, presumably from Henty & Constable, was flown from Tangmere in drop tanks beneath three Spitfire Mk.IXbs, the latter landing at 'B4'.[67]

Eleven days after the invasion started, another Canadian unit, 416 Squadron RCAF, commenced ale runs from Tangmere, heading to the newly-built 'B2' airfield at Bazenville, just three miles from Gold Beach. Sadly, reports came back that the beer tasted of Avgas.

Jeffrey Quill, who we have already encountered in this book, once recalled some of the modifications required to fly beer across the Channel: 'After D-Day in 1944, there was a problem about getting beer over to the Normandy airfields. Henty and Constable (the Sussex brewers) were happy to make the stuff available at the 83 Group Support Unit at Ford near Littlehampton. For some inexplicable reason, however, beer had a low priority rating on the available freight aircraft. So we adapted Spitfire bomb racks so that an 18-gallon (82-litre) barrel could be carried under each wing of the Spitfires which were being ferried across from Ford to Normandy on a daily basis.

'We were, in fact, a little concerned about the strength situation of the barrels, and on application to Henty and Constables for basic stressing data we were astonished to find that the eventuality of being flown on the bomb racks of a Spitfire was a case which had not been taken into consideration in the design of the barrels. However, flight tests proved them to be up to the job. This installation, incidentally, was known as Mod XXX Depth Charge.'[68]

64: Bishop Otter College Drawings

Tangmere's D-Day Era Operations Room

One of the consequences of the bombing of Tangmere on 16 August 1940, was the decision to relocate the station's Operations Room, with a new home for it being found at St James School in Chichester. As the war progressed, however, it became apparent that this location was not large enough to handle the increasing number of sorties and patrols being undertaken by the Tangmere Sector.

As a result, in preparation for Operation *Overlord* a further move was planned. This time the Operations Room was to be housed in a lecture hall at Bishop Otter College, less than a mile away. Bishop Otter College, now part of the University of Chichester campus, had been requisitioned in 1942, with staff and students being evacuated to Stockwell College in Bromley. Some of the early RAF occupants of the college were WAAFs working in the Operations Room at St James.

With construction work completed, the move to Bishop Otter was finalised on 15 February 1944. The Operations Room there was run along the lines of similar facilities elsewhere in the UK. A special observation gallery was constructed from where senior officers could observe two large plotting tables, which were manned twenty-four hours a day by specially-trained WAAFs. The staff were divided into four watches of about thirty, each supervised by an

Two drawings depicting the Tangmere Operations Room at Bishop Otter College during 1944. (*Tangmere Military Aviation Museum*)

RAF Sergeant. A watch lasted four hours during the day and eight hours at night. A large board indicated squadron availability for duty.

The Bishop Otter Operations Room was fully manned until the end of 1944. The senior controller for this period was Wing Commander Douglas Hampton Grice. Having served in the Territorial Army, and more specifically the Artists Rifles, Grice had volunteered for the RAF on a short service commission. Having trained as a fighter pilot, he was shot down on three occasions within a matter of weeks; once in the Battle of France, in early July 1940, and also during the Battle of Britain. The latter occurred on 15 August 1940, when he was shot down off Harwich. Having suffered burns to his face, he was subsequently treated by the famous plastic surgeon, Dr Archibald McIndoe – though he would not become a member of the Guinea Pig Club.

By the end of 1940, Grice had been posted to RAF Biggin Hill as a Controller. He was a Controller at Northolt from June 1941 until February 1942, Senior Controller at North Weald until December 1943, and then the Senior Controller at Tangmere until August 1945.

In January 1945, the Bishop Otter site became an Emergency Operations Room. At this point it was responsible for directing fighter aircraft to intercept flying bombs crossing the South Coast.

It is stated that no less than fifty-six Allied squadrons were controlled by the personnel in the Bishop Otter Operations Room on 6 June 1944. These squadrons were operating from some eighteen airfields, the area involved being from Friston in the east, to Lee-on-Solent in the west and as far north as Northolt.

A drawing depicting the Operations Room in St James School, Chichester, where it had been located since the bombing of Tangmere in 1940. (*Tangmere Military Aviation Museum*)

65: Newspaper Cutting of a Rear-Gunner's Survival

Safely Landed at Tangmere

For many of the aircraft diverted to RAF Tangmere, safely touching down on the runway itself might well have been a matter of life or death. One stark example of this is provided by the dramatic events of the morning of 17 July 1944.

In the early hours, fourteen Lancasters from 300 (Polish) Squadron – the only Polish squadron that operated Lancasters – took off from RAF Faldingworth to attack German positions in the area of Émiéville near Caen. One of the Lancasters was a Mk.III, which, with the serial number JA922, carried the code letters 'BH-J'. Airborne at 04.16 hours, it was over the target area by 06.05 hours – at which point the Lancaster was bracketed by 'predicted flak', forcing the crew to abandon their mission.

One of the anti-aircraft shells nearly claimed the life of the rear gunner, Flight Sergeant F. Zentar. What happened was subsequently described by the mid-upper gunner, Flight Sergeant J. Derewienko:

'Three seconds before we bombed a shell burst just to the right of the rear gunner. When

The Sunday Post, July 23, 1944.

Suspended Upside Down From Plane Flying Over Channel

Blown out of his plane by blast from an A.-A. shell a rear-gunner hung head downwards from his turret, held only by one foot, all the way back from Caen to England.

It was more than an hour before the Lancaster landed and, as it touched down, the rear-gunner, a Pole, only just managed to swing his head clear of the ground.

He is now in hospital recovering from shock but he was not seriously injured.

The Lancaster was one of more than a thousand aircraft which attacked German fortified positions near Caen on the morning of July 18.

The story is told by the mid-upper gunner, a 22-year-old Polish flight sergeant.

turret. The engineer is a strong man and he supported the rear-gunner and gave him one end of the rope.

I had to grip the engineer with my free hand while still presing the valve with the other, and I was afraid he would fall out, too. But the rear-gunner managed to tie the rope round himself and then we fastened it firmly to the inside of the aircraft.

We found an airfield soon after we crossed the English coast. As the Lancaster touched down, the rear-gunner managed to swing to one side and keep his head out of the way of the ground. He was bleeding from the ears and mouth but was not badly hurt, although suffering

The headlines of the story detailing Flight Sergeant F. Zentar's amazing survival, as they appeared in the Sunday Post *on 23 July 1944.*

the shell burst, the blast swung the [rear] turret beyond its usual position, ripped open the door at the gunner's back and sucked him out of his seat. He fell backwards, finishing up head downwards, but with his left foot somewhat jammed. That was the only thing that saved him.

'I broke a hole in the vision panel and pressed a valve which moves the turret, so as to turn it back and jam his leg firmly. I was afraid of breaking his leg, but something had to be done. Then I leaned over and held his shoes, but they began to slip off. I clawed at his trousers but they began to tear.

'As we flew on over France I hung on to him somehow however, and kept on holding the valve at the same time. The Germans were still firing at us and the Pilot had to throw the aircraft about.

'When we got over the Channel I shouted for help, and the Flight Engineer [Sergeant J. Pialucha] got a rope [from the dinghy] which we dropped out from the turret. The Engineer supported the rear-gunner and gave him one end of the rope. I had to grip the engineer with my free hand while still pressing the valve, and I was afraid he would fall out too. But the rear-gunner managed to tie the rope round himself and then we fastened it firmly to the inside of the aircraft.

'We found an airfield soon after we crossed the English coast, got permission to land, [and] signalled that we had a wounded rear gunner. We landed very well indeed; it was wonderful. As the Lancaster touched down, the rear-gunner managed to swing to one side and keep his head out of the way of the ground. When we stopped he was bleeding from the ears and mouth, but he was not badly hurt, though suffering from severe shock.'[69]

JA922 touched down at Tangmere at 07.11 hours. As Derewienko's account indicates, the Lancaster touched down with its full bomb load, including eleven 1,000lb bombs and four 500lb bombs. For his part, Zentar soon found himself in the care of Tangmere's sick bay.

66: Special Duties Pilot's Maps

Double Lysander Operation From Tangmere

It was not only the Spitfires based at Tangmere that were kept busy supporting the Allied landings in France, but also the Lysanders of 161 (Special Duties) Squadron. The maps we have included here were prepared by Flight Lieutenant George Turner for his part in Operation *Palais* that was to be undertaken on the night of 7/8 July 1944.

Operation *Palais* was a double pick-up sortie in which Turner flew Lysander V9738. He became airborne from Tangmere at 22.40 hours. He was followed five minutes later by Captain

The maps used by Flight Lieutenant Turner during Operation *Palais*. They were donated to Tangmere Military Aviation Museum by Group Captain Hugh Verity DSO, DFC. The smaller map, twice the scale of the larger map, provided greater detail of the last leg of Turner's flight to Luzillé.

66: SPECIAL DUTIES PILOT'S MAPS

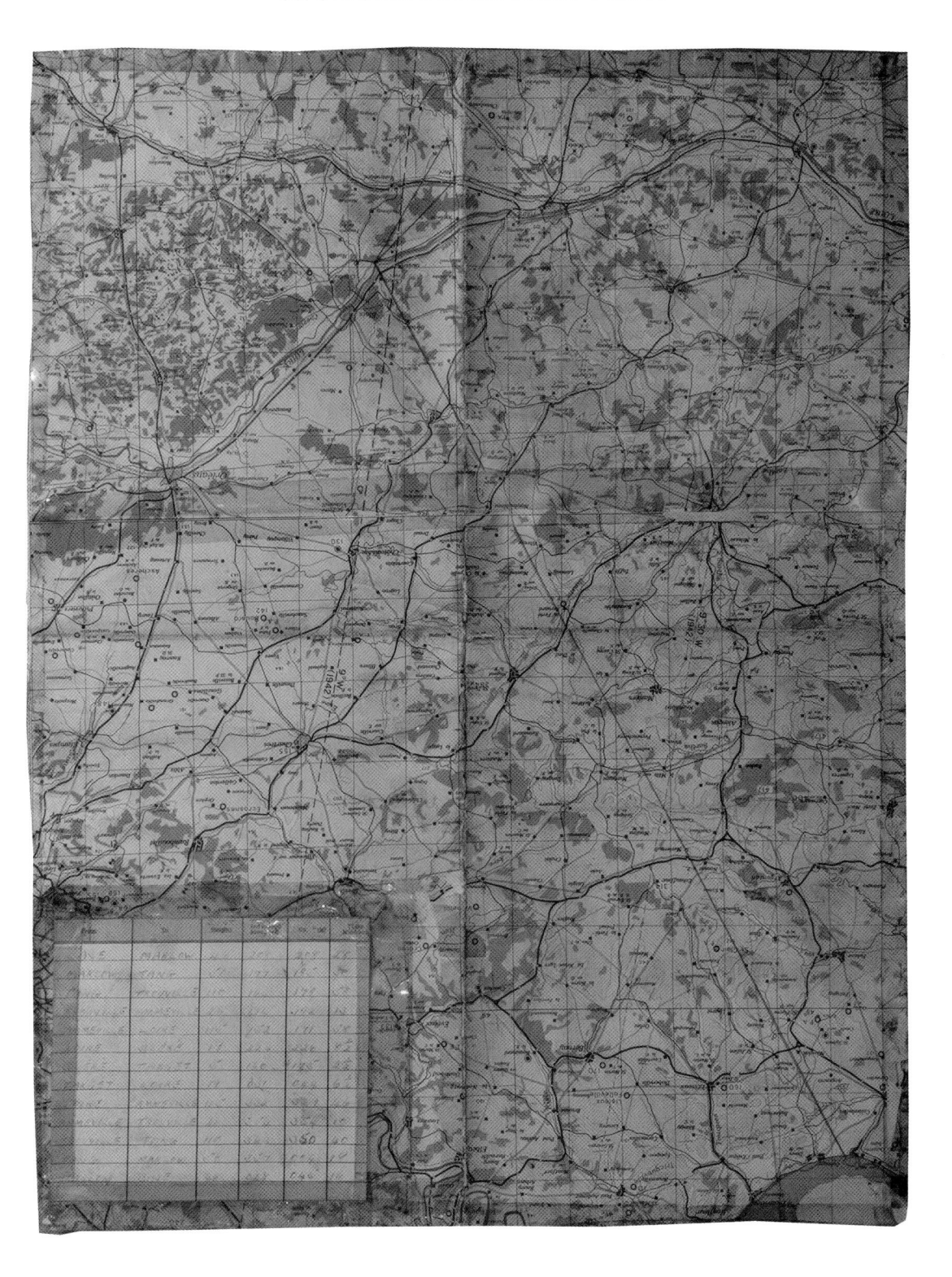

Per Hysing-Dahl in Lysander V9490. Both men would have relied heavily on their maps and their own navigational skills to find their destinations in the dark. One of the other pilots on the squadron, James McCairns, later wrote the following on the subject:

'Our map-making was an elaborate affair and would have caused any navigation officer or storekeeper to have a fit. Because we travelled such long distances, sometimes our track would involve using four or even five large sheets of maps. Obviously it was impractical to carry these and study them in the front cockpit of a Lysander, so we used to join all the sheets together, draw our track line, and mark off on this each 50 miles as a navigational aid. Afterwards we would mark off perhaps 50 miles on either side of the original track and cut down these lines, leaving us with a single sheet roughly twelve inches wide and perhaps thirty inches long. This would be carefully folded into five-inch sections each mounted on cardboard, making a very stiff, compact and easily accessible map. Sometimes, especially when the weather was bad, or the field difficult to find, those maps were given much hard wear – the cardboard stiffening was most necessary.'

Returning to the events of the night of 7/8 July, Turner reached his destination, an improvised landing ground near the village of Luzillé in the Indre-et-Loire Department in central France at 01.45 hours. Having landed, he delivered three passengers and five packages, before loading three people and two parcels for the return. He touched down back at Tangmere at 05.10 hours.

Hysing-Dahl's flight, however, ended in disaster. His Lysander was hit by Allied anti-aircraft fire while passing over the Normandy beaches and although he skilfully ditched his aircraft, one of his passengers drowned and a second died just after being rescued.

Four pilots from 161 (Special Duties) Squadron pictured in the garden of 'The Cottage' at Tangmere. They are (left to right): Flying Officer J.A. McCairns, Squadron Leader Hugh Verity, Group Captain Percy Charles 'Pick' Pickard (Squadron Commander), Flight Lieutenant Peter Vaughan-Fowler and Flying Officer Frank 'Bunny' Rymills. In front of Pickard sits his sheepdog Ming, and to the right, Rymill's spaniel Henry.

67: Royal Visit To RAF Tangmere

Letter from Second Tactical Air Force

As its Operations Record Book notes, the events of 14 July 1944 represented 'a Red Letter day in the history of Tangmere'. The reason for this statement was the visit by the King and Queen, the details for which were provided in briefing documents that accompanied the letter seen here. It was sent by Air Vice-Marshal T.W. Elmhirst, Air Officer i/c Administration at the Second Tactical Air Force, to the COs of RAF Tangmere and RAF Hartford Bridge, the latter also being inspected on the same date.

The royal party arrived at Tangmere by car with a motorcycle escort. The ORB goes on state: 'At 11.30 hours they were greeted outside the Officers Mess by Group Captain W.J. Crisham. Their majesties then drove to the Perimeter where numerous officers were decorated. After the Investiture their Majesties inspected R.A.F. and W.A.A.F. personnel and then visited the Dispersals. Lunch was taken in the Officers Mess ...The Royal party left the Station at 14.00 hours.'

The Royal visit was duly reported upon in the national press. The *Daily Record*, for example, carried the following account in its edition the following day: 'Pilots and air crews now fighting in the Battle of France were decorated by the King at open-air investitures yesterday. Fighter planes were hurtling through the sky on their way to and from the Normandy battle areas when the King and Queen visited two R.A.F. stations of the Second Tactical Air Force. Some of the pilots decorated have also been fighting flying bombs.

'Airmen and W.A.A.F.s were drawn up three sides of a square when the King and Queen arrived at the first air station [Tangmere], and Norwegian Spitfire crews formed up in front of their planes. One Norwegian told the Queen that on Thursday he received a letter from his mother in Norway, the first for two and a half years.'

One War Correspondent, Louis Wulff, also noted that 'the first pilot decorated was Group-Captain J. Cunningham, night fighter ace, who received a second bar to D.S.O.'. He also added that 'two heroes of the "pin-point" raid on a house in the Hague were among the 120 pilots and air crew members decorated'.

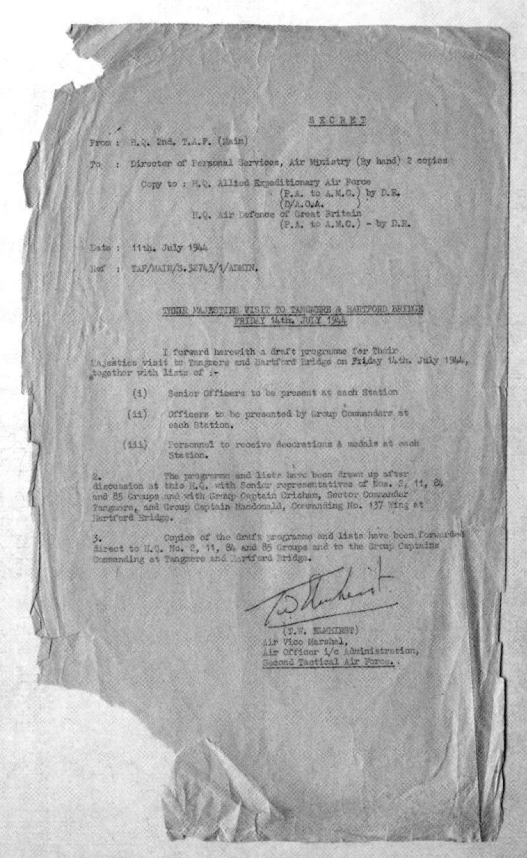

Air Vice-Marshal T.W. Elmhirst's letter regarding the Royal visit to Tangmere. (*Mark Hillier Collection*)

The King inspects a party of WAAFs at Tangmere on 14 July 1944. (*Historic Military Press*)

The Queen chats with a Norwegian pilot during the visit to Tangmere. (*Historic Military Press*)

68: Operation *Exodus*

Former Prisoners of War Return Home

As the war in Europe drew to a close, many prisoners of war who had been in German hands were being liberated from camps as the Allies advanced ever deeper into the heart of the Third Reich. These men, some of whom had been interned since 1940, were at last free. Yet they were still hundreds of miles from home, with many suffering from illness, fatigue and starvation. As ex-PoWs flooded into collection points throughout Europe, it was clear that a swift method of repatriation was needed; thankfully a combined British-American planning committee to manage such a scenario had established in London in 1944.

Consequently, a fleet of transport aircraft and bombers was assembled with the aim of flying the long-suffering men home. What was appropriately called Operation *Exodus* began on 3 April 1945, with the PoWs being flown back to receiving centres established at airfields across the UK, among the main ones being locations such as Cosford, Ford, Heathrow, Oakley, and Dunsfold.

Tangmere would also play a part in *Exodus*. The initial arrivals at Tangmere occurred on 10 May 1945, as the Operations Record Book entry for that date reveals: 'We received our first batch of liberated Prisoners of War which arrived during the evening in Lancasters of Bomber Command and there was certainly no lack of volunteers from the Station personnel to assist in looking after the ex Prisoners of War and arranging for their despatch to the Reception Camps.'

Former PoWs disembarking from Avro Lancasters at Tangmere in May 1945. (*Tangmere Military Aviation Museum*)

With good weather the next day, Tangmere saw all of its flying activities cancelled, 'due to the fact that 95 Lancasters of Bomber Command put in during the course of the afternoon and evening with more liberated Prisoners of War'.

This pace was maintained on the 12th: 'The usual Saturday night Dance was cancelled as Lancasters were arriving during the afternoon and evening with liberated Prisoners of War.' Even more Lancasters, flying in 'from Germany', landed on the 13th.

A variation in the *Exodus* flights on 14 May saw the PoWs being carried by Transport Command. 'Liberated Prisoners of War continued to arrive. This time in Dakota aircraft, and once again there was no lack of willing volunteers to assist in looking after them.'

No further mention of PoWs landing at Tangmere can be found in the station's ORB, though the following reference to Operation *Exodus* appears in the entry for 2 June 1945: 'The many volunteer helpers on the aerodrome who devoted their evenings to welcoming the returning prisoners-of-war, have been extremely gratified by a number of letters which have been sent to the Commanding Officer by some of the men who landed at Tangmere. All the letters speak very highly of the efficiency of the organisation which greeted them at Tangmere and of the happy and informal manner in which all necessary checking and distribution [was] carried out.'

One former PoW, Leslie Frith, later described the emotions that his return home stirred: 'A glorious sight and one which at times I had thought I would never see again. It was overwhelming. A week ago we were all starving to death, just waiting for the end, and now suddenly we were crossing the English coast and we were home again. I cried with sheer joy.'[70]

At the height of Operation *Exodus*, sixteen aircraft were arriving from Europe every hour bringing over 1,000 people per day into British receiving centres. By the time that *Exodus* was completed, at the end of May 1945, a total of 354,000 ex-prisoners had been brought home by Allied aircraft.

Allied bombers at Tangmere on 28 March 1944. A hand-written note on the rear states that this view was taken from the mid-upper turret of one bomber, with at least two Halifaxes and one B-24 visible in the distance. (*Courtesy of the Andy Saunders Collection*)

69: Captured Junkers Ju 88 Night Fighter

The Enemy Aircraft Flight at Tangmere

One unusual Luftwaffe survivor to pass through RAF Tangmere in 1945 was the Junkers Ju 88 R-1 night fighter seen here. Its journey to Tangmere began on the night of 9 May 1943. That evening, the aircraft, coded D5+E3 and operated by IV/NJG 3, took off from Aalborg, Denmark, on what outwardly appeared to be a normal patrol. However, two members of the three-man crew had made the decision that they were going to defect to the Allies; it is stated that the pair may have been British agents.

Once airborne, the pilot, Oberleutnant Heinrich (or Herbert) Schmitt, landed at Kristiansand, Norway, to refuel. The Ju 88 then took off again, ostensibly to commence its patrol over the Skagerrak. The defecting crew instead flew west to Scotland, holding the third crewmember at gunpoint. The aircraft was detected by British radar as it approached the Scottish coast and two Spitfires from 165 Squadron were scrambled. They intercepted the intruder one mile inland, whereupon the Ju 88 lowered its undercarriage, waggled its wings and dropped flares, signalling its crew's intent to surrender.

The Spitfires escorted the Ju 88 to RAF Dyce, where it received slight damage from the airfield's anti-aircraft guns while attempting to land. The capture of this aircraft was of great intelligence value at the time, as it was fitted with the latest UHF-band FuG 202 Liechtenstein BC radar.

The RAF Museum's unusual Tangmere visitor on display. (*Courtesy of Robert Mitchell*)

Given the RAF serial number PJ876, the Ju 88 was extensively test flown and used for trials over the months that followed. One of its last flights was made on 4 May 1945. With Flight Lieutenant Doug Gough at the controls, PJ876 was flown to RAF Tangmere, where it was handed over into the care of the Enemy Aircraft Flight of the Central Fighter Establishment. At this point it was given the code letters EA-11.

Having remained at Tangmere, it is noted by the RAF Museum that EA-11 was 'probably selected for preservation by the Air Historical Branch at Tangmere in July 1946'. It never flew again, which perhaps explains why it has survived to this day.

In September 1954, and again in September 1955, this Ju 88 was displayed on Horse Guards Parade, London, as part of the annual Battle of Britain week events. The aircraft was restored in 1975 and fitted with a replica of its characteristic Matratze 32-dipole radar antenna array, as all of its radar equipment had been removed during the war. In August 1978 it moved by road to the RAF Museum.

70: Tangmere's 'Enemy Aircraft Circus'

The Central Fighter Establishment

Oberleutnant Heinrich Schmitt's Ju 88 was only one of a number of captured enemy aircraft that could be seen at Tangmere as the war in Europe drew to a close. This remarkable gathering was, as already mentioned, operated by the Enemy Aircraft Flight, which, in turn, formed part of the Central Fighter Establishment.

Though the exact date varies between sources, the original nucleus of the CFE was formed at Tangmere in September 1944. It then moved to Wittering, where it was formally opened on 1 October 1944 as part of No.12 Group. Having absorbed the Fighter Leaders School on 27 December 1944, the CFE returned to Tangmere on 15 January the following year. Many of its instructors and commanding officers were well known aces in Fighter Command, Douglas Bader being just one of them.

The CFE's main task was 'to increase the efficiency of the fighter aircraft and the man who flies it, in all the roles in which the day and night fighter can be used'.[71] Important parts of CFE were the Fighter Leaders' Schools. There were two – a Day Fighter Leaders' School, and a Night Fighter Leaders' School. Their main purpose was to ensure that those who passed out successfully were 'fitted in every way' to command a squadron or wing.

It was Bader who, in June 1945, arrived back at Tangmere to command the CFE. According to Paul Brickhill in *Reach for the Sky*, his

Messerschmitt Me 110C, coded 5F+CM of 4(F)/14, pictured under guard at Home Farm, Goodwood, following its crash-landing there on 21 July 1940. (*Historic Military Press*)

The same Me 110 in RAF markings, and with the serial number AX772, pictured later in the war. (*Andy Saunders Collection*)

biography of the famous wartime ace, it was Air Commodore Dick Atcherley, the former Schneider trophy pilot, who declared: 'Douglas, I want a man to run the Fighter Leader School at Tangmere. It's a Group Captain's job. Would you like it?'

Brickhill takes up the story: 'He [Bader] answered with feeling, "Yes please". Eager for the comfort of the harness again, he cancelled the rest of his leave and in early June drove nostalgically to the well remembered Tangmere. He should have known better. The place looked the same, but that was all that remained of the old days. The tactics were new, the faces were new; above all the atmosphere was new. It seemed to have turned upside down.'

The transformation that greeted Bader included some of the aircraft. The use of captured enemy types by what was often nicknamed the 'Enemy Aircraft Circus' formed an integral part of the CFE's testing, evaluation and teaching processes. Another of the inventory of former Luftwaffe aircraft that graced the runways and dispersals at Tangmere in 1945 was a Messerschmitt Bf 110C-5. 5F-CM of 4(F)/14, that had been captured relatively intact during the Battle of Britain after being brought down by RAF fighters on 21 July 1940.

Following its recovery, the Bf 110 was initially transported to the Royal Aircraft Establishment (RAE) at Farnborough. Following extensive examination, it was repaired using parts culled from other Bf 110 losses and returned to the air. After handling trials with the RAE, it was flown to the Air Fighting Development Unit at Duxford, having been allocated the serial number AX772, on 13 October 1941.

On 5 March 1942, AX772 was transferred to No.1426 (Enemy Aircraft) Flight with whom it flew on a number of flying demonstrations and tours until moving to the Enemy Aircraft Flight of the Central Flying School at Tangmere on 31 January 1945. In operating from there with the CFE, AX772 had returned almost to the spot where it had first arrived in the UK in 1940, for it had come down at Home Farm in Goodwood, just some five miles or so north of Tangmere.

71: Wartime Legends Meet Again

Bader and Galland Reunited as Roles Reversed

Understandably, there are many famous or well-known pilots associated with RAF Tangmere. Indeed, notes Tangmere's ORB on 24 May 1945, 'There is an old saying that if one stands at Charing Cross for long enough, one will see everyone in the world go by at one time of another. Life in the C.F.E. at Tangmere is rather like that. Certainly one meets all the personalities of Fighter Command and, on most days, at least one famous pilot drops in to renew old friendships.'

One famous aviator associated with Tangmere was Group Captain Sir Douglas Bader, who we have already encountered. Having been forced to bale out over St. Omer on 9 August 1941, Bader, was soon to meet one of his equally famous adversaries, Oberstleutnant Adolf Galland. During the Battle of Britain, Bader had commanded 242 Squadron, flying Hawker Hurricanes, whilst Galland took charge of III/JG 26, eventually replacing Gotthard Handrick as commander of JG 26. By the summer of 1941, JG 26 was one of the main fighter forces facing Bader's Tangmere Wing in the skies over northern France.

In the days that followed Bader's capture he found himself being entertained by Galland and his fellow officers – an event at which a number of now famous photographs were taken. Galland even permitted Bader, under escort, to sit in the cockpit of a Messerschmitt Bf 109. Bader, in a semi-serious way, was recorded as asking if his hosts wouldn't mind if he took it on a test flight around the airfield. To this, Galland replied: 'If I grant your wish, I'm afraid you'll escape, and I should be forced to chase after you. Now we have met, we don't want to shoot at each other again, do we?'[72]

After that meeting, Galland and Bader parted ways, the latter heading off into captivity, initially being held in Oflag VIB at Warburg. The RAF Museum takes up the story:

'After three months in Stalag Luft III, Bader was moved to Stalag Luft VIIIB at Lamsdorf, from which he made another attempt to escape. He and four others joined a working party outside the camp, intending to make their way towards the Polish border. The alarm was raised when a Luftwaffe officer called at Lamsdorf to visit Bader and he was found to be missing; he was arrested and returned to Lamsdorf.

'A few days later Bader was transferred to Colditz Castle – Oflag IVC. With typical boldness, he told the Germans that he expected "to travel first class and be accompanied by a batman and an officer of equal rank." Colditz was thought to be escape-proof, and Bader remained there – making life difficult for his captors – until the camp was liberated on 15 April 1945.'[73]

As Bader returned to the UK to pick-up his life again, in a reversal of roles it was Galland's turn to begin a stint as a prisoner of war – he had been captured by American troops in May 1945. During his imprisonment, Galland was to be interrogated at length on Luftwaffe fighter tactics – a period during which he found himself at RAF Tangmere, and more specially the Fighter Leader School, in July 1945. There, in a strange twist of fate, he met Bader once again, though this time it was the latter who was the host.

Galland, on the left in the foreground holding the cigar, with Bader, to his left, in August 1941. Note that Bader's replacement prosthetic leg has been delivered by this time. Their next meeting would come four years later, almost to the day. (*Mark Hillier Collection*)

This occurred on 12 June 1945: 'General Galland and Oberst-Leutnant Baer, of the Luftwaffe, arrived under escort at the Tactics Library and were interrogated by leading flying and technical officers of the C.F.E. The Question Committee consisted of Group Captain Bader, Wing Commander Johnston and Wing Commander Raabjoesn. The questioning continued until nearly midnight and elicited some most interesting information.'

Of renewing his acquaintance with Bader, Galland later wrote the following: 'I saw him four years later. In 1945 I was taken to Air Force Interrogation Camp No.7 at Latimer in North London as an American Prisoner of War, and from there was driven to Tangmere aerodrome, near Chichester, where RAF group leaders were in conference, amongst them Wing Commander Bader, who had returned to England.

'This time I stood in front of him as a prisoner and he offered me his box of cigars. Our roles were reversed. Bader concerned himself in the most charming way about my personal comfort, but next morning he suddenly vanished again, as he had done once before.'[74]

Section Six

The Cold War

72: Tangmere's Type T2 Hangars

Entering the Fast Jet Era

By the end of the war, RAF Tangmere found itself without any proper hangars. In particular, the three Belfast Truss hangars, whose origins stretched back to the First World War, had suffered from the attentions of the Luftwaffe; the roof of the last survivor collapsed during a storm on 17 November 1944.

In the early post-war period, the hangar requirements for an operational RAF fighter base were set at a minimum of four Type T2 hangars. The design of the T2 can be traced back to the start of the Second World War and the introduction of large-span heavy bomber aircraft. To accommodate the newer designs entering service, the Air Ministry, in collaboration with Teesside Bridge & Engineering Ltd., developed a series of end-opening hangars known as the Type 'T'. Created by the architect A.E. Cotton, the first design in this series, the 'T1' (an example of which can still be seen at Goodwood), was, like the latter T2s, erected using a series of standard steel-fabricated lattice wall and roof units of welded-and-bolted construction. The complete framework was clad with galvanised corrugated iron.

By 1946, at least one T2 had been erected at Tangmere, in this case on the base of the earlier middle Belfast Truss structure on the north side

An aerial view of the three T2 hangars at Tangmere taken by Mark Hillier in January 2011. (*Mark Hillier Collection*)

of the airfield. Three further T2 hangars had been completed by 1950, the fourth of which was erected across the airfield on the east boundary close to Aldingbourne Church.

John Richardson was working for Short Brothers in 1962, and recalls his time servicing aircraft such as the Canberra and Vickers Varsity, 'plus any other temp visitors', at Tangmere: 'The Aircraft were involved in some sort of listening [to] and recording of signals up around the North Sea. They would be away for a few days, and when they returned I recall seeing such places as Gardermoen and Skydstrupp in the Form 700s …

'There is no recollection of being cold in the hangars, although it was drafty with the doors open. They never stayed open for long! So the heating must have been acceptable inside. I don't think there was ever more than two Canberras in the hangar at any one time. So there was always plenty of room to work in. Care had to be taken when jacking up to keep the aircraft level, and we all mucked in with that task. Cleanliness of the hangar floors may have suffered, as staffing levels were much less than the RAF would have had on site.

'Servicing the Canberras was fairly straight forward, and we followed strict RAF procedures from the relevant APs [Airforce Publications]. Signing off as necessary for all work done.

One of the trickiest jobs, also perhaps the most dangerous, was checking the explosive bolt circuits. Also for the wing tip tanks. There was another explosive bolt for the control column snatch unit. This was necessary to force the column forwards so that the pilot didn't loose his legs when ejecting.

'It was not unknown for full drop tanks to end up split open on the hangar floor when testing the bolt circuits. It's surprising just how far that much jet fuel will spread very quickly. Luckily, it never happened to me.

'We had a couple of emergencies while I was at Tangmere. A US Air Force Voodoo returning to UK from Germany declared a low fuel situation. He came in very fast and hit the up-slope of the north end of the runway, and immediately lost his main wheels. Fire crews were quick on the scene and by the time we got out there on the tow tractor, the pilot was being helped out of his cockpit. I recall that he was exceptionally pale. And looked no more than a teenager. (I was the ripe old age of 24 then). The Voodoo was recovered to the westernmost hanger, where a team of USAF ground crew set about some repairs.'[75]

After the RAF left Tangmere, the three remaining T2 hangars were used for storage by West Sussex County Council. They were finally demolished in August 2015.

73: RAF High Speed Flight is Reformed

Tangmere Becomes Home to Record Breakers

The RAF High Speed Flight had been formed by the summer of 1927, its primary purpose being to develop and pilot aircraft for setting world speed records and competing in prestigious international air races, particularly the Schneider Trophy. The High Speed Flight was also part of the RAF's efforts to conduct speed-related aviation research, develop advance aeronautical technology and maintain British leadership in aviation innovation. Until the High Speed Flight was established, the setting of faster and faster air speed records had been dominated by the USA and France.

By the time war broke out in 1939, new records had been laid down on fifty-two occasions. Only four of these were set by a British pilot. In fact, the Flight was officially dissolved in 1931, shortly after the RAF won the Schneider Trophy outright by securing three consecutive victories.

Squadron Leader William Waterton (left) and Flight Lieutenant Neville Duke (right) enquire at the Met. Office at Tangmere about flying conditions, 13 August 1946. The original caption states, 'The RAF High Speed Flight, led by Group Captain E.M. Donaldson, is awaiting favourable weather for its attack on the world speed record of 606.25 mph. Mechanics have been hard at work at Tangmere Aerodrome, near Chichester, Sussex, fitting the specially-built Rolls-Royce gas turbine engines into the Gloster Meteors which will be used for the record attempt over a three-kilometre course off Littlehampton. The aircraft which Group Captain Donaldson will fly in the record bid had its engine installation completed yesterday ... [Here] Section Officer Mary Crichton gives the[m] the "gen" from the weather chart.' (*Historic Military Press*)

73: RAF HIGH SPEED FLIGHT IS REFORMED

Members of the RAF High Speed Flight at Tangmere in 1946. They are, left to right, Flight Lieutenant Neville Duke, Squadron Leader W.A. 'Bill' Waterton, and Group Captain E.M. 'Teddy' Donaldson. (*Historic Military Press*)

By the time that the Second World War had ended, with the introduction of jet aircraft into service, attention once again turned to the question of setting new air speed records. For the British, this was spurred on by the fact that the first official post-Second World War air speed record, of just over 606 mph, had been set by Group Captain Hugh Wilson, at the controls of Gloster Meteor EE454 *Britannia*, on 7 November 1945. At this point the UK found itself holding all three official world speed records – land, sea, and air. It was now a question of pride that these should be defended.

By the summer of 1946, the RAF's reformed High Speed Flight was posted to Tangmere. Both its Commanding Officer, Group Captain E.M. 'Teddy' Donaldson, and its first Gloster Meteor arrived at the airfield on 21 June. Donaldson had been instructed to make his attempts between 1 August and 7 September in the hope of 'stealing a march on the Americans'.

The Tangmere historians Reginald Byron and David Coxon explain how the Sussex airfield was selected: 'In choosing the course, which for practical reasons would need to be over water, Donaldson studied the RAF's meteorological records for the previous 50 years, looking for a place with high mean summer temperatures and suitable wind force and direction … He chose Littlehampton, between Worthing and Bognor Regis.'[76] Naturally, the nearby RAF Tangmere made the ideal base.

Efforts at secrecy failed, and word of what the High Speed Flight was hoping to achieve,

151

in particular the breaking the 1,000 km/h, or 623 mph, barrier, leaked out. On 12 July, the Air Ministry invited some sixty reporters and correspondents to Tangmere for a briefing, during which they were introduced to Donaldson and his two main pilots, Squadron Leader William Waterton and Flight Lieutenant Neville Duke. From then on, as preparations continued apace and the course prepared, the Flight, its pilots, and Tangmere remained well and truly in the limelight.

Group Captain E.M. Donaldson, CO of the RAF High Speed Flight, 'checking up on the controls at Tangmere Aerodrome of the Special Meteor IV to be used for the attack on the world speed record of 606.25mph'. (*Historic Military Press*)

74: Gloster Meteor F4, EE549

Tangmere's Part in a World Speed Record

By the summer of 1946, the RAF's High Speed Flight at Tangmere was ready to mount its next assault on the world air speed record. This was carried out successfully on 7 September 1946.

'The world air speed record was broken yesterday by Group Captain Edward Donaldson …,' reported *The Sunday Post*. 'His average speed was 616 m.p.h. This was announced by Air Marshal Sir James Robb, C.-in-C., Fighter Command, at eight minutes past two this morning [8 September].'

Returning to the events of September 1946, *The Sunday Post*'s account continues as follows: 'Piloting a second Meteor over the two-mile course off the Channel coast was Squadron-Leader William Waterton, Canadian-born of Irish parents. His average speed was 614 m.p.h. Yesterday's record bid was unexpected, and was daringly attempted in the face of unfavourable weather conditions. Holidaymakers rushed from hotels, boarding houses, beach huts and chalets to watch the planes flashing past.

'It was a breathless moment as the first Meteor came into view. First it was no larger than a seabird in the west. The next moment it was flashing by. Then, in the twinkling of an eye, it dissolved in the distance. So fast was the plane that it flew in ghost-like silence as it sped barely 200 feet above the waters of the English Channel. Only after it had passed was the noise of its 12,000 h.p. Rolls Royce motors heard …

As part of the RAF 100 anniversary celebrations, EE549 was exhibited on Horse Guards Parade in London – where this photograph was taken. Normally, EE549 is on display at Tangmere Military Aviation Museum. (*Courtesy of Steve Knight*)

A close-up of the commemorative plaque that is on the port side of EE549's cockpit. (*Courtesy of Alan Wilson*)

The only damage to either machine was a small crack, half an inch in length, in the surface of the rudder of Group Captain Donaldson's plane.'

The aircraft that Teddy Donaldson flew on 7 September 1946, was Gloster Meteor EE549. Built in 1946 specially for the RAF's High Speed Flight, to achieve the highest possible speeds EE549 had been modified by removing its cannon and strengthening its canopy. It was delivered to Tangmere on 7 August. Before Donaldson's record-setting flight, test pilot Roland Beamont took EE549 to its compressibility limit of 632 mph, though this had not been carried out under official record conditions.

Following its time with the High Speed Flight, EE549 was used as a gate guardian at RAF Innsworth from 1961 to 1967. It was then restored and, in 1971, passed into the permanent care of the RAF Museum. In 1992, it was loaned to Tangmere Military Aviation Museum, where it remains on show to this day.

Despite having just broken the world record, it would seem that the team at Tangmere was hungry for more as *The Sunday Post* went on to note: 'Group Captain Donaldson said if the temperature to-morrow was appreciably higher, they would attempt to improve on yesterday's speeds. "We were about 16 degrees Centigrade short of the temperature we wanted. You can add one mile per hour for each degree Centigrade. So you can add m.p.h. to yesterday's, and that will give you our speeds in the best conditions."'

It was the Americans, however, who finally exceeded 1,000 km/h in a Lockheed P-80R Shooting Star on 19 June 1947.

Gloster Meteor EE549 pictured by a dispersal hut at Tangmere in the summer of 1946. (*Historic Military Press*)

75: The 'Tangmere Times'

Life on the Airfield After WW2

As pointed out on the contents page of this festive edition of *Tangmere Times*, dated December 1948, it was 'published at RAF Station Tangmere, Sussex, for personnel of the Royal Air Force, and anyone interested in the welfare of the same, under the supervision of P.O. Edwards'. As would be expected, its thirty-two pages are packed full of details of life on the station at the time.

The main event affecting the RAF in the winter of 1948 was the six-month-old Berlin Airlift. Though Operation *Plain Fare*, this being the name given to the British participation, was being played out on the Continent, Tangmere was not untouched, as one writer in *Tangmere Times* noted: 'Very few of the personnel of this station have been directly affected by the Berlin Air Lift, but most of us have been indirectly affected by having to stay in the RAF for an extra three months. Most of us have had a "bind" during the past few months about having to do this extra piece of service, especially as we are not directly helping with the Air Lift, but by filling positions in the hangar, control tower, fire section, or orderly room, we are allowing some man of similar rank and trade to hold a corresponding position at one of the Air Lift stations in Germany.'

Many of those stationed at Tangmere in the early part of the Cold War remember the station dog, a white bull terrier named Crippen. However, as was pointed out in the 'Rumblings' section of this issue of *Tangmere Times*, Crippen had only just survived to see the Christmas celebrations: 'The other day our trusty old friend Crippen was strolling along near the static water tank and he even decided to have a swim or he

The front cover of the December 1948 issue of *Tangmere Times*. (*All Historic Military Press*)

fell in. But sometime later he was found floating around on the surface. Help was sought and the old warrior was fished out and given artificial respiration and as you all know is still around.'

Other snippets on the same page included the following: 'One evening not so long ago a [Douglas C-54] Skymaster touched down from the States. The crew naturally made their way to the Station Dance but did not stay and quite a number of disappointed sighs were heard from the weaker sex.'

One of the images of the airfield in our featured issue of 'Tangmere Times' – in this case it is captioned as 'Main Street, Tangmere'.

There was also news of another farewell: 'This month the Royal Air Force will say goodbye to the Tiger Moth as a trainer. The Tiger Moth is now been replaced by monoplanes. In their day hundreds of thousands have been taught to fly in the Tiger Moth, which has been in use for 17 years.'

Another hang-over from the Second World War was the matter of salvage, as 'The Salvage King' wrote: 'To most of us this Salvage business is a "bind". We had it during the war and, like the poor, it has been with us ever since. At first it was "Save paper for this" and "Save scrap for that – Bombs, Bullets and Battleships". Now it is save Dollars.

'To most of you Salvage means no more than the days fatigues with the Salvage Section, for which leave qualifies one. Or the sight of an eager Salvage "bod" into whose ready sack vanishes the contents of the waste paper basket. By themselves, these few pounds may appear insignificant, but when they have been multiplied by the number of sections visited, and by the number of visits made in one year, we find that last year Tangmere saved 5 tons of paper and cardboard. When this has been multiplied by the number of units in the RAF you can obtain some idea of the wood-pulp, i.e. Dollars, saved …

'So, remember when you complain about the cost of cigarettes, tobacco and food, that it is within everyone's power to help themselves. If we have to spend Dollars on the wood-pulp, there is obviously less to spend on food and tobacco. Therefore, save waste paper – all you have to do is ring Ext. 127 and we will gladly pay you a call.'

A 'fog-bound' Dakota at Tangmere. The 'Rumblings' section explained that the 'most notable visitors this month were the C-in-C Coastal Command, Air Marshal John Baker, and Air Vice Marshal F.L. Hopps, who arrived during the fog, accompanied by several staff officers, in a 24 Squadron Dakota: 'We are not quite sure whether the pilot really meant to land at Tangmere; we understand that G.C.A. talked him into it.'

76: Portrait of Colonel Robin Olds USAF

First Peacetime Non-Commonwealth CO of an RAF Squadron

During its existence, RAF Tangmere was the location for a number of 'firsts'. One of these, in the years after the Second World War, was when an operational RAF Squadron, in this case No.1 Squadron, was placed under the command of a non-Commonwealth citizen for the first time in peacetime. That officer was the USAF's Major Robin Olds, who arrived at Tangmere under the auspices of a post-war RAF/USAF officer exchange programme on 20 October 1948.

A Second World War veteran who had twelve 'kills' to his name, with a further 11.5 aircraft destroyed on the ground, Olds had been awarded the Silver Star, both the American and British DFCs and the French *Croix de Guerre* by the time he arrived on No.1 Squadron. The latter was, at the time, equipped with Gloster Meteor F.4s.

Olds later recalled his arrival at the Sussex airfield: 'Tangmere was, as the RAF would say, pissing with rain on that late October day in 1948.

Colonel Robin Olds pictured in Southeast Asia in 1967. Olds commanded the 8th Tactical Fighter Wing at Ubon Royal Thai Air Force Base, Thailand, during the Vietnam War, from September 1966 to September 1967. He shot down four North Vietnamese MiGs. Having attained the rank of Brigadier General, Olds finally retired from the USAF in June 1973, and passed away in 2007. (*USAF*)

Meteors of No.1 Squadron arranged behind squadron personnel at RAF Tangmere. Robin Olds can be seen on the left of the front row. (*Courtesy of the Andy Saunders Collection*)

Ragged gray clouds caught in trees and blurred nearby buildings. And it was damp, thoroughly damp. Not your normal kind of rain-wet damp, but damp right through to your clothes, down in your shoes, between your shoulder blades. It was the sort of damp that made mockery of a trench coat and made me wish for fireplace and a hot glass of something.'[77]

After his abrupt and somewhat inauspicious introduction to the winter weather at Tangmere, it was only a matter of hours before he was allowed to take one of the squadron's Meteors up for a familiarisation flight. After some brief instructions from the Commanding Officer, not all of which entirely made sense to the American pilot, he was given permission to continue: 'Yank, this Tangmere Flying Control. Turn left from your present position and taxi east.'

It was an instruction that left Olds somewhat perplexed: 'Making a left turn put me out in the middle of the flying field. Nothing but grass. With rain puddles. And much splashing.'

Refusing to give in, Olds pushed on: 'That expanse of macadam on my right ... oops, starboard ... was obviously the missing runway. I taxied on east till I saw the end, turned onto it, and held the brakes ...

'Well, I thought, here goes nothing, and released the brakes ... I pushed the throttles forward, made sure I was aligned, glanced inside for the engine and oil gauges, couldn't find them, and peered through the heavy front glass at the runway ahead. The Meteor IV accelerated smoothly and the stick grip came alive.'[78] Moments later Major Olds was airborne from Tangmere for the first time.

It was the start of a unique year-long relationship that the American Ace enjoyed with the Royal Air Force, No.1 Squadron, and, of course, RAF Tangmere. Such was Olds' abilities and skills that by the time his exchange had come to an end, he had become the squadron's commanding officer.

77: Hurricanes Return to Tangmere

'Angels One Five'

This photograph shows pilots from a Hurricane-equipped Portuguese squadron being welcomed by RAF officers following their arrival at Tangmere in July 1951. On the left is Group Captain T. Pritchett, Tangmere's Commanding Officer.

The Hurricanes' imminent arrival was, unsurprisingly, a big news story at the time. The following was reported in the *Coventry Evening Telegraph* on Saturday, 14 July 1951: 'Over London and parts of Southern England during the coming week, aeroplanes of an

The Portuguese pilots at Tangmere after their journey from Espinho. (*Historic Military Press*)

almost forgotten type will be seen once more. Five Hurricanes from the Portuguese Air Force are coming to this country to take part in a film called *Hawks in the Sun* which deals with the Battle of Britain. It was, of course, the Hurricanes and Spitfires that wrought such havoc with the German Air Force.

'The planes are expected to arrive at the Tangmere R.A.F. station on Monday on a goodwill visit to the R.A.F. Their arrival will be a sequel to a world-wide search by the Air Ministry and the firm that manufactured the 'planes for an operational group of these veteran 'planes of the last war. Although some 10,000 Hurricanes were made in Britain during the war, only two airworthy craft have been found here after intensive searches. Thus the 'planes from Portugal will be disguised to appear once more as R.A.F. fighters and they will be converted by camouflage experts from four-gun Hurricanes to eight-gun Battle of Britain types.

'It is extremely unlikely that a group of these aircraft will ever again be seen in flight over Britain in any number. The Portuguese pilots who fly these 'planes before the film cameras will thus not only be reliving history, they will also, in a sense, be making it.'

The Portuguese Hurricanes took off from their base at Espinho on 13 July. Equipped with long range fuel tanks under their wings they were guided to Tangmere by an Avro Anson, making stopovers at Logrono and Bordeaux.

Though the report states that the film was called *Hawks in the Sun*, it was in fact released under the name *Angels One Five*. The first British post-war production to deal with the events of the Battle of Britain, the name *Angels One Five* was a play on the wartime radio procedure that indicated an altitude of 15,000 feet.

In the end, the film featured three Hurricanes from British sources and five from the Portuguese Air Force. The latter, Nos. 544, 554, 600, 601, and 624, were all Mk.IIc aircraft. The three from the UK were two Mk.Is supplied by the RAF, P2617, which we have already encountered, and L1592. All eight were painted in the colours of 56 Squadron and were based at RAF Kenley for the filming, the aerial scenes of which were mainly completed between 20 and 27 July. *Angels One Five* was released in March 1952.

A Gloster Meteor of No.1 Squadron taxiing past the Watch Office at RAF Tangmere in the late 1940s, early 1950s. (*Historic Military Press*)

78: 'Fighter Station Supreme'

The Memoirs of Wing Commander H.R. Allen DFC

Having joined the RAF on a short service commission in June 1939, Hubert Raymond Allen served throughout the Second World War. One of 'The Few', having been a Spitfire pilot with 66 Squadron in the Battle of Britain, 'Dizzy' Allen opted to remain in the RAF after the war. He was the only officer ever to have commanded both of Tangmere's premier squadrons, two units whose history is inextricably linked with that of the airfield – the 'terrible twins' as he referred to them. These were No.1, of which he was the CO from January to October 1946, and 43 Squadron, which he commanded from December 1949 to February 1952.

A graduate of the RAF Staff College, Allen retired on 1 January 1965, with the rank of Wing Commander. In the years that followed, Allen wrote a number of books detailing the various stages of his RAF career. It is one of these publications, *Fighter Station Supreme: RAF Tangmere*, that features as our next 'object'. As the subtitle indicates, much of the book, which was first published in 1985, concerns Allen's time at Tangmere, predominantly during the burgeoning Cold War.

Allen dedicated the book 'To the Memory of RAF Tangmere, in the optimism that those who believed that Biggin Hill was the crack Station in Fighter Command think again'. In his opening chapter, Allen revealed a little more of his feelings for the Sussex airfield: 'The RAF Fighter Station at Tangmere could hardly be likened to a retreat where one could get away from it all, though that was eminently possible. Sudden death could claim you if your aircraft made a hole in the ground because of technical failure or German bullets. But that applied to most fighter stations based in southern England, so it can be left out of the argument.'

The cover of Wing Commander H.R. Allen DFC's *Fighter Station Supreme*.

Having completed six tours of duty at Tangmere, Allen was confident that few people would known the airfield 'so intimately as I did'. In conclusion, he wrote, 'During my twenty years service with Fighter Command I served at every major station … I can mention Biggin Hill, Kenley, West Malling, Hawkinge, Manston, Gravesend, Hornchurch, North Weald, Duxford, Coltishall – even Exeter to make the point. But there never was and never will be a station so attractive as Tangmere.'

79: RAF Tangmere's Badge

Approved July 1953

Even now, in the twenty-first century, heritage, customs and traditions help define and shape the professionalism of the United Kingdom's armed forces. For the RAF, this includes the adoption of a squadron or unit badge.

Established to record and preserve the history of these emblems, which are often referred to incorrectly as the 'crest', the RAF Heraldry Trust provides some interesting background information: 'Mottos and devices had been in use with many units, especially the flying squadrons, since the earliest days of the RAF; during the 1920s many units designed, and employed, unofficial squadron badges – in many cases these became the basis for the official badge.'

The Trust goes on to point out that 'the badge, once awarded, becomes a central part of the unit's identity, appearing on correspondence, aircraft or other equipment, as the major motif upon the Squadron Standard, and in a host of other uses. All RAF units, from Command size downwards, are entitled to apply for such a badge.'

That entitlement, however, was, and still is, subject to two main provisions. These were that the squadron or unit had 'been in existence for at least 2 years – and likely to stay in existence', and that it had 'a status and function which can justify the sanction of a badge'.

'The initial step was to submit, via the appropriate "chain of Command", a draft sketch of the motif and motto to the RAF Inspector of Badges, at the College of Heralds, including a statement of how the design/motto were arrived at – i.e. the origin and significance. The Inspector would then make his suggestion as to amendments such that the design followed the precepts of heraldry and the motto made sense. This latter point was important as most chosen mottos were in Latin and few squadrons boasted high grade Latin scholars amongst their number. Along with the draft, the unit had to send 15 guineas for the Inspector's fee!'[79]

What is perhaps surprising is that RAF Tangmere did not formally apply for authorisation for a badge until February 1953. The all-important approval, following the design's acceptance by the RAF Inspector of Badges and sanction by the Chief of the Air Staff, was given by the recently-crowned Queen Elizabeth II in July that year.

A commercially produced example of RAF Tangmere's station badge. (*Historic Military Press*)

79: RAF TANGMERE'S BADGE

Tangmere's badge followed the well-established pattern of an edged circle surmounted by a crown, with a scroll at the base – in this case it was a St Edward's Crown, more often referred to as the 'Queen's Crown'. The design itself consists of two pommelled and hilted swords in *saltire*, the latter, also called St Andrew's Cross, being a heraldic symbol in the form of a diagonal cross, behind a *passant-guardant* Lion. The swords represented the day and night fighter role of the Station, whilst the lion was taken from the Arms of the nearby City of Chichester. The motto, emblazoned on the scroll, is 'Attack to Defend'.

Meteors at Tangmere pictured from the control tower. Note the blister hangar that can be seen in the background. (*Courtesy of the Andy Saunders Collection*)

The fate of one of Tangmere's Meteors, in this case VT257 of 43 Squadron. Mechanical failure forced Flight Lieutenant A.G.C. Farley to make a crash landing at Tangmere on 19 December 1949. (*Courtesy of the Andy Saunders Collection*)

80: Hawker Hunter WB188

Tangmere's Part in a World Speed Record in 1953

As it transpired, Group Captain Teddy Donaldson's new air speed record would only stand for just over nine months – it fell to the Americans once again on 19 June 1947. Indeed, for the eight years after EE549 achieved 616 mph, the Americans would officially smash the air speed record a total of six times. The RAF duly set out to reclaim the prize.

Tangmere was once again selected as the base for the new attempt, and Squadron Leader Neville Duke was handed the task. For the flight, Duke choose Hawker Hunter WB188. Ordered in June 1948 as one of three Hunter prototypes, WB188 was flown in July 1951 by Hawker's Chief Test Pilot – none other than Duke himself. In early 1953, WB188 was fitted with side-mounted airbrakes, extra fuel tanks in the wings and a new reheated version of the Avon RA.7R engine capable of 7,130lbs thrust dry and 9,600lbs with reheat lit. She had also been fitted with a sharply pointed nose cone fairing and windscreen fairing – at which point she became known as the Hunter Mk.3.

Unlike in 1946, for this series of attempts the three kilometre course only had marker buoys to indicate its beginning and end. This did not overly concern Duke, for, as he himself noted, he had 'flown the course a couple of hundred times already!'

Following in the footsteps of EE549, WB188, seen here, arrived at Tangmere in 1992 where she remains on permanent loan, allowing visitors the opportunity of seeing together two of the most important historic airframes in the UK. (*Courtesy of Robert Mitchell*)

80: HAWKER HUNTER WB188

The altimeter from WB188 was presented to Neville Duke for his participation in what was an important occasion in British aviation history. Like the aircraft it came from, it is also on display at Tangmere Military Aviation Museum.

It was on 30 August 1953, that Duke took off from Tangmere for his first record attempt. The first practice runs went well. Then, on the last, WB188's engine began to run intermittently. The attempt was abandoned.

A further bid was made on 1 September 1953. It too ended in failure. 'I took off from Tangmere on to course, dropping the nose to build up speed rapidly,' Duke later recalled. 'Coming down first from 1,000 feet I lined up on the marker flares seven miles away. I caught a glimpse of Bognor pier and my indicated airspeed was registering 550 knots. I switched on reheat. There was a surge of acceleration, followed by a loud bang.

'The Hunter flipped over in a vicious roll to starboard, and a force of six and a half "g" crushed down on my ribs and nearly blacked me out. Beach and sea had swum into the place of the sky and were coming closer every second. I cut off the reheat, thrust over the stick, and came out of the roll, right way up, at about 200 feet. I looked out at the wing and saw part of the undercarriage leg sticking through a jagged hole in the wing surface. The aerodynamic stresses and strains of the high speed had sucked out the undercarriage leg and smashed it through the wing like a cannon shell.'[80] Duke was able to land at Dunsfold.

Undeterred, Squadron Leader Duke was soon back at Tangmere with a repaired WB188. His next attempt took place on 7 September – and was met with success. After fifteen minutes in the air, Duke returned to Tangmere having achieved a mean average over four runs of 727.63 mph.

WB188 pictured at Tangmere at the time of the attempts on the air speed record. (*Courtesy of the Andy Saunders Collection*)

81: Rustington Memorial

Commemorating Two World Records

Located on the seafront at Rustington, a short distance to the east of Sea Lane, can be found a plaque commemorating the two air speed records that had been set by aircraft operating from RAF Tangmere.

Further detail of Squadron Leader Duke's 1953 attempt was provided by *The Surrey Comet* in its edition of 9 September that year: 'Squadron Leader Neville Duke, Hawker's Chief Test pilot, created a new world air speed record when he flew his Hawker Hunter jet fighter at an average of 727.6 mph. He made four runs over the course between Rustington and Kingston Gorse on the Sussex coast and on the first attained a speed of 738.8 mph. He said it was much easier to keep level when flying low. During two of his runs he flew at a height of only 50 feet above the sea.'

A similar report appeared in *The Daily Herald*: 'During the afternoon, while the figures for his [Duke's] first run were being worked out, he was told that the air was calmer over the three-kilometre course. Without waiting for the results, he took off again from Tangmere RAF station, near Chichester, in the bright red Hunter. On the first run he broke the record, too. His speed was 726.9 mph.

The plaque commemorating new air speed records set in 1946 and 1953. (*Historic Military Press*)

81: RUSTINGTON MEMORIAL

Group Captain 'Teddy' Donaldson passing a timing station on the high speed run course in EE549 in September 1946.

'Holiday-makers gasped as the machine rocketed along the shore, almost disappearing before the sound of its Rolls Royce Avon engine could be heard. Regulations for the record demand that Duke fly no higher than 300 ft. But he kept the Hunter well down over the choppy sea.

'After he landed. Duke said: "It was a nice ride. It was bumpy as the wind was gusty. At times felt like driving car over rutted field." His 33-year-old wife Gwen listened to the flight from the control tower at Tangmere. She heard his voice over the radio, "Beginning run one," "Beginning run two." And when he came in over the airfield and did tour victory rolls she ran to the control room's roof and waved.'

Another correspondent, writing for the *Belfast News-Letter*, described how Duke's runs appeared from the ground – including the area where the plaque stands today. 'Swimmers, holiday-makers in yachts and rowing boats, and thousands of people packing the beaches over a 15-mile stretch of the Sussex coast, watched as the Hunter flashed by 1,000 yards out from the shore on the first flight. Hundreds of others watched from cars parked along the coast road. Most of them had waited since the middle of the morning. They heard the whine and roar of the Rolls Royce Avon engines two seconds after the machine had passed them.'

82: Tangmere's Headline Departure

A Front-Page Royal Story

It was at about 19.30 hours on the evening of Wednesday, 28 July 1954, that a Royal Canadian Air Force VIP transport, the unique Canadair C-5 serial 17524 (later 10000), climbed into the air from Tangmere's runway and, quickly disappearing in to the low cloud, set course for the North Atlantic. On board was the Duke of Edinburgh at the start of a three-week tour of Canada.

The Duke had arrived at Tangmere in company with the Queen. 'Shortly before the Royal party arrived,' reported the *Portsmouth Evening News* on 29 July, 'a heavy downpour sent the crowds scurrying for shelter. But as the large saloon car drove along the [runway] tarmac, the rain stopped.

'The Queen and the Duke shook hands with the Station Commander, Group Capt.

The Queen and Prince Philip being greeted by Tangmere's Station Commander, Group Captain John Kent DFC & Bar, AFC, on their arrival. (*Tangmere Military Aviation Museum*)

82: TANGMERE'S HEADLINE DEPARTURE

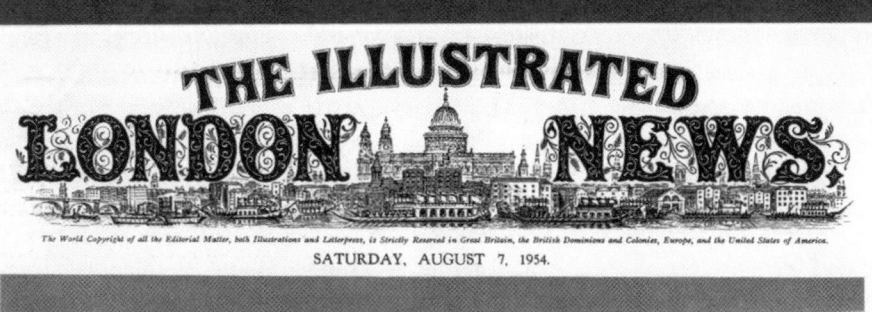

The front page of *The Illustrated London News* of 7 August 1954, showing the Queen leaving the RCAF Canadair C-5 VIP transport on the runway at Tangmere. (*via Historic Military Press*)

John Kent, who welcomed them, the crew and mechanics of the plane, and three members of the Royal Canadian Mounted Police, who will form part of the Duke's escort while he is Canada, were presented to the Queen and the Duke ... After the crew, who are under Wing Commander B.H.A. Harrison [some accounts state Morrison], of the Royal Canadian Air Force, had been presented, the Queen entered the plane with her husband. After a few minutes, she climbed down the gangway steps. The Duke watched her from the plane.'

Operated by 412 Squadron RCAF, to which it was delivered on 21 June 1950, the C-5 was a larger version of the civil Canadair North Star then in service with Trans-Canada Airlines. With a DC-6 undercarriage and Pratt and Witney radial engines, it was a one-off hybrid. The author Peter Pigott has described the C-5 as being, at the time, 'the most luxurious of any aircraft in Canada, if not the world'.[81]

The C-5 was divided into two main sections. The main compartment, designed to seat twenty-four passengers, was followed by the gallery, as well as a washroom and cloakroom. Major M. Joost once described the area beyond: 'It is in the rear compartment that luxury was the byword. Here there was seating for thirteen. It had its own private washroom with hot and cold water. The furniture consisted of two divans, a semi-circular lounge, an executive desk with swivel chair, a filing cabinet, and a telephone to talk to the captain.'[82]

Once the Queen had bid farewell to Prince Philip, she alighted from the C-5 – a moment which provided the front-page illustration used by *The Illustrated London News* and seen here.

'She walked over to her car,' continued the *Portsmouth Evening News*, 'and waved through the window until the giant plane was airborne. She then drove to the Officers Mess, and after spending a few minutes chatting with officers, left for Arundel. As the car left the station, the Royal Standard, which was flying from the flagstaff during the visit, was lowered.'

83: Gloster Meteor Pilot's Logbook

Squadron Leader Jeremy Mudford, Based at Tangmere in 1950s

One of the pilots who might well have been on the airfield when the Queen passed through Tangmere in August 1954 was Squadron Leader Jeremy 'Jerry' Mudford.

Having completed his pilot's training on types such as the North American Harvard, a complex radial piston engine aircraft with retractable undercarriage, Mudford converted to jet power on the Gloster Meteor III at RAF Driffield. Jerry arrived on his first posting to 34 Squadron at RAF Tangmere in 1954, the unit being equipped at the time with the Meteor F8 fighter.

Jerry's logbook reveals that his first three flights at Tangmere were in a two-seat Meteor T7, before he undertook his first solo flight in one of the squadron's Meteor F8s, in this case WB109, for an hour's sector reconnaissance. The intention of the latter was to assist in familiarisation of Tangmere's local air space, features and surrounding airfields. Throughout the following three months, Jerry undertook formation flying, as well as tactics and gunnery training.

Despite the part it played in Tangmere's post-war service, the Meteor was far from a vice-less aircraft. Indeed, the Meteor had a high loss rate, with 150 crashes in 1952 alone and 436 fatal accidents between 1944 and 1986.[83] In speaking with Mark Hillier, Jerry recalled one issue that the Tangmere Meteor pilots faced:

The RAF Form 414, or Pilot's Logbook, that belonged to Squadron Leader Jeremy Mudford. Some of his entries for 1954 can be seen here. (*Mark Hillier Collection*)

Gloster Meteors, more specifically Mk.IVs of 266 Squadron, at RAF Tangmere in April 1948. (*Historic Military Press*)

'In a fighter aeroplane you always kept your speed up as long as you possibly could, so that when you come into your base you would fly in at anything up to 300 knots at low level. This would make it difficult for an enemy to attack you. Then you would close the throttles, pull round, pull the air brakes out to slow your speed down, and then, when you got within undercarriage speed, which was 175 knots, you put the undercarriage down and kept turning all the way round to the runway. That required quite a bit of skill.

'Quite a number of people got killed in the circuit after they put the undercarriage down and the aircraft dived into the ground. 'If you really had some bank on and you put the undercarriage down, the aeroplane was not only turning already, it also developed a yaw because one leg came down before the other. When it developed a yaw, the airflow came over the airbrake and shielded the elevator, so no elevator control left – and you lost control. You went in with the aeroplane. So, in 1954 we stopped flying the Meteor for three months because so many people were being killed.'[84]

A Meteor NF.12, in this case WS716/B, of 25 Squadron, pictured landing at RAF Tangmere in April 1958. (*Historic Military Press*)

84: Supermarine Spitfire Mk.LF XVI TE311

A Tangmere Gate Guardian

The Battle of Britain Memorial Flight, or the BBMF, was inaugurated at RAF Biggin Hill on 11 July 1957. It was initially called the RAF Historic Aircraft Flight and consisted of three PR Mk XIX Spitfires and the RAF's last airworthy Hurricane, LF363. It was then called the Battle of Britain Flight before a final renaming, in 1969, to what it is known as today, BBMF.

Between 1959 and 1965 the flight had one Spitfire (PM631) and one Hurricane (LF363) on its strength. Now, as a 'museum without walls', it maintains eleven historic and irreplaceable aircraft: a Lancaster, a C-47 Dakota, two Hurricanes, a pair of de Havilland Chipmunk training aircraft, and five Spitfires. One of the latter is Spitfire Mk LF XVIe TE311.

Built at Castle Bromwich, TE311 was taken on charge by the Air Ministry on 8 June 1945, exactly one month after VE Day, being delivered to No.39 Maintenance Unit at Colerne eight days later – at which point it was promptly put in storage. In October, TE311 was allocated to the Empire Central Flying School's Handling Squadron at RAF Hullavington. It only remained with the unit for four months before being passed on to 33 Maintenance Unit at RAF Lynham. This Spitfire's last posting was

Spitfire Mk LF XVIe TE311 at its post at RAF Tangmere's main gate at some point between 1955 and 1967. (*Tangmere Military Aviation Museum*)

Spitfire TE311 landing at RAF Coningsby following a display as part of the Battle of Britain Memorial Flight in April 2015. (© *MoD/Crown Copyright, 2024*)

to No.1689 Ferry Pilots Training Flight at RAF Aston Down. In all, with spells on the ground and long periods in storage, TE311 was only flown for a total of only about twelve months. When it was transferred to non-effective stock in December 1954, it had just thirty hours 'on the clock'.

In August 1955, with her wings well and truly clipped, TE311 was placed at the main gate of RAF Tangmere. She remained there, welcoming visitors and staff alike, until 1967. At that point, TE311 was one of a number of aircraft loaned for the filming of *Battle of Britain*. Altered to represent a high-back Spitfire, TE311 was restored sufficiently to taxi under its own power for ground scenes.

Once filming was complete, TE311 did not return to Tangmere, but was allocated to RAF Benson, before assuming a variety of exhibition roles. It was put up for disposal in 1999, but the BBMF managed to convince the MoD that this airframe may still be of use, albeit initially as a source of spares. Then, in 2002, a ten-year rebuild to flying condition was commenced, led by Chief Technician Paul Blackah MBE. Finally, in October 2012, Tangmere's former gate guardian took to the air again for the first time in fifty-eight years.

85: RAF Javelins Gather at Tangmere

A 'First' For Fighter Command

A formation of twenty-seven RAF Gloster Javelins, in nine 'vics' of three, can be seen here on Tangmere's Runway 25, prior to taking-off to participate in a flypast at Farnborough, on 28 August 1957. The first nine aircraft were from 46 Squadron, the second nine from 23 Squadron and the third nine from 141 Squadron.

An aerial view of the twenty-seven Javelins at Tangmere on 28 August 1957. The shadow of the Javelin from which the image was taken can be seen, along with four standby aircraft on the operational readiness platform to the right. (*Tangmere Military Aviation Museum*)

Another Gloster Javelin FAW.9, in this case XH890/M of 23 Squadron, pictured at Tangmere in September 1961, the height of the Cold War. (*Historic Military Press*)

The world's first twin-jet delta-wing fighter aircraft, the Javelin was designed to intercept bombers at high altitudes and speeds, and was the RAF's first all-weather interceptor aircraft. The Javelin's delta wing and large tailplane allowed for effective manoeuvrability at high speeds and control at low landing speeds

The leader of the formation seen here was Wing Commander Harry White of 46 Squadron. White was a Second World War veteran who had joined the RAF and initially flown as a Sergeant Pilot before receiving a Short Service Commission in 1941. His postings were to 534 Squadron and then to 141 Squadron, flying Beaufighters in the night fighter role. White took part in bomber support operations using *Serrate* as well as AI radar to protect the night bombers from prowling Luftwaffe fighters. By the end of the war, his claims stood at twelve destroyed and four damaged. Having also been awarded a DFC and two Bars, White went on to attain the rank of Air Commodore after twenty-two years of service.

Returning to the gathering seen here, the Javelin in the centre of the fifth-row back was that of Flight Lieutenant Fred Butcher, the Deputy Leader of 23 Squadron, and his navigator, Flight Lieutenant Benny Baronowski. The Javelin of Squadron Leader 'Dizzy' Gladstone, CO of 23 Squadron, can be seen in the centre of the fourth row back. The Javelins met up with an equal sized formation of Hunters to carry out the flypast.

86: Donald Campbell's Bluebird-Proteus CN7

Another Record-Breaker at Tangmere

By the end of the 1950s, and into the early 1960s, Tangmere's status was gradually diminishing – a situation exacerbated by the disbandment of the airfield's three fighter squadrons in the summer of 1958. Nevertheless, there were still odd moments of excitement that punctuated an increasingly humdrum existence.

One of these came in April 1962, with the arrival, albeit temporarily, of the Bluebird-Proteus CN7, one of a long line of speed machines associated with the Campbell family. Already the holder of the Water Speed Record, Donald Campbell had set himself a new challenge – to achieve a speed of 400mph on land. With technical and financial support from across British industry, Campbell had two brothers, Ken and Lew Norris, design the vehicle that he would use to hopefully reach this target. The existing record, of 394 mph, was held by John Cobb in the Railton Mobil Special.

Though RAF Tangmere is known for its aviation history, its connection to Campbell's record-breaking ambitions is a notable chapter in its history. The Bluebird-Proteus CN7 is seen here in its final form, on display at the National Motor Museum, Beaulieu. (*Courtesy of VanWiel*)

The resulting Bluebird-Proteus CN7 was powered by a Bristol-Siddeley Proteus gas turbine engine, as used in airliners, which drove all four wheels. However, this massive and expensive project, costing an estimated £1,000,000 to build, was initially beset with problems, being delayed due to mechanical issues and accidents, including a significant crash at Bonneville Salt Flats in 1960.

It was as development continued after the crash that a site for further testing was sought. It is worth nothing that this testing followed CN7's initial public demonstration at Goodwood Circuit in July 1960 and preceded another demonstration at Goodwood in July 1962.

Three factors ultimately led Campbell's team to RAF Tangmere for this work. The chief of these was Tangmere's expansive and flat tarmac runways, which provided a controlled environment ideal for testing high-speed vehicles. At the same time, Tangmere was easily accessible and logistically convenient for Campbell's team and support personnel. Lastly, as a military site, the airfield offered the necessary privacy for testing such an ambitious and secretive project – and, of course, local residents would also have been used to the sound of turbine engines in action.

As a proving ground, Tangmere was used for a number of CN7's shakedown runs, Campbell's team performing lower-speed trials to evaluate the car's systems, including its steering, suspension, and braking. Such tests allowed engineers to refine the car's performance, including its aerodynamics and turbine engine response. Importantly, Tangmere's flat runway surfaces helped ensure all systems were operating correctly before the next set of serious attempts on the world record took place on natural surfaces like Lake Eyre in Australia.

Bluebird-Proteus CN7's time at Tangmere would ultimately prove instrumental in Campbell's success. Though bad weather meant that his record attempts in 1962 and 1963 had to be abandoned, he finally attained a new world record of 403.10 mph at Lake Eyre in South Australia on 17 July 1964. The CN7 was the first car to officially set a Land Speed Record in excess of 400mph.

Donald Campbell's Bluebird-Proteus CN7 undergoing testing on the runway at RAF Tangmere. Unfortunately, Campbell's record was short lived. Rule changes soon meant that jet-propelled cars could be used. Indeed, by the end of 1964, the record had been broken five times and was 133mph faster. And of CN7, when asked if he enjoyed driving it during the record attempts, he simply replied: 'No, it was awful, the car slewed all over the track.' (*Courtesy of the Andy Saunders Collection*)

87: Freedom Scroll

Cementing Tangmere's Links With The City of Chichester

In September 1958, Wing Commander Dennis 'Hurricane' David arrived at Tangmere as the station's new Commanding Officer. One of The Few, David had flown from Tangmere during the Battle of Britain, having been posted to 213 Squadron as 'B' Flight Commander on 16 September 1940.

During his time as Tangmere's CO, David struck up a relationship with the then mayor of Chichester, William Pope. 'He had been an airman in the MT (Motor Transport) section during the war,' recalled Dennis, 'and was stationed at Tangmere. One day we were reminiscing about the special relationship that had always existed between the city and RAF Tangmere, and I suggested that it would be a wonderful idea to cement the relationship by awarding the Freedom of the City of Chichester to Tangmere. Bill was at once enthusiastic, and said he would like to push this through while he was still mayor.'[85]

Councillor Pope was as good as his word. During a council meeting on 6 January 1960, it was 'unanimously resolved that in recognition of Tangmere being one of the oldest stations in the Royal Air Force, mindful of its fame as a fighter station during the Great War of 1939–45, and in appreciation of the long and cordial association of the City and that Royal Air Force Station, the Council do confer upon the Royal Air Force Station, Tangmere the honorary Freedom of the City of Chichester'.

The ceremony itself took place on 5 May 1960. 'The parade assembled at Prior's Field,' recalled Dennis, 'where the presentation of the beautiful illuminated Freedom Scroll took place. On behalf of the station, I presented the city with a silver statue of a young pilot of the 1940 era.'

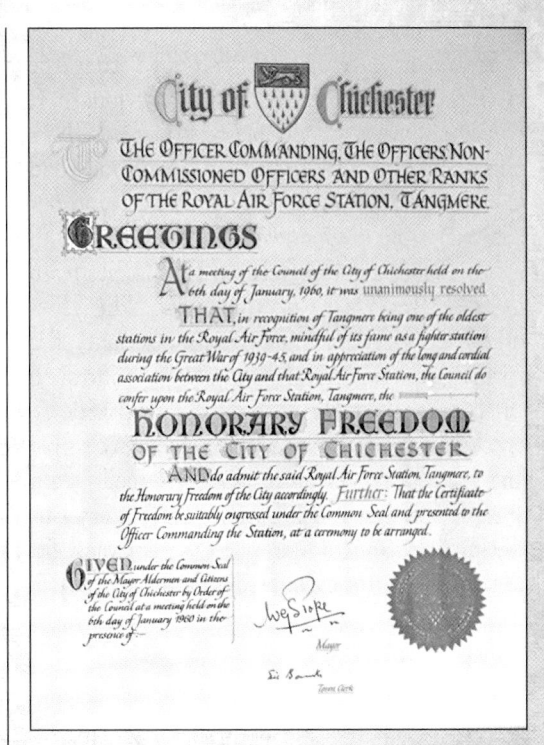

The Freedom Scroll for RAF Tangmere.

In his speech, Mayor Pope noted that, 'We are all conscious of the great service that airmen from the Tangmere Wing rendered to this country in the Battle of Britain. This decisive victory was not achieved without cost in human life. They lie at rest in village churchyards and cemeteries in and around our City. We all owe them a great debt which can bever be repaid.'

These words were followed by the presentation of the Freedom Scroll. The following account was published in the *Bognor Regis Observer* on 13 May 1960: 'As the RAF scroll bearer party took the scroll from the dais and trooped in

The Freedom Scroll being paraded after its presentation on 5 May 1960. (*Courtesy of the Andy Saunders Collection*)

front of the parade in slow time the climax came to the ceremony. With a roar of power, five Canberras forming the letter "T" for Tangmere; eight Hawker Hunters in a figure 1, the symbol of No. 1 Squadron, and finally two heroes of the war, a Hurricane and Spitfire, flew past. There was a hush of awe over the park as the two seemingly frail craft sped low overhead casting their shadows on the grass. In a flash memories of war time days returned.'

88: The Unicorn Public House

A Blue Plaque Remembers a Tangmere Favourite

In the same year that the ties between Chichester and RAF Tangmere were reinforced, one existing link was lost. Though a public house had existed on the site of the Unicorn Inn for hundreds of years, the art-deco style building that the wartime personnel at RAF Tangmere, along with those at its satellites of Westhampnett and Merston, came to know and love was built in Chichester's Eastgate Square in 1937.

During the Second World War, the landlord of the Unicorn Inn was Arthur King, an individual who became well known for his warm hospitality

The art-deco building that was the home of the Unicorn Inn during the Second World War. (*Courtesy of Robert Mitchell*)

towards servicemen and women. Group Captain Johnnie Johnson was one of King's patrons who later wrote: 'When the flying was over we drank pints of beer in the "Unicorn" at Chichester and formed warm ties with the affable host, Arthur King, who was such a good friend to countless fighter pilots based at Tangmere during the war.'

Another pilot with similar views to Johnson was Flight Lieutenant Colin Hodgkinson. In the whole of the Second World War, only two men served as operational fighter pilots in the RAF after losing both legs. Douglas Bader was one, and his story is well-known – indeed, he has been described as 'one of the Royal Air Force's most famous pilots'. The other was Colin Gerald Shaw Hodgkinson.

Born in Wells, Somerset, in 1920, Colin Gerald Shaw was accepted for pilot training as a midshipman in the Fleet Air Arm in 1938. However, he was grievously injured in a flying accident whilst training in May 1939. Colin awoke in hospital to find that his right leg had been amputated at the thigh, whilst his remaining left leg was severely injured. His face was also damaged and he had trouble with the sight in one eye. In the weeks that followed, Colin's left leg refused to heal. Coolly, calculatingly, he made his decision: 'Chop it off … Chop the damned thing off and let's be rid of it!'

Colin was serving in 610 (County of Chester) Squadron when he first encountered the Unicorn and its proprietor: 'Arthur, solid, beaming and discreetly paunchy, would have served admirably as the model for the jovial "mine host" of an eighteenth century coaching print. The only touch out of character was the attitude of subservience. Arthur was subservient to nothing and no-body if it wasn't to the idea that he had been brought into the world to serve, coddle, advise and generally spoil the "fighter boys" of the Tangmere Wing. Unfortunately for Arthur his heart was bigger than his stock books. He lent too much money, gave too many rounds "on the house", threw too many parties – without ringing up the till –in his back parlour. Anyone who flew from Tangmere during the war will remember Arthur with gratitude.'[86]

Even in the post-war era, pilots from Tangmere were still drawn to the Unicorn. Robin Olds was among them: 'We finally arrived in front of a two-story structure with a sign proclaiming it to be the Unicorn … I unfolded myself [from the car], stretched my cramped legs as unobtrusively as possible, and entered the "Ol Uni" behind my two new friends. It turned out the old pub had been a favorite hangout for the Battle of Britain pilots flying out of Sussex. The walls of the upstairs bar held photographs and marvellous drawings of young faces with dates and names. These men were already legends when I entered the war in 1944. I saw Sailor Malan, Cocky Dundas, Douglas Bader, Ginger Lacey, Stanford Tuck, and others, all heroes to me as a young cadet back in 1940. I had to admit, I still held them in awe.'

Having been a part of life at RAF Tangmere for more than twenty years, the Unicorn closed its doors for the last time in 1960. Clues to the building's past are revealed by a Blue Plaque that can be seen on the wall today.

89: Hawker P.1127 Crash-Landing

A Forerunner to the Harrier Jump-jet

During the summer of 1958, Tangmere was transferred from Fighter Command to 90 (Signals) Group, which, later in the year, was renamed RAF Signals Command. In simple terms, this formation was responsible for control of the RAF's signals units from 1958 to 1969.

This move resulted in a somewhat more sedate existence for Tangmere, though there was still aircraft present, including Canberras from 245 Squadron, Varsities of 115 Squadron, and, as we shall shortly explore in more detail, Whirlwind helicopters from 22 Squadron.

Among the routine operations of these aircraft at Tangmere, there were still the occasional moments of excitement. One such event took place on 30 October 1962.

That morning, Hugh Merewether, one of Hawker's test pilots, took off from Dunsfold at the controls of XP972, the third prototype Hawker P.1127. The deputy chief test pilot at Hawker's airfield at Dunsfold at the time, Merewether was one of the test pilots who, through projects such as the P.1127, pioneered the vertical and short take-off and landing techniques that led to the production of one of

The third prototype Hawker P.1127, XP972, pictured on the ground at Tangmere after Hugh Merewether's crash-landing on 30 October 1962. (Tangmere Military Aviation Museum)

Work to recover XP972 pictured underway at Tangmere. Note the Vickers Varsity that can be seen in the background. (*Courtesy of Chris Budgen*)

the RAF's most successful and enduring combat aircraft, the Harrier.

As soon as he was airborne, Merewether turned to the south and headed towards the English Channel to undertake a series of high-speed manoeuvring exercises. Once there, things soon went wrong. During a high-G turn at 3,000 ft, XP972's engine suffered a catastrophic failure when the engine compressor blades came into contact with the engine casing, which, in turn, sparked a fire. Rather than eject and abandon his aircraft, Merewether made the split-second decision to try and put it down.

Despite a total loss of power, Merewether successfully executed a successful dead stick landing at Tangmere. 'Rather than eject,' noted *The Daily Telegraph*, 'he managed to crash-land at RAF Tangmere, thus allowing the engineers to investigate the failure fully'. For his achievements, Merewether was awarded the Queen's Commendation for Valuable Services in the Air, and the Guild of Air Pilots and Navigators Derry and Richards Memorial Medal.

At the time. John Richardson was a civilian aircraft engineer working on a ground radio calibration flight at Tangmere. He once recalled the events that day: 'While working at RAF Tangmere late in 1962, we were attending to our normal routine on the flight line, looking after the Canberras' and Varsities' pre- and post-flight inspections. Suddenly someone said, "What's that?", and there on the south side of the airfield, on or near the perimeter track, was one of the early Hawker P.1127 jets.

'We had neither heard nor received any warning of an emergency, but the fire crew were quickly on the scene. We later heard that the aircraft had suffered an engine failure while on a test flight, and that the pilot had skilfully managed to reach Tangmere, despite a complete loss of power.'[87]

Though Merewether had managed to reach the relative safety of Tangmere, he had been forced to put XP972 down with the undercarriage only partially extended. Though he was unhurt, the extent of the damage to airframe was such that it was deemed beyond repair and written off.

Section Seven

The End of an Era

90: Slides of Tangmere's Whirlwinds

Air Sea Rescue Helicopters of 22 Squadron

Originally formed in 1915 as an aerial reconnaissance unit, 22 Squadron was reformed as a helicopter unit at Thorney Island on 15 February 1955. Equipped with the Westland Whirlwind, the squadron, which then comprised four detached flights, was tasked with providing Search and Rescue (SAR) coverage across a large area of the south and south east, as well as Wales.

In May 1961, one of the flights, which were all operating the Whirlwind HAR.2, was deployed to Tangmere. It was the start of a hectic period for the unit. Indeed, it was announced on 1 November that year that 22 Squadron had completed its 1,000th operational sortie on rescue, potential rescue or casualty evacuation duties since becoming a SAR unit in 1955. At the time the squadron was commanded by Squadron Leader G.L. Verran, whose headquarters was at St Mawgan, alongside Tangmere, the other detachments were based at Chivenor, Valley and Manston.

An example of the work undertaken by Tangmere's Whirlwinds was provided by the *Birmingham Daily Post* on 6 January 1962. Under the headline 'Helicopter Rescues 8 Soldiers', the paper reported the following: 'Eight young soldiers were taken off an assault craft which broke down in the Solent, last night, by an RAF helicopter which landed them unhurt at Gosport.

'The helicopter from 22 Squadron, RAF Tangmere, took off after reports that the assault craft with a party of youths on board was missing. A Naval spokesman at Portsmouth said that the helicopter sighted the craft between Gosport and Lee-on-Solent. On board were eight soldiers

The slides of views of 22 Squadron's Tangmere-based Westland Whirlwinds and personnel, all of which are believed to have been taken during a group visit to the airfield in 1963. (*All images Historic Military Press*)

from the first training battalion, Royal Army Service Corps, at Aldershot. Before a Naval torpedo recovery vessel, sent from Portsmouth, could reach the scene, the helicopter had taken off the soldiers in twos and threes and landed them safely.'

On 2 May 1962, one of the Tangmere-based Whirlwinds undertook a civilian casualty evacuation. This time it was the *Coventry Evening Telegraph* that carried the news: 'An RAF air-sea helicopter of 22nd squadron at Tangmere brought a critically ill child to the Atkinson Morley Hospital in West Wimbledon today from Rye, Isle of Wight. The child, a ten years old girl, is suffering from severe head injuries from a cliff fall. The helicopter landed only 50 yards from the main operating theatre.'

A Westland Whirlwind of 22 Squadron takes off from Tangmere.

Two of the Whirlwinds operated by 22 Squadron's Tangmere Flight. Nearest the camera is the HAR.10 variant with the serial number XP354.

Visitors to Tangmere with a member of 22 Squadron in its briefing room.

The rescues kept on coming. On 13 May 1962, for example, another of Tangmere's helicopters rescued 'a man and his son from a speedboat marooned on a mud-bank off Hayling Island, Hants … They were taken to the RAF at Thorney Island.'

Not every scramble, however, resulted in a successful SAR sortie. Again, it was the *Birmingham Daily Post*, this time in its edition of 25 June 1962, that reported the story: 'An RAF helicopter from Tangmere joined boats in a fruitless search last night for [a young male, aged 17] who was swept out to sea at Littlehampton. The youth was with a coach-load of young people from London. He went for a swim with two companions and was later seen waving, and shouting "help".'

It had seemingly been a hectic day for the crews of 22 Squadron. The same article concluded with the news that, 'Earlier, two miles along the coast at Rustington, two canoeists were rescued by an RAF helicopter when their canoe overturned.'

During the latter part of 1962, 22 Squadron's HAR.2s were replaced by the HAR.10 variant, of which a total of sixty-eight were built. The introduction of the HAR.10 saw a significant increase in the capability of the RAF's SAR helicopters: 'They continued to be operated as

Two further views of XP354, this time taken whilst the helicopter was hovering low over Tangmere. First flown on 23 March 1962, this Whirlwind was delivered to the RAF the following month. It was scrapped in 1999.

A newspaper cutting showing a Whirlwind from 'Tangmere rescuing children from a ledge under Seaford Head' on 29 June 1962. The original caption goes on state that '30 schoolchildren from Plumstead Common Congregational Church were cut off by the tide near Seaford Head, Sussex. Some of them were rescued by coastguards, but 17 of them were lifted to safety by an RAF helicopter.'

Visitors to Tangmere being shown around a 22 Squadron Whirlwind.

before, but with up to a 30% increase in fuel/pay load, the aircraft had a greatly enhanced range and was able to respond more successfully to a wider range of task'.[88]

Tangmere's new Whirlwinds were soon as busy as their predecessors, as events in the Channel on Friday, 4 January 1963, testify. 'The five members of the crew of a Belgian trawler leaped to safety from their blazing ship …' noted one report.[89] 'Three jumped into the sea with a raft and were picked up by an RAF helicopter. The others were able to jump across to a lightship after the trawler, the *Dom Bosco*, from Ostend, had gone alongside.

'Shipping was warned to approach the drifting trawler with caution, as her engine room was full of gas. After the fire was put out by firemen from Chichester and Selsey, taken out by the Selsey lifeboat and the Tangmere helicopter, the trawler was taken in tow for Portsmouth by the Admiralty fire-fighting tug *Confiance*.

'The three who were rescued from the raft were flown to RAF Tangmere, where medical officers said that there was "nothing very wrong with them." One of the survivors said that they were "very pleased to see the helicopter approaching" when they were in the raft. "This has been our first experience of being rescued by a helicopter, and our first acquaintance with the RAF. It was very nice – but we do not want to do it every day."'

In July 1963, 22 Squadron, including its Tangmere flight, received the annual award of the Guild of Air Pilots and Air Navigators. The announcement stated that the squadron, 'whose yellow helicopters have become famous for rescue flights', won the Brackley Memorial Trophy 'for outstanding flying contributions to the operational development of air transport'.

Tangmere's association with the RAF's Search and Rescue helicopters ended in 1964, when 22 Squadron's Whirlwinds were moved to Thorney Island.

91: Royal Flying Lesson Images

Prince of Wales' First Flight

On Tuesday, 30 July 1968, a nineteen-year-old Prince of Wales flew an aircraft for the first time. The flight in a dual-control Chipmunk T10 trainer, which lasted roughly thirty minutes and took place under the auspices of the Queen's Flight, was made from Tangmere.

In the 'World News' section of its edition of 8 August 1968, *Flight International* informed its readers of the royal flying lessons: 'At RAF Tangmere last week Prince Charles was given air experience in a Chipmunk, with Sqn Ldr Philip Pinney, an instructor at the Central Flying School, as pilot. He first flew on Tuesday, July 30, then on subsequent days except for Wednesday [July 31].

'The purpose of these flights was to see whether he has an aptitude for flying. If he has, he will be given a course of instruction. The Chipmunk in which the prince flew … was one formerly piloted by Prince Philip; it had been in storage for two years.'

To mark the Prince's first landing at Tangmere, Wing Commander A.E. Schofield, Tangmere's then Acting Station Commander, presented a Station badge to the Royal pupil.

David Cole recalls how he obtained a series of pictures of the Prince of Wales taking to the air: 'Fifty years ago I was a youngish newspaper photographer working in West Sussex. I was told by a friend that Prince Charles was learning to fly at Tangmere. I approached the authorities at Tangmere (by turning up at the main gate and simply asking!) and was given permission to take some long-distance images.

'I was the owner of a 400mm Novoflex lens and a Nikon camera and I captured the pictures you can see here. The legendary Fleet Street

The Prince of Wales and Squadron Leader Philip Pinney taking off in de Havilland Chipmunk WP903 towards the west, from Tangmere's main runway. In the background can be seen one of the wartime T2 hangars. (© David Cole, 01798-342716)

The Prince of Wales in the cockpit of WP903. (© David Cole, 01798-342716)

Picture Editor of *The Daily Mirror*, Simon Clyne, asked to use the images. He subsequently persuaded me to leave Sussex for Fleet Street where I spent more than forty years as a news photographer finishing as a Night Picture Editor on Murdoch's *Sun*.'[90]

The Prince must have displayed the required aptitude, for he subsequently made his first solo flight from RAF Bassingbourn on 14 January 1968, by which time he had completed fourteen-and-a-half hours' instruction.

On 2 August, a year to the day since his third flight from Tangmere, the Prince was presented with his Preliminary Flying Badge by the Air Officer Commanding-in-Chief RAF Training Command. Although the badge was normally only presented to members of University Air Squadrons, of which the Prince was not a member, it was felt that its award to him would be recognition of the fact that he had completed all the air and ground syllabus required. In the twelve months since his first flight with Squadron Leader Pinney, a New Zealander, his Royal Highness had logged more than eighty hours on the Chipmunk.

The Prince of Wales and Squadron Leader Philip Pinney discussing a flight at Tangmere. (© David Cole, 01798-342716)

Delivered to the RAF on 1 November 1952, the aircraft in which the Prince of Wales learnt to fly from Tangmere, de Havilland Chipmunk T10 WP903, is still operational, albeit with the civilian registration G-BCGC. Regularly seen on the air show circuit, it still features the red warning lamp, commonly referred to as the 'Parrot', which was a specific modification for its Royal service. (*Courtesy of Andrew Thomas*)

92: Champagne Glass From a Guest Night

RAF Tangmere's Last Formal Evening

Dining in is a formal military ceremony for members of a regiment, unit, or base, which includes a dinner, drinking, and other events, all with the aim of fostering camaraderie. RAF dining in nights are well-known for their formality, but also for their raucousness and eccentricity as the evening progresses. Guest nights and ladies' nights were similar events but, with local guests and dignitaries also being invited, things were generally being tamer and more controlled than a traditional dining in night.

Wing Commander H.R. 'Dizzy' Allen DFC, who we have already encountered, recalled how the facilities at Tangmere were particularly suited to such events. 'The dining hall at Tangmere,' he wrote, 'with its parquet floor and the raised stage which contained the band, gave plenty of room for dancing and a buffet'.[91] It was there that a dining in night was held in 1950, though Allen decided to use the evening as an opportunity to make a point on what he considered was 43 Squadron's imminent and misplaced move north to RAF Leuchars in Scotland.

One of the guests that night was the Commander-in-Chief Fighter Command, Air Marshal Sir Basil Embry. It was after Embry's speech about the impending move of the squadron that, in Allen's own words, 'the fun and games started': 'The doors were flung open and someone threw Cockie [43 Squadron's mascot – a cockerel] into the room. He flew around squawking, landed with unerring precision on the top table in front of the C-in-C, left some droppings and walked out again. Bagpipes wailed, and Dusty Miller marched in wearing kilts, playing a lament. Behind him six bearers dressed in top hats and black suits carried a coffin draped in the black and white chequered flags of No 43 Squadron. The cortège walked slowly round the tables, behind the top table and out through the doors. Percy then entered in his chef's uniform and tall white hat carrying an evil-smelling haggis on a silver salver and put it on the top table in front of the C-in-C.'[92]

The champagne glass from Tangmere's last guest night that Barry Shears presented to Tangmere Military Aviation Museum.

The last ever guest night held in Tangmere's Officers' Mess took place in 1968. The guest list that night was a mixture of serving officers, ex RAF officers and a large number of wives and girlfriends. It was decided to mark the occasion by arranging champagne glasses in a large pyramid and to carefully pour champagne down the pyramid.

Flight Lieutenant Paul Moore was given the delicate task of pouring the champagne, which he successfully did, and the cold fizzing liquid overflowed down the stems of the glasses to the ones below. This continued until all sixty glasses in the pyramid were full. The pyramid was finally dismantled, and each glass was passed to the assembled guests for them to drink.

One of the champagne glasses from that stack was presented to the Museum in 2012 by Barry Shears. An engineering officer at Tangmere who was present that night, Barry recalled discovering it in his car the following morning. As to how it got there, he has absolutely no idea!

A formal night underway at RAF Tangmere in the Cold War era; unfortunately the exact nature of the event, or the date on which it occurred, is unknown. (*Courtesy of the Andy Saunders Collection*)

93: A 'Royal Tangmere Incident'

Prince Charles' Continuation Flying Training

On 2 February 1970, the Prince of Wales passed the necessary Board of Trade examinations for his Private Pilot's Licence after graduating to a twin-engine Beagle Bassett, flying mostly from RAF Oakington near Cambridge. Later that year the Prince was in a Bassett when he was involved in what *Flight International*, in a news story published on 6 August, described as a 'Royal Tangmere Incident'.

'While Prince Charles was carrying out some continuation flying training at RAF Tangmere on July 30 in a Beagle Basset,' *Flight International*'s account noted, 'the aircraft and a Piper Aztec came into close proximity. Prince Charles' flying instructor filed an air-miss report stating that the other aircraft was seen at a range of 400yd in front of, and 200ft-300ft below, the Basset. The aircraft were on diverging tracks and no avoiding action was necessary.

'The Aztec was carrying passengers to the Goodwood horse racing meeting and was under the control of Goodwood air traffic. Goodwood lies within the combined Military Air Traffic Zone around Tangmere and Thorney Island, but the Aztec was guided so as to avoid the Tangmere circuit. The pilot was aware of the use of Tangmere that morning and is reported to have seen the Basset taking off.

'Flying training by members of the Royal family is not subject to "purple airspace" procedure, but a system of notification to military airfields is in force and where adjacent civil airfields are likely to be affected they are informed by the appropriate military ATC authority.'

It is quite likely that Prince Charles was flying Beagle B.206 Basset XS770, seen here, during the 'Royal Tangmere Incident'. This aircraft is often referred to as the 'Regal Beagle' from its time with the Queen's Flight providing multi-engine instruction to Prince Charles. This view of XS770 was taken while it was arriving at RAF Fairford in July 2003 to participate in the Royal International Air Tattoo. (*Courtesy of Chris Lofting*)

94: Tangmere Closure Programme

The End of an Era, 16 October 1970

Shortly after 18.00 hours on the evening of Friday, 16 October 1970, the sounds of the Last Post rippled out across the runways at Tangmere. As the bugler brought his rousing salute to a close, the Station's RAF Ensign was gently lowered towards the ground for the last time.

As the spectators returned to their seats, the ranks of military personnel present, having been called to attention, turned and, as instructed, marched off in slow time, accompanied by the Queen's Colour Squadron and the Central Band of the Royal Air Force playing *Auld Lang Syne*. Tangmere, officially at least, was no longer an RAF airbase.

The official programme for the closing ceremony included a short history of RAF Tangmere. Helpfully, this included a description of the base's final role:

'In the past six years Royal Air Force Tangmere has been the home of No. 38 Group Support Unit, which provides facilities or the Royal Air Force in its world-wide operations. It has also been pleased to share its accommodation and responsibilities with a Royal Navy Unit and two Army units – formerly Nos. 22 and 48 Air Despatch Squadrons of the Royal Corps of Transport, which train all Air Despatch personnel for the Army, and, currently, No. 244 Signals Squadron (TAS) of the Royal Corps of Signals, which has shared the support commitment of the Unit on a truly joint-Service basis, as part of the Tactical Communications Wing.'

Amongst the many guests present for the closing ceremony was *The Times*' correspondent Geoffrey Wansell. He subsequently penned the following report: 'A single Spitfire flew across the Royal Air Force Station at Tangmere, near Chichester, this evening to mark the closure of one of the best-known Battle of Britain stations. Tangmere's fighter squadrons accounted for more than 300 enemy aircraft between August and October 30 years ago, when the battle was at its height. By September 1944, the base had raised its tally to 866 aircraft destroyed. 252 probably destroyed and 440 damaged. The station was heavily bombed in a raid on August 16, 1940, but the attackers lost 25 aircraft.

'As Last Post sounded today to the lowering of the R.A.F. Ensign, and the Spitfire dipped its wings in salute, memories of Douglas Bader and Peter Townsend, who flew from Tangmere, and of men like them, had hardly dimmed. Air Vice-Marshal Denis Crowley-Milling, AOC 38 Group[93], who had flown as Bader's wing man from Tangmere, could hardly have failed to be moved.'

The front cover of the programme produced for Tangmere's closure ceremony. (*Historic Military Press*)

RAF TANGMERE — STATION COMMANDERS

Major W. V. Strugnell MC	March	1918
Flight Lieutenant H. L. Nunn DSC DFC	June	1925
Flight Lieutenant T. G. Bowler	April	1926
Wing Commander J. H. S. Tyssen MC	November	1926
Squadron Leader E. O. Grenfell MC DFC AFC	October	1928
Wing Commander J. B. Graham MC AFC	December	1928
Wing Commander R. M. Drummond OBE DSO MC	November	1931
Wing Commander G. C. Pirie MC DFC	June	1933
Wing Commander E. G. Hopcraft DSC	August	1934
Wing Commander R. B. Mansell OBE	February	1935
Wing Commander L. H. Slatter OBE DSC DFC	August	1935
Wing Commander C. W. Hill	April	1937
Group Captain K. R. Park MC DFC ADC	December	1937
Group Captain F. Sowrey DSO MC AFC	June	1938
Group Captain C. H. Nicholas DFC AFC	August	1939
Wing Commander I. A. Bertram	October	1939
Wing Commander C. L. Lea-Cox	February	1940
Group Captain J. A. Boret OBE MC AFC	July	1940
Group Captain A. B. Woodall OBE	April	1941
Group Captain C. H. Appleton DSO DFC	January	1942
Group Captain H. D. McGregor DSO	September	1942
Group Captain W. J. Crisham	May	1943
Wing Commander P. R. Walker DSO DFC	February	1944
Wing Commander N. J. Starr DFC	September	1944
Group Captain D. M. Somerville	October	1944
Wing Commander J. A. O'Neill DFC	November	1944
Air Commodore R. L. R. Atcherley OBE AFC	January	1945
Air Commodore G. D. Harvey	September	1945
Wing Commander R. J. Hardiman DFC	October	1945
Wing Commander C. H. Dyson MBE DFC	May	1946
Wing Commander W. G. Clouston DFC	June	1946
Wing Commander G. S. A. Parnaby OBE	September	1947
Group Captain T. O. Prickett DSO DFC	August	1949
Group Captain S. C. Elworthy CBE DSO DFC AFC	December	1951
Group Captain J. A. Kent DFC AFC	March	1953
Group Captain E. A. Whiteley CBE DFC	November	1955
Group Captain R. I. K. Edwards DFC AFC	April	1956
Wing Commander H. E. Walmsley DFC	June	1958
Wing Commander W. W. T. Ritchie OBE AFC	August	1958
Group Captain W. D. David CBE DFC AFC	September	1958
Group Captain P. A. Hughes DFC	May	1961
Wing Commander E. R. Dutt AFC	October	1963
Wing Commander P. D. J. Wood DFC	February	1965
Wing Commander D. Gray AFC	April	1968

The rear page of the programme which contains a list of the base's commanding officers. (*Historic Military Press*)

95: ATC Cadet's Logbook

Gliders at RAF Tangmere

Having previously been based at White Waltham, No.623 Gliding School moved to Tangmere on 1 July 1963. Operating the Slingsby TX Cadet Mk.3 and Sedburgh T21, the school's primary aim was to give air cadets their first taste of flying, with winch launch gliders, through to training them up to a standard where they could undertake their first solo.

One of those cadets, identified as Paul F, describes his experiences of flying at RAF Tangmere: 'Once in the mid-seventies I spent 30mins on Sunday morning soaring a T21B Sedburgh under the instruction of a chap called Paddy Edwards, who was one of the ATC gliding school instructors at RAF Tangmere. We

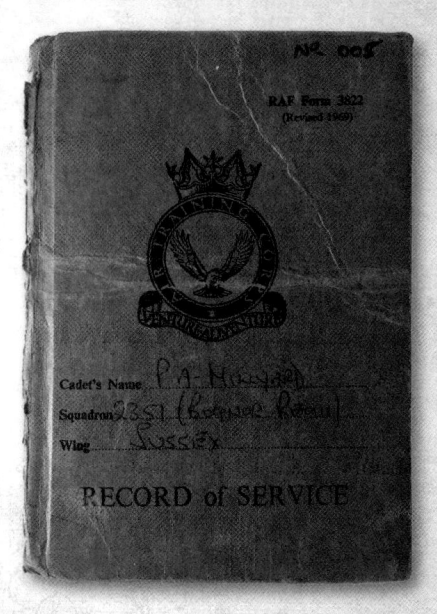

The logbook of Sergeant Peter Millyard of 2351 (Bognor Regis) Squadron ATC showing some of the flights he undertook from Tangmere in No.623 Gliding School's gliders. (*Courtesy of Peter Millyard*)

Sergeant Peter Millyard on duty in the control caravan at Tangmere in the 1970s. Note some of No.623 Gliding School's gliders in the background. (*Courtesy of Peter Millyard*)

were only supposed to do simple circuits that morning, but Paddy hadn't flown for a week or two, and sensed the soaring would be good, so he went for it (no two way radios to call us back in those days).

'As we climbed, the South Coast was an ever expanding landmark. Paddy handed control to me and then took my camera which I had been allowed to take up with me. Winding the strap tightly round his left arm, he got me to set the camera up and then stuck his arm out over the rim of the cockpit into mid-air. I then had to concentrate on flying the glider and also indicate which way he should point the camera to try and guess when to say "fire".

'We just about got things sorted as the wind noise died to a whisper, and Paddy quickly re-took control and dropped the nose a few degrees in pitch, back to a more normal attitude. Luckily the resulting photo (no chance of seeing the image immediately afterwards to check in those days) was Okay when the film came back from the developers a week later.

'Eventually we had to call it a day and head back to Tangmere. Paddy decided to lose height quickly by spinning the glider, and, after a couple of short spins during which time I had no idea which way was up, but loved the g-forces, and during which I clung tightly to my camera, we dropped back into the circuit …

'In those days Tangmere was free from glasshouses, and still had both runways intact. Plus it still had fifties-style concrete wall blast pens, and the domestic site was very much intact.'[94]

96: A Sedburgh T21 of No.623 Gliding School

Tangmere's Last Permanent RAF Unit

The arrival of No.623 Gliding School at Tangmere was reported on in local newspapers. The *Bognor Regis Observer*, for example, carried the following announcement in its edition of 11 October 1963:

'Cadets of the Hampshire and Sussex branches of the Air Training Corps will soon have more opportunities for flying with the opening of a gliding school at Tangmere. The school began at the weekend with the training of 20 instructors and should soon be properly underway. There are already four gliders, and flying will take place all day on Saturdays and Sundays under the guidance of Flight Lieut. W. Virling [should be Verling]. The school will cater for Air Cadets in the whole of the Southern District, but the Chichester branch is particularly lucky to be so near to it.'

The importance of gliding centres such as that at Tangmere was revealed in the *Eastbourne Gazette* of 2 December 1964: 'A party of 12 cadets from Eastbourne Squadron of the Air Training Corps gained first-hand experience of gliding when they visited RAF Tangmere. This is the base of No. 623 Gliding School, which operates specifically for the ATC. All the cadets received

One of No.623 Gliding School's Sedburgh T21s pictured flying over the Cold War blast pens at Tangmere. This particular glider, serial XN148, is listed a number of times in our previous item, Sergeant Peter Millyard's logbook. (*Courtesy of Ben Newman*)

two launches and it was generally agreed by the boys that this was by far the most exhilarating method of flying.

'Cadets waiting their turn to take to the air took over the duties of the ground crew which included retrieving and fixing the launching cables to the gliders, preparing them for launching and Aldis lamp signalling. Further visits to Tangmere are scheduled for cadets of the Eastbourne Squadron who are clocking-up a considerable number of flying hours.'

Despite its value, and the importance of training and enthusing future pilots, No.623 Gliding School was disbanded in November 1974. Its loss finally sealed Tangmere's fate, and any further links with the British military, for it was both the last RAF unit permanently based there and the last flying unit to ever operate from the airfield.

Another view of a glider in the air over the eastern end of Tangmere. (*Courtesy of the Andy Saunders Collection*)

97: Building 116

The Only Surviving H-block at Tangmere

Until 1983, some thirty-seven acres of barracks, administration buildings and assorted workshops remained derelict until bought by developers. In the years that followed, housing soon spread around the site of the airfield, a process which saw most of the original RAF buildings being demolished – though a few have thankfully been saved.

One of the most important of these survivors is Harvey Court in Neville Duke Way. Granted protection as a Grade II Listed building in April 2007, Historic England's description for Harvey Court stresses the importance of what was known by the RAF as Building 116: 'It was built to Air Ministry design 8/84 in 1938 as part of the late 1930s expansion of RAF Tangmere, when the base was modified and improved to form a permanent station with accommodation for an additional squadron. Originally one of three H-blocks on the base, Building 116 is now the only remaining example and is believed to be the only surviving accommodation block from the former airbase. It is remarkably complete both externally and internally where its plan-form, fixtures and fittings provide a fascinating insight into accommodation for airmen at this Battle of Britain fighter station … Building 116 provided accommodation for three non-commissioned officers and seventy-two other ranks with eighteen to a room.'[95]

Building 116, or Harvey Court, as it appears today. Note the bomb or bullet damage that has scarred the walls. Hooks in the wall that were used to hang camouflage nets can also be seen by visitors. (*Courtesy of Robert Mitchell*)

97: BUILDING 116

Some of the original RAF signage that can still be seen on the walls of Building 116 – in this case it reads 'OC 4 Sqdn'. (*Courtesy of Robert Mitchell*)

When it was inspected as part of the process for its listing, it was noted that 'each of the four wings, to the north west, north east, south west and south east, contains a large dormitory except for the north west room which was allocated for a sitting room on the original plan. Central west-east range has a central corridor with borrow-light windows, flanked by ablutions, NCO accommodation, and other domestic rooms (such as laundry rooms).'

There was also a 'small basement level air raid shelter with blast door to stairs up and escape hatch leading out of the building to the east. This contains original benches, lighting, space for a W.C., an escape tunnel with a vertical ladder to a hatch outside the building, and graffiti such as squadron numbers and names and ranks – e.g. "RAF Squad 43" and "LAC [Leading Aircraftsman] Webb".'

In time, planning permission was sought, and granted, for the conversion of Building 116 into eleven luxury flats. Interestingly, one of these flats was converted in such a way as to retain the original open plan layout of the existing sleeping quarters as used in the war. An original laundry cupboard with fold-down ironing board has also been preserved, though it was moved from its original location in the first floor laundry room to one of the block's new communal areas.

A view of some of Tangmere's buildings which were photographed at around the time of the airfield's closure. (*Courtesy of the Andy Saunders Collection*)

98: The Former Spitfire Club

Tangmere's Preserved Airmen's Institute and Chapel

At the time of writing, just three of the buildings built by, or for, the RAF at Tangmere had been given listed status in the years since the airfield closed. Two of these, the Watch Office and Building 116, we have already covered. The third structure that has been protected for future generations is the former Spitfire Club (see also Item 10).

Originally an airmens' institute and chapel, it is thought that the Spitfire Club, which can today be seen off Jerrard Road, was built around 1920. One of the main reasons that the listed status was granted is that the building was considered to be 'a well-designed and early example of the neo-Georgian style favoured by the Ministry of Defence for RAF buildings during the inter-war expansion period of the Royal Air Force'.

It was in the Spitfire Club that an important gathering took place in September 1980. The intention of those present was to discuss the possibility of setting up a museum at Tangmere, for which the list of attendees was certainly impressive. Those present included the likes of Lord Balfour of Inchrye, Jim Beedle and Alan Pollock, who between them represented all the main eras of Tangmere and the RAF's history.

A First World War veteran with seven 'kills' by the time the Armistice came round, Harold

The former NAAFI building at RAF Tangmere, which is now known as Spitfire Court. (*Courtesy of Robert Mitchell*)

98: THE FORMER SPITFIRE CLUB

The blue plaque on the wall of Spitfire Court which alludes to its past and the fact that it is one of the oldest of RAF Tangmere's buildings to have survived. (*Courtesy of Robert Mitchell*)

Balfour, who had also been awarded the Military Cross and Bar, remained in the RAF until 1926. He subsequently entered politics and, in 1938, was appointed Under Secretary of State for Air, a position he held throughout the Second World War. Lord Balfour had frequently been a visitor to RAF Tangmere.

For his part, Jim Beedle, an ex-Halton apprentice who was a member of groundcrew on 43 Squadron, had served at Tangmere during the Second World War. He had been present during the big Luftwaffe attack on 16 August. Meanwhile, Pollock, a Cold War pilot with 43 Squadron, the very same that Lord Balfour served in during the First World War while flying Sopwith 1½ Strutters, had flown one of the last jet fighters to use Tangmere. The occasion for the latter had been the celebrations to mark the RAF's 50th anniversary in April 1968; Flight Lieutenant Pollock was flying a Hawker Hunter FG9 of 1 Squadron at the time.

Returning to the meeting in the Spitfire Club, it concluded with the decision being taken to establish a working group that was given the challenge of finding suitable premises that might be able house the intended museum. Including local residents and RAF veterans, the group, as we shall discover, set about its task with great enthusiasm under the leadership of the erstwhile Jim Beedle.

A former road sign for RAF Tangmere that was saved for posterity following the airfield's closure. Like so many of the objects in this book, it can be seen today in Tangmere Military Aviation Museum.

99: RAF Tangmere Memorial

Unveiled by Group Captain Douglas Bader

In the aftermath of 623 Gliding School's departure from Tangmere, and amid a gradual decay of the site, and while there was already talk of a museum being established, a group of local residents raised the idea of erecting a permanent memorial to the airfield. This, it was said, would commemorate RAF Tangmere and 'remind future generations about the role played by the aerodrome in the defence of the nation'.

A suitable home for the memorial was found on the small village green at the junction of Church Lane and Tangmere Road, a site that is a short distance from where the original main gate was located. The dedication ceremony took place on Saturday, 18 December 1976, with the actual unveiling being carried out by Group Captain Douglas Bader CBE, DSO & Bar, DFC & Bar, DL, FRAeS.

Among the many serving RAF personnel, veterans and local dignitaries present was Air Chief Marshal Sir Hugh Saunders. A First World War ace, Saunders remained in the RAF climbing through the ranks in the inter-war period. He was made Air Officer Commanding No.11 Group on 28 November 1942, a role in which he had direct operational control of RAF Tangmere. He remained in this post until November 1944.

Representing the families of fallen airmen, the parents of Wing Commander Brendan Eamonn Fergus 'Paddy' Finucane were also present. Having flown from Tangmere while serving in 65 Squadron, Finucane became the youngest wing commander in the RAF's history – he had yet to reach his 22nd birthday at the time. Finucane did not return from a fighter sweep over France on 15 July 1942; he was forced to ditch into the Channel and was subsequently posted missing.

The RAF Tangmere Memorial Stone. (Historic Military Press)

Not only does Tangmere proudly remember its links with the RAF through the memorial and St Andrews Church, but also through many of the road names around the village. At least eleven of the roads are, for example, named after RFC and RAF holders of the Victoria Cross. This includes Bishops Road, in honour of Captain William Avery 'Billy' Bishop VC, Cheshire Crescent, that is named after Group Captain Geoffrey Leonard Cheshire VC, or Nicolson Close, that remembers the only Fighter Command VC holder, Flight Lieutenant James Brindley Nicolson.

Other roads have been named after famous or important RAF aircraft. Among those most relevant to Tangmere are Hawker Close, Lysander Way, Merlin Close (a reference to the Rolls-Royce Merlin engine) and Spitfire Court.

100: Tangmere Military Aviation Museum

The Airfield's History Lives On

By 1981, the efforts of the working group set up in the Spitfire Club in September 1980 had yielded results. That year the Parish Council offered to donate some accommodation, thereby ensuring that the history of RAF Tangmere is also commemorated in perpetuity by the presence of Tangmere Military Aviation Museum. The story is taken up by the Military Aviation Heritage Network's website:

'In 1981 the Parish Council donated the new museum two large SECO prefabricated huts which had been built in the late 1940s. The huts were in very poor condition, derelict, vandalised and covered in brambles.

'Work started on the buildings in late 1981 and an ambitious opening date target of June 1982 was set. Many thought this impossible but on 6 June 1982, the Tangmere Military Aviation

An aerial photograph of Tangmere Military Aviation Museum in its early years. Note the perimeter track that can be seen on the left. The Hawker Hunter that is visible is believed to be E-412, which was an F.51 originally built for the Royal Danish Air Force. Having been re-acquired by Hawkers after its service in Denmark, E-412 ended up on display at the Tangmere Military Aviation Museum, at one point being painted up as a 43 Squadron RAF aircraft with the serial number XF314. In due course, E-412 moved to the now-defunct Front Line Aviation Museum on the Isle of Wight. (*Courtesy of Peter Amos*)

RAF veteran Joe Roddis, a member of 234 Squadron's groundcrew in the Britain of Britain, being shown around Tangmere Military Aviation Museum by author Mark Hillier's son George. Joe, who remembered Tangmere from his wartime service – in fact, it was from there that he flew out to Normandy in an RAF Dakota after D-Day – always enjoyed his visits to the museum. (*Mark Hillier Collection*)

Museum opened its doors to the public for the first time.'[96]

The museum's chairman at the time of opening was none other than Jim Beedle. The SECO huts that formed the original basis of the museum are known to have been used variously as a radio repair workshop and well as been occupied by the Joint Services School for Linguists (JSSL). A blue plaque on the wall by the museum's main entrance, which was unveiled by the RAF Linguist's Association in 2007, confirms the latter. It states: 'Between 1959 and 1965 the Joint Services Language School was located at RAF Tangmere. Here linguists were trained for covert work, their vigilance contributing to national security during the Cold War.' The primary languages taught by the school at the time were Russian, Mandarin, Polish and Czech.

During the ceremony on 6 June 1982, the Museum was officially opened by Marshal of the Royal Air Force Sir Dermot Boyle. Having enlisted in the RAF in 1922, Sir Dermot was the first person ever to rise from the rank of aircraft apprentice to the highest rank of Marshal of the Royal Air Force. He was commissioned as a pilot officer in 1926 after training at the Royal Air Force College Cranwell, and reached his final rank in 1958. Aside from his remarkable rise through the ranks, Boyle is also noted for his influence on shaping the RAF during a critical period in its history when he oversaw its modernization during the early Cold War period, a time when it adapted to the nuclear age and the emergence of new technologies. Like Hugh Saunders, who attended the unveiling of the memorial stone, Boyle had also been made Air Officer Commanding No.11 Group, this time in July 1945, when he replaced Saunders' successor.

Over time, Tangmere Military Aviation Museum has expanded to become the fascinating visitor attraction that it is today, exhibiting the history of aircraft and personnel involved in military aviation with a particular reference to RAF Tangmere. Now one of the UK's leading aviation museums, Tangmere is, as this book hopefully shows, home to an impressive display of historic aircraft and has a unique collection of aviation memorabilia stretching from the First World War through to the Cold War. Among the many attractions are numerous interactive displays, aircraft cockpits, and simulators for visitors to experience.

It goes without saying that a visit is highly recommended. For more information please see: www.tangmere-museum.org.uk

Source Information and Notes

1. Information panel on display in Tangmere Military Aviation Museum.
2. Ken Rimell, 'The First Pilot Who Found Tangmere', *Sussex Views*, November 2012, pp.34–5.
3. ibid.
4. Reginald Byron and David Coxon, *Tangmere – Famous Royal Air Force Fighter Station* (Grub Street, Grub Street, 2013), pp.15–6.
5. John Goodwin, *The Military Defence of West Sussex* (Middleton Press, Midhurst, 1985), pp.76–7.
6. See John H. Morrow Jnr. and Earl Rogers (Eds.), *A Yankee Ace in the RAF: The World War I Letters of Captain Bogart Rogers* (University of Kansas Press, Lawrence, 1996).
7. Byron and Coxon, *op. cit.*, p.20.
8. Dennis Winter, *First of the Few: Fighter Pilots of the First World War* (Viking, London, 1982).
9. *Chichester Observer*, Wednesday, 5 June 1918.
10. *Derbyshire Advertiser and Journal*, Saturday, 30 March 1918.
11. A.F.C. Hillstead, *Those Bentley Days* (Faber & Faber, London, 1953), pp.35–6.
12. *Chichester Observer*, Wednesday, 10 September 1919.
13. For a full account, please see Reginald Byron and David Coxon, op. cit.
14. The National Archives (TNA), T 161/212.
15. Paul Francis, *British Military Airfield Architecture* (Patrick Stephens, Sparkford, 1996), p.16.
16. Byron and Coxon, op. cit., p.24.
17. Jimmy Beedle, *The Fighting Cocks: 43 (Fighter) Squadron* (Pen & Sword, Barnsley, 2011), p.43.
18. *Aeroplane*, 15 April 1926.
19. Jimmy Beedle, op. cit., p.48.
20. Byron and Coxon, op. cit. p.32.
21. Michael Shaw, op. cit, p.54.
22. Located on the seafront at Aldwick, to the west of Bognor Regis, Craigwell House was owned at the time by the industrialist and politician Sir Arthur du Cros. The house is famously remembered for the arrival of King George V for a period convalescence that lasted from 9 February to 15 May 1929. The house was demolished during 1938 and 1939 following a fire.
23. For more information on this impressive aircraft and HAC's work, please see: www.historicaircraftcollection.ltd.uk.
24. Air Chief Marshal Sir Frederick Rosier GCB, CBE, DSO, *Be Bold* (Grub Street, London, 2011), pp.25–6.
25. Alfred Price, *The Spitfire Story* (Haynes, Sparkford, 2010), p.47.
26. Quoted from Quill, Jeffrey Quill, *Spitfire: The Amazing Personal Story of a Spitfire Test Pilot and RAF Fighter* (Arrow, London, 1985), pp.89–90.
27. For more information, please see: www.derelictmisc.org.uk
28. Michael Shaw, *No 1 Squadron* (Ian Allan Ltd, London, 1986), p.62–3.
29. Paul Richey, *Fighter Pilot* (Cassell, London, 2001), pp.19–21.
30. TNA, AIR 27/411.
31. TNA, AIR 50/90–91.
32. Riley, Gordon, *Hawker Hurricane Survivors* (Grub Street, London, 2015), p.16.
33. For more information, please visit: www.pillbox-study-group.org.uk
34. Quoted from the excellent website www.scramblebell.co.uk.
35. TNA, AIR 28/815; RAF Tangmere Operations Record Book.
36. Speaking on 'Tangmere Revisited', a BBC documentary produced in 1985.
37. Letters in the Tangmere Military Aviation Museum's archives.
38. Ron London survived the attack unscathed and later volunteered to become a member of aircrew. Serving with 227 Squadron, Flying Officer Ronald London was the pilot of Avro Lancaster PB646, coded 9J-P, on the night of 6 December 1944. He and his crew had been tasked to attack the railway yards at Giessen, Germany. His was one of ten aircraft that failed to return; Ronald and his crew are buried in Hannover War Cemetery.
39. There were also five to the RCAF, seven to the RAAF, two to the RNZAF and two to the SAAF. See Michael Maton, *Honour The Air Forces: Honours and Awards to the RAF and Dominion Air Forces During World War II* (Token Publishing, Exeter, 2004).
40. *The London Gazette*, Issue 34986, 5 November 1940.
41. Air Vice-Marshal Sandy Jonstone, *Enemy in the Sky: My 1940 Diary* (William Kimber, London, 1976), pp.96–7.
42. Interview dated 6 July 2003, Tangmere Military Aviation Museum archives.
43. Andy Saunders, 'He Died for England', *Aeroplane*, February 2004, p.24.
44. ibid.
45. Quoted from the Battle of Britain Monument website: www.bbm.org.uk/airmen/Fiske.htm.

46. From: www.601squadron.com/billy-fiske-window2.html
47. Vice-Marshal Sandy Jonstone, op cit, p.96.
48. Quoted by Hector Bolitho in *Combat Report* (B.T. Batsford Ltd, London, 1943), pp.86–8.
49. TNA, AIR 28/815.
50. Quoted from www.chichesterpost.co.uk.
51. Jeff West, *Spitfires and Spots* (Published by James West, New Zealand, 2018), p.77.
52. Norman Franks, *Frank 'Chota' Carey* (Grub Street, London, 2006).
53. TNA, AIR 27/985/10.
54. Interview with Martin Mace, circa 1998.
55. Interview with Mark Hillier.
56. TNA, AIR 27/956/1.
57. ibid.
58. Quoted from www.tangmere-museum.org.uk/westland-lysander-mk-iii-sd/.
59. 'Karel Kuttelwascher, My Uncle', a personal memoir by Mimi Kuttelwascher Chanova in *Tangmere Log Book*, No.12, Summer 2013.
60. Hugh Verity, *We Landed By Moonlight: Secret RAF Landings in France 1940–1944* (Ian Allan Ltd, Shepperton, 1978), pp.20–1.
61. Barbara Bertram, *French Resistance in Sussex* (Barnworks Publishing, Pulborough, 1995), p.35.
62. Quoted from www.henryadams.co.uk/news/643/the-secret-life-of-tangmere-cottage.
63. Desmond Scott, *One More Hour* (Hutchinson, London, 1989).
64. For more information, please see: www.historicengland.org.uk/listing/the-list/list-entry/1403165
65. TNA, AIR 27/144/21.
66. TNA, AIR 28/815.
67. For more information, please see: www.thirstyswagman.com
68. *Air International*, September 1976, and *Aviation News*, 8–21 April 1994, quoted on www.westerhambrewery.co.uk.
69. TNA, AIR 27/1658.
70. John Nichol and Tony Rennell, *The Last Escape* (Penguin, London, 2003), p.348.
71. TNA, AIR 64 series.
72. Adolf Galland, *The First and the Last* (Methuen, London, 1955).
73. For more information, please see: www.rafmuseum.org.uk/research/online-exhibitions/douglas-bader-fighter-pilot
74. Adolf Galland, op.cit.
75. Quoted from, www.dunsfoldairfield.org/type-t2-hangars
76. Byron and Coxon, op cit, p.223.
77. Robin Olds, *Fighter Pilot: The Memoirs of Legendary Ace Robin Olds* (St. Martin's Press, New York, 2010), pp.180–1.
78. ibid, pp.185–6.
79. Quoted on the RAF Heraldry Trust's website: www.rafht.co.uk
80. See Martin Bowman, *The Hunter Story* (The History Press, Stroud, 2009).
81. Peter Pigott, *Royal Transport: An Inside Look at the History of Royal Travel* (Dundurn Group, Toronto, 2005), p.156.
82. ibid, p.157.
83. For more information, please see Nick Carter, *Meteor Eject! – Recollections of a Pioneer RAF Jet Pilot of the 1950s and 60s* (Woodfield Publishing, 2000).
84. Interview with Mark Hillier, 2021.
85. Dennis 'Hurricane' David, *My Autobiography* (Grub Street, London, 2000).
86. Colin Hodgkinson, *Best Foot Forward: The Autobiography of the RAF's other Legless Fighter Pilot* (Frontline Books, Barnsley, 2017).
87. Interview with Mark Hillier.
88. Quoted from: www.22squadronassociation.org.uk.
89. *Birmingham Daily Post*, 5 January 1963.
90. Correspondence with the authors, 19 January 2018.
91. Wing Commander H.R. Allen DFC, *Fighter Station Supreme: RAF Tangmere* (Granada, London, 1985), p.160.
92. ibid, p.186.
93. Air Vice-Marshal Crowley-Milling had only recently returned from the United States, where, from 1967 to 1970, he had served as the Commander RAF Staff and Principal Air Attaché in Washington, to take up command of the RAF's 38 Group. Whilst in America, Crowley-Milling had been responsible for setting up the arrangement under which the US Navy began to operate Harriers.
94. Quoted from www.key.aero/forum/historic-aviation/60266-vintage-gliders
95. See https://historicengland.org.uk/listing/the-list/list-entry/1391924?section=official-list-entry.
96. Quoted from: www.mahn.org.uk/events/tmam-at-40-exhibition.